An Intermediate Course

# Taiwan Today

今日台灣

中級漢語課程

**Third Edition**

鄧守信 Shou-hsin Teng
National Taiwan Normal University

孫珞 Lo Sun Perry
University of Puget Sound

Cheng & Tsui Company
Boston

16 15 14 13 12 11 10     2 3 4 5 6 7 8 9 10

Third edition 2009

**Published by**
Cheng & Tsui Company, Inc.
25 West Street
Boston, MA 02111-1213 USA
Fax (617) 426-3669
www.cheng-tsui.com
"Bringing Asia to the World"™

ISBN 978-0-88727-564-7

Library of Congress Cataloging-in-Publication Data

Teng, Shou-hsin.
Taiwan today : an intermediate course / Shou-hsin Teng, Lo Sun Perry. -- 3rd ed.
p. cm.
Text in Chinese with traditional/simplified characters, English, and pinyin.
Parallel title and statement of responsibility also in Chinese.
Includes indexes.
ISBN 0-88727-564-8 (pbk.)
1. Chinese language--Textbooks for foreign speakers--English. 2. Taiwan--Problems, exercises, etc. I. Perry, Lo Sun. II. Title.

PL1129.E5T46 2008+
495.1'82421--dc22

2008062325

All illustrations and photographs are courtesy of the authors except the following: p. 90, photo of subway ( http://flickr.com/photos/ayustety); p. 93, photo of books (http://www.flickr.com/photos/lemuelinchrist); p. 164, photo of rally (http://flickr.com/photos/princeroy); p. 221, (http://www.flickr.com/photos/63138333@N00).

Printed in the United States of America

# Publisher's Note

The Cheng & Tsui Chinese Language Series is designed to publish and widely distribute quality language learning materials created by leading instructors from around the world. We welcome readers' comments and suggestions concerning the publications in this series. Please contact the following members of our Editorial Board, in care of our Editorial Department (e-mail: editor@cheng-tsui.com).

# Audio Recordings

Users of this textbook have access to downloadable audio files that correspond to this third edition of *Taiwan Today*. These audio recordings contain texts, vocabulary, grammar, and selected exercises for each lesson, spoken by native speakers. To download the audio files, simply register your product key at the publisher's website:

1. Visit the Cheng & Tsui download center at **www.cheng-tsui.com/downloads** and follow the instructions for creating a user account.
2. Register your product key.
3. Download the audio files.
4. For technical support, please contact support@cheng-tsui.com or call 1-800-554-1963.

If you have purchased a used copy of this book or one without a valid product key, you may purchase a new key via our website (www.cheng-tsui.com) or by contacting our customer service department at 1-800-554-1963.

MENU-MEHE

# Contents

# Introduction

This text is not a passive reader. Rather, *Taiway Today* invites students to actively participate in the process of acquiring skills in intermediate modern Chinese—from listening and speaking to reading and writing. While the main texts of this volume are presented in a written style, most of the exercises are in spoken form. We intend the texts to serve as jumping-off points for extended and active conversation and discussion in the classroom.

This newly revised and expanded third edition features two brand new lessons—Lessons 13 and 14--along with audio material for each lesson that provides students with the native pronunciation of texts, vocabulary, grammar structures, and select exercises (see page iv for details about downloading the audio). Lessons 7 and 12, about Taiwan's educational system and China-Taiwan relations respectively, have been revised to keep students informed about significant changes in Taiwanese society. With these added and updated materials, students' understanding of Taiwanese culture will develop as their language skills improve.

We have also added parts of speech for each new vocabulary item in this edition. The system of parts of speech used in this volume departs significantly from the traditional systems found in other textbooks but is familiar to those in Chinese linguistic circles. The glosses to each part of speech and the examples given ought the make the new system fairly transparent. It is our belief that parts of speech not only should be given but also should be taught in class. If any users of this textbook, whether instructors or learners, wish to obtain further information on the new system, you may contact the authors in care of the publisher at editor@cheng-tsui.com.

Since the focus of this book is on Taiwan, information is primarily presented in traditional Chinese characters and the language usage reflects that of contemporary Taiwan. To accommodate learners of simplified Chinese characters, we have added simplified character versions of texts, new vocabulary words, grammar examples, and exercises. (The simplified versions of supplementary vocabulary words, which do not appear in the texts, are provided in the index.) Wherever differences in language usage exist in contemporary speech, we have presented the Taiwan usage in the traditional text and the Mainland China usage in the simplified text. Such differences in regional usage are indicated by dual vocabulary entries in the vocabulary lists; readers may also refer to the "Contrastive Vocabulary" chart in the Supplementary Materials for Lesson 12 for a list of words that reflect regional variations in usage. Finally, we've added a bopomofo–pinyin conversion chart to introduce learners to the phonetic transcription system used in Taiwan.

# Course Overview

This text is geared to intermediate Chinese language students, i.e., those currently in the second semester of their second year of Chinese language study and who undergo five hours of classroom instruction per week. It can follow or be used concurrently with an intermediate conversational textbook, and should precede the introduction of authentic materials at the third year level. We have tailored the language used in this volume so that it can serve as a bridge between textbooks and authentic materials.

A typical semester in an American college lasts fifteen weeks, but trimming the semester by vacations, holidays, and examinations leaves twelve solid weeks of instruction. *Taiwan Today*, Third Edition, includes fourteen lessons from which teachers can choose. Where semester schemes vary, instructors will find this book quite expandable by working extensively with the supplementary materials included at the end of each lesson.

# Components of the Lessons

### Texts

The fourteen lessons in this volume introduce students to some common topics about today's Taiwan, such as the separation of Taiwan from Mainland China and the state of Taiwan's economy. The lessons also cover traditional themes, such as religions in China. However, instructors are urged to make use of the book's contents as points of departure and to extend the scope of discussion to cover China as a whole.

Each narrative is deliberately short so that students do not spend a whole week working on the text. Instead, the authors encourage users to talk about the topics in class discussions that go beyond the narrative texts.

### Grammar

A common assumption in the field of teaching Chinese as a second language is that learning "grammar" is a task for first-year students and instructors. We take a different stance in this book and demonstrate that there is plenty of intermediate-level grammar to cover, even towards the end of the second year. Some grammatical points introduced here are used in advanced-level colloquial speech and some are literary but commonly used in daily conversation by educated native speakers.

We also believe that students using this book should fine-tune their mastery of the modern language by being able to compare one grammatical usage with another of the same linguistic element. Therefore, many grammatical elements covered in this book are given an integrated presentation at the risk of repetition.

Brief grammatical definitions are followed by sentences illustrating usage. Immediately thereafter, students are invited to try out their understanding of the grammar presented by completing sentences and English-to-Chinese translations. Instructors are encouraged to devise extra sentences or applications, time permitting.

### Exercises

The exercises constitute the core of this book. They are varied in nature and in purpose. Some items take half an hour to complete and some require a couple of days or longer. Students may find that they must invest a great deal of time and energy on this component of the book, and it may be necessary for their instructors to spend an equal amount of time, or longer, to go over corrections and assist in student presentations. However, we hope that the work will be rewarding.

Some themes of the exercises are borrowed from Western language pedagogy and some are indigenous to Chinese culture. We understand that students or instructors will not find all the exercises beneficial or practical. Variations of themes are therefore encouraged. For instance, Role Play may be impractical for a very large or a very serious class, but suggested topics can be easily adapted to controlled composition. Though some of the exercises are more lighthearted in nature, none are to be taken as games. There is a linguistic intent behind each type of exercise.

### Supplementary Materials

The concluding section of each lesson consists of sub-topics related to the main passage, presented in systematically organized tables. Some present rather valuable information that may not be otherwise available to students (for instance, the uniquely Chinese terms used to describe the effects that certain foods have on the body). It is entirely at the instructor's discretion as to how to work with such materials. We intentionally do not give explanations of these tables, and not all of the items are translated into English. They can even be discussed in English so that important cultural information is understood.

Some tables, charts, or pictures included in this section are, however, directly related to sections of the vocabulary or exercises. Where this is the case, a brief note within the lesson directs readers' attention to the supplementary materials.

### Video Materials

The *Taiwan Today* program does not include video materials. Fortunately, a wealth of material is available from the archives of the former Public Television Corporation of Taiwan, as well as the Taiwan Public Television Service. See page 259 for a list of suggested video materials and contact information for PTS. Because these are authentic video clips, the language used in documentaries is advanced and, thus, English may be necessary from time to time to guide students.

# Acknowledgments

This volume is the product of a project funded by Tunghai University, Taichung, Taiwan, under the general editorships of Shou-hsin Teng, formerly with the Department of Asian Languages and Literatures, University of Massachusetts, Amherst, and currently with the Institute of Chinese as a Second Language, National Taiwan Normal University, Taipei; and Feng I-chien, Chinese Department and Director of Chinese Language Center, Tunghai University.

The team that undertook the project consisted of the following members:

| | |
|---|---|
| 蘇文伶 Su Wen-ling | *University of Illinois, Chicago* |
| 邢璐 Luh Hsyng Nelson | *University of California, Irvine* |
| 孫珞 Lo Sun Perry | *University of Puget Sound, Washington* |
| 艾安竹 Andrew Abel | *University of Massachusetts, Amherst* |
| 馮以堅 Feng I-chien | *Chinese Language Center, Tunghai* |
| 鄧守信 Shou-hsin Teng | *National Taiwan Normal University* |

All of the members are affiliated with Tunghai University and University of Massachusetts, Amherst in some way. While in the process of compilation, *Taiwan Today* was used by students attending the UMass-at-Tunghai Summer Program. We are grateful for the feedback and suggestions of both the students and their teacher.

Shou-hsin Teng
November 2008

# Taiwan Today

第 一 課

# 去 公 園 學 功 夫

## 繁体課文 Traditional Text

如果你希望了解一下中國人常做的運動，最好就是哪一天大清早到公園去走一趟。早晨在公園裡運動的，男女老少都有。一走進公園你可能就會聽到一陣音樂；順著聲音走過去一看，原來是一群婦女正在那兒做健美操。旁邊也許還有人練習跳舞。比較安靜的是一群專心打太極拳的人，其中多半是年紀在四、五十歲以上的。你若是有興趣的話，也可以在一旁跟著學習。還有一些不常見的中國功夫；也許是一位老太太在舞劍，或是一個年輕人兩手抱著一棵大樹在練功。當然公園內也有不少慢跑和散步的人們。樹下也總是坐著兩三位老人，有的在下棋，有的提著鳥籠，讓心愛的鳥也出來呼吸呼吸新鮮空氣。許多公園裡還有球場跟游泳池，因為網球、羽毛球、籃球和游泳都是中國人非常喜愛的運動。

## 简体课文 Simplified Text

如果你希望了解一下中国人常做的运动，最好就是哪一天大清早到公园去走一趟。早晨在公园里运动的，男女老少都有。一走进公园你可能就会听到一阵音乐；顺着声音走过去一看，原来是一群妇女正在那儿做健美操。旁边也许还有人练习跳舞。比较安静的是一群专心打太极拳的人，其中多半是年纪在四、五十岁以上的。你若是有兴趣的话，也可以在一旁跟着学习。还有一些不常见的中国功夫；也许是一位老太太在舞剑，或是一个年轻人两手抱着一棵大树在练功。当然公园内也有不少慢跑和散步的人们。树下也总是坐着两三位老人，有的在下棋，有的提着鸟笼，让心爱的鸟也出来呼吸呼吸新鲜空气。许多公园里还有球场跟游泳池，因为网球、羽毛球、篮球和游泳都是中国人非常喜爱的运动。

## 生詞 Vocabulary

| | | | | | |
|---|---|---|---|---|---|
| 1. | 了解 | 了解 | liǎojiě | *Vst.* | to understand |
| 2. | 運動 | 运动 | yùndòng | *N.* | exercise, sports; *Vi.* to exercise |
| 3. | 大清早 | 大清早 | dàqīngzǎo | *N.* | early morning |
| 4. | 趟 | 趟 | tàng | *M.* | verb measure, indicating number of times something is done, often in reference to a trip of some kind |
| 5. | 少年<br>老少 | 少年<br>老少 | shàonián<br>lǎoshào | *N.* | young people<br>the old and the young |
| 6. | 陣 | 阵 | zhèn | *M.* | measure, referring to a brief occurrence/encounter with both inception and termination understood |

| | | | | | |
|---|---|---|---|---|---|
| 7. | 音樂 | 音乐 | yīnyuè | *N.* | music |
| 8. | 順著 | 顺着 | shùnzhe | *Prep.* | following |
| 9. | 聲音 | 声音 | shēngyīn | *N.* | sound, noise |
| 10. | 原來 | 原来 | yuánlái | *Adv.* | one realizes that ...; it turns out that ... |
| 11. | 群 | 群 | qún | *M.* | measure, referring to a group of people or animals |
| 12. | 婦女 | 妇女 | fùnǚ | *N.* | women |
| 13. | 健美操<br>健康<br>美麗 | 健美操 | jiànměicāo<br>jiànkāng<br>měilì | *N.*<br>*Vs.*<br>*Vs.* | fitness exercise<br>fit and healthy<br>pretty, beautiful |
| 14. | 跳舞 | 跳舞 | tiàowǔ | *V-sep.* | to dance |
| 15. | 安靜 | 安静 | ānjìng | *Vs.* | quiet |
| 16. | 專心 | 专心 | zhuānxīn | *Adv., Vs.* | attentively |
| 17. | 太極拳 | 太极拳 | tàijíquán | *N.* | shadow boxing, *Taichi* (*See chart in "Supplementary Materials" for this lesson*) |
| 18. | 其中 | 其中 | qízhōng | *Loc.* | among which, therein |
| 19. | 多半 | 多半 | duōbàn | *N.* | the majority, the greater part |
| 20. | 年紀 | 年纪 | niánjì | *N.* | age |
| 21. | 以上 | 以上 | yǐshàng | *N.* | over, more than, above |
| 22. | 興趣 | 兴趣 | xìngqù | *N.* | interest |
| 23. | 一旁 | 一旁 | yīpáng | *N.* | (to/at) one side |
| 24. | 功夫 | 功夫 | gōngfū | *N.* | *kungfu*, a martial art |
| 25. | 舞劍 | 舞剑 | wǔjiàn | *V-sep.* | a style of *kungfu*, involving dancing with a sword |
| 26. | 抱 | 抱 | bào | *V.* | to hold or carry in the arms; to hug |
| 27. | 棵 | 棵 | kē | *M.* | measure for trees |
| 28. | 樹 | 树 | shù | *N.* | tree |
| 29. | 散步 | 散步 | sànbù | *V-sep.* | to take a walk, to stroll |
| 30. | 下棋 | 下棋 | xiàqí | *V-sep.* | to play Chinese chess *(See chart in "Supplementary Materials" for this lesson)* |
| 31. | 提 | 提 | tí | *V.* | to carry in one hand |
| 32. | 鳥籠 | 鸟笼 | niǎolóng | *N.* | birdcage |
| 33. | 呼吸 | 呼吸 | hūxī | *V.* | to breathe |
| 34. | 新鮮 | 新鲜 | xīnxiān | *Vs.* | fresh |
| 35. | 空氣 | 空气 | kōngqì | *N.* | air |

| | | | | | |
|---|---|---|---|---|---|
| 36. | 球場 | 球场 | qiúchǎng | *N.* | courts, field (for various ball games) |
| 37. | 游泳池 | 游泳池 | yóuyǒngchí | *N.* | swimming pool |
| 38. | 網球 | 网球 | wǎngqiú | *N.* | tennis |
| 39. | 羽毛球 | 羽毛球 | yǔmáoqiú | *N.* | badminton |
| 40. | 籃球 | 篮球 | lánqiú | *N.* | basketball |

# 文法 Grammar

Each pattern below is illustrated by sample sentences. When blanks are provided, complete the sentences. When English sentences are provided, give Chinese counterparts.

## 1. 最好 zuìhǎo: (Adv.) it is imperative that, it is advisable that, it is best that

a. 你如果要身體健康，最好天天運動。
（你如果要身体健康，最好天天运动。）
If you want to be healthy, it is best to exercise every day.

b. 上課的時候，最好專心聽老師講課。
（上课的时候，最好专心听老师讲课。）
It is advisable to pay close attention to the teacher's lecture when attending class.

c. 明天要參加運動會的學生，最好 练习运动 ______________ 。
（明天要参加运动会的学生，最好 ______________________ 。）

d. 想多了解中國文化，最好 ______________________ 。
（想多了解中国文化，最好 学习中国文化 ______________ 。）

## 2. 哪 nǎ: (Indefinite pronoun) Question words such as 哪 can be used to refer to unspecified subjects or objects. （什麼 'something'; 誰 'someone'; 哪 . . . + noun 'some. + noun.'）

a. 我餓死了，想吃點什麼。
（我饿死了，想吃点什么。）
I am starved, I'd like to have a little something to eat.

b. 我們走错路了，誰去問問路吧。
（我们走错路了，谁去问问路吧。）
We've taken the wrong road. Someone should go ask for directions.

c. 我希望哪一天能到非洲去玩一趟。
(我希望哪一天能到非洲去玩一趟。)
I hope that someday I can take a trip to Africa.

d. Can someone lend me a car for the weekend?
谁可以在周末借一辆车给我?

e. Can I help you with something?
有什么我可以帮你?

### 3. 一陣 yízhèn: (Measure) referring to a brief occurrence/encounter with both inception and termination understood

a. 下了一陣大雨，天氣涼快多了。
(下了一阵大雨，天气凉快多了。)
After the rainstorm, the weather became much cooler.

b. 窗外一陣鳥叫聲把我吵醒了。
(窗外一阵鸟叫声把我吵醒了。)
A sudden chirping of birds by the window woke me up.

c. ______________________，我覺得很舒服。
(下一阵雨的时候睡觉，我觉得很舒服。)

d. 我坐在公園休息的時候，聽到______________________。
(我坐在公园休息的时候，听到一阵孩子叫声音。)

### 4. 順著 shùnzhe: (Prep.) following; going along with/down

a. 順著這條路一直走，差不多十五分鐘就到了。
(顺着这条路一直走，差不多十五分钟就到了。)
By following this road, you will get there in about 15 minutes.

b. 總是順著別人的意思，不一定是最好的法子。
(总是顺着别人的意思，不一定是最好的法子。)
Always going along with other people's opinions is not necessarily the best way.

c. A：請問，到羽毛球館怎麼走？
(请问，到羽毛球馆怎么走？)
B: 顺着这条路一直走。

d. 父母的意見跟我的不同的時候，______________________。
(父母的意见跟我的不同的时候，最好跟父母的意见。)

## 5. 原來 yuánlái:

(A) *(Adv.) indicating that one has realized something one didn't know before*

a. 我以為早晨公園裡很安靜，原來有那麼多人在那裡運動。
（我以为早晨公园里很安静，原来有那么多人在那里运动。）
I thought it would be quiet in the park in the morning; actually there are many people who exercise there.

b. 難怪他身體這麼好，原來他天天運動。
（难怪他身体这么好，原来他天天运动。）
No wonder he is so healthy; he exercises every day.

c. 他聽見外面有聲音，走過去一看，原來（是）____________。
（他听见外面有声音，走过去一看，原来（是）鸟叫的声音。）

d. 我以為網球場離公園很遠，原來________________。
（我以为网球场离公园很远，原来网球场离公园很近。）

(B) 原來的：*(Adj.) original, former.* 原來：*(Adv.) originally, formerly.* (*Note that only in the* (B) *usage is* 原來 *interchangeable with* 本來.)

a. 他還是喜歡在原來的地方打太極拳。
（他还是喜欢在原来的地方打太极拳。）
He still likes to do *Taichi* at the same old place.

b. 那個公園原來只是散步的地方，現在又加了游泳池。
（那个公园原来只是散步的地方，现在又加了游泳池。）
That park was originally only a place for people to take walks. Now a swimming pool has been added.

c. ________________，現在他對中國已經有很深的了解了。
（他原来不了解中国，现在他对中国已经有很深的了解了。）

d. ________________，現在他的健康情況已經好多了。
（他的健康情况不好，现在他的健康情况已经好多了。）

## 6. 其中 qízhōng: (Localizer) of whom, of which, among whom, among which（其 qí: (Pron.) it, they, its, their ... [referring to an antecedent]）

a. 他的作品很多，其中有一半已經翻譯成英文了。
（他的作品很多，其中有一半已经翻译成英文了。）
He has written many books, half of which have been translated into English.

b. 我們學校有五百個學生，其中女學生占百分之六十。
（我们学校有五百个学生，其中女学生占百分之六十。）
There are five hundred students in our school, of whom sixty percent are female.

c. 早晨在公園裡運動的人很多，其中＿＿＿＿＿＿＿＿＿＿。
（早晨在公园里运动的人很多，其中 多半是年老的人 。）

d. 大學生熱愛的運動有許多，＿＿＿＿＿＿＿＿＿＿。
（大学生热爱的运动有许多，其中有篮球和网球 。）

## 7. 要是/如果/假如/若是...的話 yàoshi / rúguǒ / jiǎrú/ ruòshi ... dehuà: (Conditional marker, optional only if a preceding conjunction is used.)

a. 要是天氣不好的話，我們就留在家下棋了。
（要是天气不好的话，我们就留在家下棋了。）
If the weather is bad, we'll stay home and play chess.

b. 要是你想把中國功夫學好，應該向張先生請教請教。
（要是你想把中国功夫学好，应该向张先生请教请教。）
If you want to study Chinese martial arts, you should ask Mr. Chang to teach you.

c. If you like Chinese music, you should go to that concert tonight.
如果你喜欢中文声音，你今晚应该去音乐会。

d. If there are already too many people playing tennis, I'll go swimming.
如果已经有太多人打网球，我会去游泳。

# 練習 Exercises

## 1. 生詞練習 Vocabulary Drills

相似詞 Match words of similar meaning from the following two columns:

| | | | | | | |
|---|---|---|---|---|---|---|
| ( ) | 1. | 了解 | 了解 | A. | 清早 | 清早 |
| ( ) | 2. | 趟 | 趟 | B. | 老是 | 老是 |
| ( ) | 3. | 總是 | 总是 | C. | 明白 | 明白 |
| ( ) | 4. | 也許 | 也许 | D. | 如果 | 如果 |
| ( ) | 5. | 早晨 | 早晨 | E. | 可能 | 可能 |
| ( ) | 6. | 若是 | 若是 | F. | 次 | 次 |

相反詞 Match opposites from the following two columns:

| | | | | | | |
|---|---|---|---|---|---|---|
| ( ) | 7. | 安靜 | 安静 | G. | 討厭 | 讨厌 |
| ( ) | 8. | 喜愛 | 喜爱 | H. | 黃昏 | 黄昏 |
| ( ) | 9. | 清晨 | 清晨 | I. | 老 | 老 |
| ( ) | 10. | 年輕 | 年轻 | J. | 吵鬧 | 吵闹 |

## 2. 生詞填充 Fill in the blanks with the given words:

| | | | |
|---|---|---|---|
| 安靜 | 安静 | 抱著 | 抱着 |
| 功夫 | 功夫 | 原來 | 原来 |
| 球場 | 球场 | 興趣 | 兴趣 |
| 新鮮 | 新鲜 | 了解 | 了解 |
| 專心 | 专心 | 趟 | 趟 |
| 男女老少 | 男女老少 | 群 | 群 |

a. 請你們大家________一點，裡面有人開著會呢！
（请你们大家________一点，里面有人开着会呢！）

b. 游泳這個運動，________都喜歡，所以天氣一熱，游泳池邊是一家人最好的去處。
（游泳这个运动，________都喜欢，所以天气一热，游泳池边是一家人最好的去处。）

c. 王老師兩手________學生的作業慢慢地從教室走出來。
（王老师两手________学生的作业慢慢地从教室走出来。）

d. 那是一部________片子，所以演員們都得會打一點兒拳或舞一舞劍。
（那是一部________片子，所以演员们都得会打一点儿拳或舞一舞剑。）

e. 山上的空氣當然比城市裡的________，因為樹木比較多。
（山上的空气当然比城市里的________，因为树木比较多。）

f. 我們才認識幾天，對他我還不太________。
（我们才认识几天，对他我还不太________。）

g. 聽說她搬家了。我們到她的新家走一________吧！
（听说她搬家了。我们到她的新家走一________吧！）

h. 雖然太陽這麼大，籃________上還是有很多人在打球。
（虽然太阳这么大，篮________上还是有很多人在打球。）

i. 他對中國音樂沒有什麼________，就聽西洋歌曲。
（他对中国音乐没有什么________，就听西洋歌曲。）

j. 十字路口站了一大________人，不知道出了什麼事了。
（十字路口站了一大________人，不知道出了什么事了。）

k. 我以為他生病了，所以沒來，________他跟朋友去跳舞了！
（我以为他生病了，所以没来，________他跟朋友去跳舞了！）

l. 太累了！沒法________工作，得先睡個覺再說。
（太累了！没法________工作，得先睡个觉再说。）

## 3. 接字遊戲 Word Train

按上一個詞寫出另一個新的詞，新詞必須包含上一詞的其中一個字，或其中一個字的同音異義字。可分組比賽，讓各組同學輪流接字，在黑板上寫出答案。

（按上一个词写出另一个新的词，新词必须包含上一词的其中一个字，或其中一个字的同音异义字。可分组比赛，让各组同学轮流接字，在黑板上写出答案。）

Form a new word using one of the two (or more) characters from the previous word or a homonym of one of those characters.

例 EXAMPLE:

中國⇨ 國家⇨ 家人⇨ 女人⇨ 女生⇨ 聲音⇨ 因為⇨ 為什麼

a. 公園 ⇨______⇨______⇨______⇨______⇨______⇨

______⇨______⇨______⇨______⇨______⇨______

b. 打球 ⇨ 籃球 ⇨______⇨______⇨______⇨______⇨

______⇨______⇨______⇨______⇨______⇨______

## 4. 說雙簧 Speak and Act

兩人一組，一人坐在椅子上表演動作，一人在椅子後面念。

（两人一组，一人坐在椅子上表演动作，一人在椅子后面念。）

Find a partner and decide who will be the speaker and who the actor. The actor performs what the speaker reads in the following narrative.

今天早上五點我就起來了！
我提著鳥籠去公園散步。
我的小鳥很喜歡叫，它會說：『你早！你早！』
公園裡有很多人在做運動。
有的人做健美操；
有的舞劍；
還有一些人在打網球、打籃球、打羽毛球、
踢足球、游泳...
有一位老先生在打太極拳。
中國功夫太容易了！
我看了一分鐘就會了。

我來教你：一個大西瓜，把它切成兩半；
一半送給你，一半我自己留著。

今天早上五点我就起来了！
我提着鸟笼去公园散步。
我的小鸟很喜欢叫，它会说：『你早！你早！』
公园里有很多人在做运动。
有的人做健美操；
有的舞剑；
还有一些人在打网球、打篮球、打羽毛球、
踢足球、游泳...
有一位老先生在打太极拳。
中国功夫太容易了！
我看了一分钟就会了。
我来教你：一个大西瓜，把它切成两半；
一半送给你，一半我自己留着。

## 5. 情況對話 Role Play

兩人一組，演出下面的角色：
（两人一组，演出下面的角色：）
Choose a partner and act out the following situations:

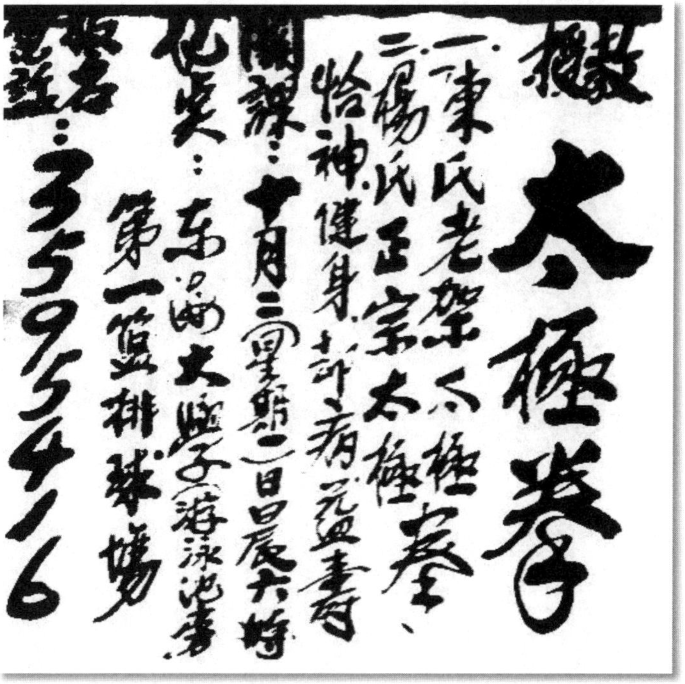


情況 （一） 清早在公園裡

**Role A:**
An American student. While taking a stroll in the park, he/she notices an old gentleman doing *Taichi.* The American is fascinated by the old man's movements, and wants to learn them. He/she approaches the old man politely and inquires about the possibility of some sort of tutorial arrangement before he/she leaves for the States next month.

**Role B:**
An old man in his eighties. He has been studying *Taichi* all his life and practices at four every morning in the park. He is willing to teach the young American, but his daughter, who lives in the States, has just given birth to a son. He has made plans to see her next week and will stay in the States for at least three months. However, he has a friend, who is also a master of *Taichi.* He can introduce the American to his friend.

## 情況（二）李和王一面吃著早飯一面談話

Mr. Lee has just finished his routine morning exercises in the park. Mr. Wang is interested in the kind of exercises people do there. Lee is an enthusiastic advocate of morning exercise and tries to convince Wang to join him in his exercises. Wang thinks it is too early for him because he has to take a two-hour bus ride to work every day, and he often works late at his office. Wang would like to exercise with Lee on Sunday mornings, so they make plans to play basketball during the coming weekend.

## 6. 作文 Composition

請說一說在你住的地方一般人常做的運動有哪些。
也說一說你最喜歡的運動是什麼。
（请说一说在你住的地方一般人常做的运动有哪些。
也说一说你最喜欢的运动是什么。）

What kind of sports/exercises do the people do where you live?
What are the most popular sports there? What is your favorite sport?

# 補充資料 Supplementary Materials

## 1. 棋和牌 Chess and Card Games

| 棋和牌 Chess & Card Games | |
|---|---|
| 象棋 xiàngqí | Chinese Chess |
| 圍棋 wéiqí | Go |
| 跳棋 tiàoqí | Chinese Checkers |
| 橋牌 qiáopái | Bridge |
| 麻將 májiàng | Mahjong |
| 西洋棋 xīyángqí | Western Chess |

Playing Go

Mahjong Players

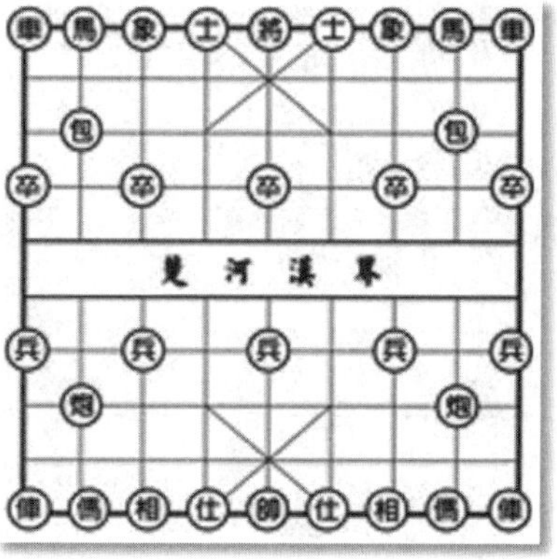

## 2. 武術 Martial Arts

| 武術 wǔshù Martial Arts | |
|---|---|
| 氣功 qìgōng | *Qigong*, art of using/focusing energy |
| 柔道 róudào | *Judo* |
| 太極拳 tàijíquán | *Taichi*, shadow boxing |
| 合氣道 héqìdào | *Aikido* |
| 空手道 kōngshǒudào | *Karate* |
| 跆拳道 táiquándào | *Taekwondo* |

跆拳道

## 3. 運動 Sports

| 運動 yùndòng Sports | | | |
|---|---|---|---|
| 棒球 bàngqiú | baseball | 慢跑 mànpǎo | jogging |
| 足球 zúqiú | football | 划船 huáchuán | rowing, rafting |
| 排球 páiqiú | volleyball | 跳水 tiàoshuǐ | diving |
| 籃球 lánqiú | basketball | 溜冰 liūbīng | skating |
| 網球 wǎngqiú | tennis | 滑雪 huáxuě | skiing |
| 羽毛球 yǔmáoqiú | badminton | 滑水 huáshuǐ | water-skiing |
| 乒乓球 pīngpāngqiú | ping pong | 曲棍球 qūgùnqiú | hockey |
| 保齡球 bǎolíngqiú | bowling | 高爾夫球 gāo'ěrfūqiú | golf |

## 第二課

# 逛夜市

## 繁体課文 Traditional Text

夜市大概是一般台灣城市裡晚上最熱鬧的地方了。天一黑一個一個的小販就開始忙著把自己的攤子擺出來。從日用品、衣服、書籍、花草到各種水果、冷熱小吃，夜市裡應有盡有。在比較大的夜市裡，連金魚、兔子、狗這樣的小動物都買得到。去逛夜市的人不但可以玩遊戲，而且還可以看看表演。

夜市裡最吸引人的地方就是商品的價錢比一般商店或百貨公司的東西便宜的多，而且買什麼都可以講一講價。不過，一分錢一分貨。地攤上的東西有時品質較低，有時是仿冒品：要是大小不合適的話，又不能退換。所以逛夜市一定得有耐心，慢慢地挑，慢慢地選。因為所有的攤子都擺在路邊，顧客往往一邊和老闆講價錢，一邊還得注意身旁的車子和行人。擠、吵和亂是夜市最大的特色了。但是去逛夜市的人都不在乎，總是提著大包小包滿載而歸。逛夜市的樂趣大概只有去逛過的人才能了解了。

## 简体课文 Simplified Text

夜市大概是一般台湾城市里晚上最热闹的地方了。天一黑一个一个的小贩就开始忙着把自己的摊子摆出来。从日用品、衣服、书籍、花草到各种水果、冷热小吃，夜市里应有尽有。在比较大的夜市里，连金鱼、兔子、狗这样的小动物都买得到。去逛夜市的人不但可以玩游戏，而且还可以看看表演。

夜市里最吸引人的地方就是商品的价钱比一般商店或百货公司的东西便宜的多，而且买什么都可以讲一讲价。不过，一分钱一分货。地摊上的东西有时质量较低，有时是仿冒品：要是大小不合适的话，又不能退换。所以逛夜市一定得有耐心，慢慢地挑，慢慢地选。因为所有的摊子都摆在路边，顾客往往一边和老板讲价钱，一边还得注意身旁的车子和行人。挤、吵和乱是夜市最大的特色了。但是去逛夜市的人都不在乎，总是提着大包小包满载而归。逛夜市的乐趣大概只有去逛过的人才能了解了。

## 生詞 Vocabulary

| | | | | | |
|---|---|---|---|---|---|
| 1. | 逛<br>逛街 | 逛 | guàng<br>guàngjiē | *Vi.*<br>*Vi-sep.* | to browse, to look around<br>to go window-shopping; stroll down a street |
| 2. | 夜市<br>市場 | 夜市 | yèshì<br>shìchǎng | *N.*<br>*N.* | night market<br>market *(See chart in "Supplementary Materials" for this lesson)* |
| 3. | 一般 | 一般 | yībān | *Vs.* | most, regular, ordinary; usually |
| 4. | 小販 | 小贩 | xiǎofàn | *N.* | peddlers, stall keepers |
| 5. | 攤子 | 摊子 | tānzi | *N.* | roadside stands |

| | | | | | |
|---|---|---|---|---|---|
| 6. | 擺 | 摆 | bǎi | *V.* | to place, arrange; to be placed or arranged |
| 7. | 日用品 | 日用品 | rìyòngpǐn | *N.* | daily sundries, daily necessities *(See chart in "Supplementary Materials" for this lesson)* |
| 8. | 書籍 | 书籍 | shūjí | *N.* | books and magazines |
| 9. | 花草 | 花草 | huācǎo | *N.* | flowers and plants |
| 10. | 各種 | 各种 | gèzhǒng | *Vs-attr.* | various, all kinds of |
| 11. | 應有盡有 | 应有尽有 | yīngyǒu jìnyǒu | *Id.* | to have all sorts of things |
| 12. | 兔子 | 兔子 | tùzi | *N.* | rabbit |
| 13. | 小動物 | 小动物 | xiǎo dòngwù | *N.* | pets (lit., small animals) |
| 14. | 遊戲 | 游戏 | yóuxì | *N.* | games; to play games |
| 15. | 表演 | 表演 | biǎoyǎn | *Vi.* | to perform; *N.* a performance |
| 16. | 吸引 | 吸引 | xīyǐn | *Vst.* | to attract |
| 17. | 商品 | 商品 | shāngpǐn | *N.* | merchandise, goods |
| 18. | 講價 | 讲价 | jiǎngjià | *V-sep.* | to bargain |
| 19. | 一分錢<br>一分貨 | 一分钱<br>一分货 | yìfēn qián<br>yìfēn huò | *N.* | to get what you pay for (i.e., cost determines quality) |
| 20. | 品質 | 品质 | pǐnzhí | *N.* | quality |
| 21. | 低 | 低 | dī | *Vs.* | low, inferior |
| 22. | 仿冒品 | 仿冒品 | fǎngmàopǐn | *N.* | pirated goods, imitations |
| 23. | 合適 | 合适 | héshì | *Vs.* | suitable, appropriate |
| 24. | 退換 | 退换 | tuìhuàn | *V.* | to return or exchange (goods) |
| 25. | 耐心 | 耐心 | nàixīn | *N.* | patience |
| 26. | 挑 | 挑 | tiāo | *V.* | to pick, to select |
| 27. | 選 | 选 | xuǎn | *V.* | to select, to choose |
| 28. | 顧客 | 顾客 | gùkè | *N.* | customers |
| 29. | 往往 | 往往 | wǎngwǎng | *Adv.* | often (the case that ...) |
| 30. | 老闆 | 老板 | lǎobǎn | *N.* | the owner (of some business) |
| 31. | 行人 | 行人 | xíngrén | *N.* | pedestrians |
| 32. | 擠 | 挤 | jǐ | *Vs.* | crowded, packed |
| 33. | 亂<br>亂七八糟 | 乱 | luàn<br>luànqī bāzāo | *Vs.*<br>*Id.* | disorderly, messy; random, reckless<br>in a mess |
| 34. | 特色 | 特色 | tèsè | *N.* | special or unique features, characteristics |
| 35. | 不在乎 | 不在乎 | bú zàihū | *Vst.* | do not care, do not mind |

| | | | | | |
|---|---|---|---|---|---|
| 36. | 滿載而歸 | 满载而归 | mǎnzài érguī | *Id.* | to return loaded with goods |
| 37. | 樂趣 | 乐趣 | lèqù | *N.* | fun, joy, pleasure |

# 文法 Grammar

Each pattern below is illustrated by sample sentences. When blanks are provided, complete the sentences. When English sentences are provided, give Chinese counterparts.

## 1. 一般 yībān: (Adj.) an average ..., most ...; (Adv.) mostly, generally

a. 現在，一般商店都不喜歡顧客講價。
（现在，一般商店都不喜欢顾客讲价。）
Most stores nowadays do not want their customers to haggle.

b. 大學商店裡只賣一般的學生用品。
（大学商店里只卖一般的学生用品。）
The university store only sells the usual student supplies.

c. 大城市一般都有二十四小時服務的商店。
（大城市一般都有二十四小时服务的商店。）
Large cities usually have stores that are open 24 hours a day.

d. 大學畢業生一般應該能認識五千字以上。
（大学毕业生一般应该能认识五千字以上。）
Usually, college graduates are able to recognize over 5,000 characters.

e. 一般用品 ________________________________。
（一般用品 ________________________________。）

f. 小動物一般都 ___________________________。
（小动物一般都 ___________________________。）

g. Most fruits are available in Taiwan.

h. Generally speaking, department stores are found only in big cities.

## 2. 一個一個的 yíge yígede: (Adj./Adv.) one by one; individually

*(Reduplicated classifiers indicating succession or accumulation.)*

a. 到了半夜，逛夜市的人就一個一個的離開了。
（到了半夜，逛夜市的人就一个一个的离开了。）
At midnight, the night market's customers begin leaving, one after another.

b. 夜市賣的小吃，他一樣一樣的吃，好像很餓似的。
（夜市卖的小吃，他一样一样的吃，好像很饿似的。）
He sampled various foods at the night market, seeming very hungry.

c. The police towed all the cars away, one after another.

d. He put the goldfish into the aquarium one at a time.

### 3. 連...都... lián ... dōu ...: (Prep ... Adv.) even, including
（連 *can precede a subject, an object, a prepositional phrase, or even a verb*）

a. 連年老的人都喜歡到夜市逛逛。
（连年老的人都喜欢到夜市逛逛。）
Even elderly people like to visit night markets.

b. 他高興得連身旁的車子都沒注意到。
（他高兴得连身旁的车子都没注意到。）
He was so excited that he didn't even notice the cars around him.

c. 她連跟自己的妹妹一起住都不太願意。
（她连跟自己的妹妹一起住都不太愿意。）
She wasn't even willing to live with her own sister.

d. 雖然想要另一種顏色，可是老板連換都不肯換。
（虽然想要另一种颜色，可是老板连换都不肯换。）
Although I wanted a different color, the owner of the store wasn't even willing to make the exchange.

e. 他連東西的價錢____________________________。
（他连东西的价钱____________________________。）

f. 連自己的錢包____________________________。
（连自己的钱包____________________________。）

g. Don't worry ! Even experts cannot tell this is a fake.

h. He's lived in Hong Kong for ten years, but he can't even count in Cantonese.

### 4. （像） xiàng + Noun1 + 這/那樣的 zhè/nàyàngde + Noun2: Such a Noun2 as Noun1.

a. （像）張老師這樣的人，世界上少有。
（[像]）张老师这样的人，世界上少有。）
People like Mr. Zhang are rare in this world.

b. 吃生魚生蝦這樣的東西，一定要特別注意衛生。
（吃生鱼生虾这样的东西，一定要特别注意卫生。）
One must pay special attention to hygiene when eating such things as raw fish and raw shrimp.

c. Some pets, such as Pekinese dogs, are extremely expensive in the United States.

d. Japanese businesses prefer to buy real estate in such large cities as San Francisco and New York.

## 5. （比）較 (bǐ)jiào: (Adv.) relatively; (Verb) to compare

a. 把東西比較比較，就看得出來那個品質較高。
（把东西比较比较，就看得出来那个品质较高。）
You'll be able to tell which has better quality after comparing them.

b. 老板跟老板娘都很客氣，但是老板比較有耐心。
（老板跟老板娘都很客气，但是老板比较有耐心）
Both the owner and his wife are nice people, but he is more patient.

c. 比較熱鬧的城市 ______________________________。
（比较热闹的城市 ______________________________。）

d. 今天老師比較了______________________________。
（今天老师比较了______________________________。）

e. Please compare the merits of night markets and regular stores.

f. White clothes suit you better.

## 6. 往往 wǎngwǎng: (Adv.) it is often the case that ...; frequently
*(Note that while 常常 refers to frequency, 往往 stresses a set pattern or a regularity.)*

a. 有的老師總是認為聰明的學生往往不太用功。
（有的老师总是认为聪明的学生往往不太用功。）
Some teachers say that bright students often do not work hard enough.

b. 逛夜市的人往往買一些不需要的東西。
（逛夜市的人往往买一些不需要的东西。）
At the night market, people often buy things that they don't need.

c. 買便宜的東西往往 ______________________________。
（买便宜的东西往往 ______________________________。）

d. 看國外報紙往往 ______________________________。
（看国外报纸往往 ______________________________。）

e. One often does not see one's own weaknesses.

f. Cheaper things usually have poorer quality.

## 7. 只有...才... zhǐyǒu ... cái ... : only ( in a single sentence ); only if (in a compound sentence)

a. 只有大熱天我才去游泳。
（只有大热天我才去游泳。）
I only swim on very hot days.

b. 只有這種魚才能生吃。
（只有这种鱼才能生吃。）
Only this kind of fish can be eaten raw.

c. 只有常做運動，身體才會健康。
（只有常做运动，身体才会健康。）
One stays healthy only if one exercises regularly.

d. 只有耐心地看，才能挑到合適的禮物。
（只有耐心地看，才能挑到合适的礼物。）
Only if you patiently search will you be able to pick out an appropriate gift.

e. 只有在夜市 ________________________ 才 ________________________ 。
（只有在夜市 ________________________ 才 ________________________ 。）

f. 只有晚上去 ________________________ 才 ________________________ 。
（只有晚上去 ________________________ 才 ________________________ 。）

g. Only local people can set up a stall at the night market.

h. One remembers Chinese characters only if one practices them daily.

9/23/14

# 練習 Exercises

## 1. 生詞練習 Vocabulary Drills

相似詞 Match words of similar meaning from the following two columns:

| | | | | | | |
|---|---|---|---|---|---|---|
| ( ) | 1. | 夜裡 | 夜里 | a. | 各樣 | 各样 |
| ( ) | 2. | 講價 | 讲价 | b. | 選 | 选 |
| ( ) | 3. | 仿冒品 | 仿冒品 | c. | 晚上 | 晚上 |
| ( ) | 4. | 挑 | 挑 | d. | 往往 | 往往 |
| ( ) | 5. | 常常 | 常常 | e. | 假貨 | 假货 |
| ( ) | 6. | 各種 | 各种 | f. | 還價 | 还价 |

相反詞 Match opposites from the following two columns:

| | | | | | | |
|---|---|---|---|---|---|---|
| ( ) | 7. | 亂 | 乱 | a. | 不二價 | 不二价 |
| ( ) | 8. | 熱鬧 | 热闹 | b. | 小吃 | 小吃 |
| ( ) | 9. | 大餐 | 大餐 | c. | 整齊 | 整齐 |
| ( ) | 10. | 講價 | 讲价 | d. | 冷清 | 冷清 |
| ( ) | 11. | 老闆 | 老板 | e. | 顧客 | 顾客 |

## 2. 找相關詞 Related Words

Select words from the right column and put them into appropriate categories as given on the left. You can put more than one word in each category.

| | | | | | | |
|---|---|---|---|---|---|---|
| ( ) | 1. | 書籍 | 书籍 | a. | 蘋果 | 苹果 |
| | | | | b. | 乒乓 | 乒乓 |
| ( ) | 2. | 日用品 | 日用品 | c. | 迷你裙 | 迷你裙 |
| | | | | d. | 餃子 | 饺子 |
| ( ) | 3. | 衣服 | 衣服 | e. | 白兔 | 白兔 |
| | | | | f. | 京劇 | 京剧 |
| ( ) | 4. | 花草 | 花草 | g. | 課本 | 课本 |
| | | | | h. | 健美操 | 健美操 |
| ( ) | 5. | 動物 | 动物 | i. | 毛巾 | 毛巾 |
| | | | | j. | 西瓜 | 西瓜 |
| ( ) | 6. | 小吃 | 小吃 | k. | 西洋棋 | 西洋棋 |
| | | | | l. | 棒球 | 棒球 |

| | | | | | |
|---|---|---|---|---|---|
| (　　) | 7. 表演 | 表演 | | m. 貓 | 貓 |
| | | | | n. 牙刷 | 牙刷 |
| (　　) | 8. 水果 | 水果 | | o. 雜誌 | 杂志 |
| | | | | p. 牛仔褲 | 牛仔裤 |
| (　　) | 9. 遊戲 | 游戏 | | q. 玫瑰 | 玫瑰 |
| | | | | r. 衛生紙 | 卫生纸 |
| (　　) | 10. 運動 | 运动 | | s. 獅子狗 | 狮子狗 |

## 3. 填充 Fill in blanks by using the words below:

| | | | |
|---|---|---|---|
| 逛 | 逛 | 換 | 换 |
| 挑 | 挑 | 擺 | 摆 |
| 遊戲 | 游戏 | 樂趣 | 乐趣 |
| 特色 | 特色 | 在乎 | 在乎 |
| 吸引 | 吸引 | 合適 | 合适 |
| 耐心 | 耐心 | 講價 | 讲价 |
| 應有盡有 | 应有尽有 | 滿載而歸 | 满载而归 |

a. 陳先生愛看書，他最喜歡_____書店；他太太愛_____街買衣服。
（陈先生爱看书，他最喜欢_____书店；他太太爱_____街买衣服。）

b. 張小姐的書桌上________了兩三張家人的照片。
（张小姐的书桌上________了两三张家人的照片。）

c. 這家商店裡_____，從吃的穿的到用的，都可以買得到。
（这家商店里_____，从吃的穿的到用的，都可以买得到。）

d. 湖邊美麗的風景________了許多遊客。
（湖边美丽的风景________了许多游客。）

e. 那部電影，十三歲以下的小孩去看不太________。
（那部电影，十三岁以下的小孩去看不太________。）

f. 她想先回家________一件裙子再去晚上的舞會。
（她想先回家________一件裙子再去晚上的舞会。）

g. 那麼多種不同的漢英字典，我不知道該________哪本。
（那么多种不同的汉英字典，我不知道该________哪本。）

h. 這首歌很有中國音樂的________。
（这首歌很有中国音乐的________。）

i. 參加比賽的運動員對輸贏當然非常________。
（参加比赛的运动员对输赢当然非常________。）

9/23/14

j. 這件事情沒有別的方法，只有________地等。
（这件事情没有别的方法，只有________地等。）

k. 老李覺得吃是人生最大的________。
（老李觉得吃是人生最大的________。）

l. 學生一聽到老師說不要上課，要玩______，都高興得叫了起來。
（学生一听到老师说不要上课，要玩______，都高兴得叫了起来。）

m. 超市裡的貨品全部是不二價，不可以________的！
（超市里的货品全部是不二价，不可以________的！）

n. 李太太最喜歡逛夜市，每次都_________。
（李太太最喜欢逛夜市，每次都_________。）

## 4. 情況對話 Role Play

兩人一組，按照下面所說的角色和情況，編演出一段對話。
（两人一组，按照下面所说的角色和情况，编演出一段对话。）
Choose a partner and act out the following roles:

情況（一） 在遠東百貨公司裡

**Role A:**
是一位顧客。昨天去遠東百貨公司逛街。那裡大拍賣，所有的貨品都打七折。就買了一件紅色的上衣。回家以後，室友說還是太貴了，在夜市可以買到比較便宜的；而且紅色不好看。所以今天又去這家百貨公司退。

（是一位顾客。昨天去远东百货公司逛街。那里大拍卖，所有的货品都打七折。就买了一件红色的上衣。回家以后，室友说还是太贵了，在夜市可以买到比较便宜的；而且红色不好看。所以今天又去这家百货公司退。）

A customer. Yesterday, he/she went to the Far East Shopping Mall to go window-shopping. There was a clearance sale, and everything was 30% off, so the customer bought a red jacket. After he/she got home, his/her roommate said that the jacket was still too expensive and that the customer could have gotten a cheaper shirt at the night market; furthermore, red was unattractive. Today, the customer has gone back to the shopping mall to return the jacket.

**Role B:**
是公司裡的售貨員。已經在那裡做了三年了，對公司的規定知道得很清楚。打折的東西一定不能退錢，但是可以換不同的顏色或是別的東西。

（是公司里的售货员。已经在那里做了三年了，对公司的规定知道得很清楚。打折的东西一定不能退钱，但是可以换不同的颜色或是别的东西。）

A salesperson at the Far East Shopping Mall. He/she has worked there for three years, and knows the company policies very well. Sale items absolutely cannot be returned, but they can be exchanged for different colors or other items.

| | | | |
|---|---|---|---|
| 大拍賣 | 大拍卖 | dà pāimài | clearance sale |
| 打折 | 打折 | dǎzhé | to be discounted |
| 打七折 | 打七折 | dǎqīzhé | 30% off |
| 規定 | 规定 | guīdìng | rule, regulation, policy |

情況（二） 在一個夜市裡，很吵

**Role A:**
是一位顧客。看到地攤上有兩個茶壺，很喜歡。問攤販價錢，是兩百元一個。覺得太貴了！而且身上只有三百五十元，想跟老板講一講價，用三百塊買兩個。

（是一位顾客。看到地摊上有两个茶壶，很喜欢。问摊贩价钱，是两百元一个。觉得太贵了！而且身上只有三百五十元，想跟老板讲一讲价，用三百块买两个。）

A customer. He/she sees that a street vendor's stall is selling two teapots that he/she likes very much. He/she asks the vendor for the price—they are 200 yuan each. He/she feels that this is too expensive. Also, he/she only has 350 yuan on her person. He/she would like to bargain with the owner and buy both teapots for NT$300.

**Role B:**
是地攤老板。知道顧客很喜歡茶壺，告訴他是很難得找到的一種，沒有一家百貨公司裡有這種茶壺。如果買兩個可以打折。可是最低的價錢一定得在一百六十以上。

（是地摊老板。知道顾客很喜欢茶壶，告诉他是很难得找到的一种，没有一家百货公司里有这种茶壶。如果买两个可以打折。可是最低的价钱一定得在一百六十以上。）

The owner of the stall. He/she knows that the customer likes the teapots very much and tells the customer that this kind of teapot is hard to find and that no shopping malls carry this kind of teapot. If the customer is buying two teapots, he/she can get a discount. But the lowest possible price is NT$160 each.

| | | | |
|---|---|---|---|
| 茶壺 | 茶壶 | cháhú | teapots |
| 難得 | 难得 | nándé | rare; hard to come by |

## 5. 作文 Composition

請解釋美國的跳蚤市場或是舊貨店。
（请解释美国的跳蚤市场或是旧货店。）
What is a “flea market” or a “second-hand store”? Please explain in Chinese.

| | | | |
|---|---|---|---|
| 跳蚤市場 | 跳蚤市场 | tiàozǎo shìchǎng | flea market |
| 舊貨店 | 旧货店 | jiùhuò diàn | second-hand shop |
| 二手貨 | 二手货 | èrshǒu huò | second-hand goods |
| 手工藝人 | 手工艺人 | shǒugōngyìrén | handicraft artist(s) |
| 手工藝品 | 手工艺品 | shǒugōngyìpǐn | handicraft goods |
| 古董 | 古董 | gǔdǒng | antiques |

## 6. 教室活動 Suggested Classroom Activity

畫圖猜謎遊戲（画图猜谜游戏）Pictionary

依班上學生人數分成幾組，每組二到六人。給每組數張白紙（或可用黑板），讓各組學生坐在一起。每組各派一代表畫圖。老師事先從本課挑選生詞寫在小紙片上。每組代表看了紙片上的生詞後即回位畫出這個生詞。如紙上的字是『人』就畫出人形讓同組同學猜這個字。先猜到正確答案的那組就得一分。每次各組派出不同的人代表畫圖。老師也可要求學生寫出正確答案。

（依班上学生人数分成几组，每组二到六人。给每组数张白纸（或可用黑板），让各组学生坐在一起。每组各派一代表画图。老师事先从本课挑选生词写在小纸片上。每组代表看了纸片上的生词后即回位画出这个生词。如纸上的字是『人』就画出人形让同组同学猜这个字。先猜到正确答案的那组就得一分。每次各组派出不同的人代表画图。老师也可要求学生写出正确答案。）

Divide the class into several teams of from 2 to 6 students each. Each team chooses a team member who will draw first. The instructor writes different vocabulary words selected from this lesson on small pieces of paper and reveals them one at a time only to the designated drawer from each team. The drawers then draw pictures representing the words and team members try to guess what the drawing is. Whichever team comes up with the correct word first will be awarded one point. The instructor may also ask that the answers be written down in characters. Students take turns drawing.

# 補充資料 Supplementary Materials

## 1. 日用品 Daily Necessities

| 日用品 Daily Necessities | | |
|---|---|---|
| 牙刷 | yáshuā | toothbrush |
| 牙膏 | yágāo | toothpaste |
| 毛巾 | máojīn | towel |
| 面紙 | miànzhǐ | facial tissue |
| 肥皂 | féizào | soap |
| 衛生紙 | wèishēngzhǐ | toilet paper |
| 洗髮精 | xǐfǎjīng | shampoo |
| 洗衣粉 | xǐyīfěn | laundry detergent |

日用品應有盡有

## 2. 市場 Marketplaces

| 市場 shìchǎng Marketplaces | | |
|---|---|---|
| 花市 | huāshì | flower market |
| 菜市場 | càishìchǎng | food market |
| 玉市場 | yùshìchǎng | jade market |
| 超級市場 | chāojí shìchǎng | supermarket (=超市) |
| 跳蚤市場 | tiàozǎoshìchǎng | flea market |
| 股票市場 | gǔpiào shìchǎng | stock market (=股市) |

Delicious Seafood!

# 第三課

# 還是小吃好

## 繁体課文 Traditional Text

隨著一家家漢堡店、炸雞店等西式餐飲店的開張，「速食」已經成為台灣都市人非常熟悉的一種飲食方式了。其實中國人本來就常常吃速食；這種中式速食一般人叫做「小吃」。

常見的小吃有餃子、包子、春捲和各式炒麵、炒飯。另外，還有不少特別的地方小吃。不同的地區口味也有所不同，比如台灣北部的炒米粉、南部的豬腳、廣東的點心和南京的臭豆腐，都是遠近馳名的。

傳統的小吃店往往店面很小，也沒有西式速食店那麼乾淨。不過因為到處可見，既經濟又方便，很受歡迎。有時就是一個小吃攤，或是擠在小巷子裡，或是擺在路邊。只要有幾張桌子凳子和簡單的廚房用具就可以開張了。店裡的服務雖然沒有大飯館的好，但是食物的口味不比大飯館的差。像這樣的小吃店或小吃攤沒有一定的營業時間，有的除了供應三餐以外，還賣消夜，直到深夜才休息。

## 简体课文 Simplified Text

随着一家家汉堡店、炸鸡店等西式餐饮店的开张，「快餐」已经成为台湾都市人非常熟悉的一种饮食方式了。其实中国人本来就常常吃快餐；这种中式快餐一般人叫做「小吃」。

常见的小吃有饺子、包子、春卷和各式炒面、炒饭。另外，还有不少特别的地方小吃。不同的地区口味也有所不同，比如台湾北部的炒米粉、南部的猪脚、广东的点心和南京的臭豆腐，都是远近驰名的。

传统的小吃店往往店面很小，也没有西式快餐店那么干净。不过因为到处可见，既经济又方便，很受欢迎。有时就是一个小吃摊，或是挤在小巷子里，或是摆在路边。只要有几张桌子凳子和简单的厨房用具就可以开张了。店里的服务虽然没有大饭馆的好，但是食物的口味不比大饭馆的差。像这样的小吃店或小吃摊没有一定的营业时间，有的除了供应三餐以外，还卖消夜，直到深夜才休息。

## 生詞 Vocabulary

| | | | | | |
|---|---|---|---|---|---|
| 1. | 隨著 | 随着 | suízhe | *Prep.* | in pace with; along with; as |
| 2. | 漢堡 | 汉堡 | hànbǎo | *N.* | hamburger |
| 3. | 炸 | 炸 | zhá | *V.* | deep-fried |
| 4. | 等 | 等 | děng | *Part.* | and so on and so forth, etc. (=等等) |
| 5. | 餐飲店<br>餐<br>飲料<br>餐廳 | 餐饮店 | cānyǐn diàn<br>cān<br>yǐnliào<br>cāntīng | *N.*<br>*N.*<br>*N.*<br>*N.* | restaurant<br>meal<br>beverage<br>cafeteria, restaurant |
| 6. | 開張 | 开张 | kāizhāng | *Vi.* | the opening (of a new business) |

| | | | | | |
|---|---|---|---|---|---|
| 7. | 速食<br>快餐 | 速食<br>快餐 | sùshí<br>kuàicān | *N.*<br>*N.* | fast food (Taiwan usage)<br>fast food (Mainland China usage) |
| 8. | 成為 | 成为 | chéngwéi | *Vpt.* | to become |
| 9. | 熟悉 | 熟悉 | shóuxí (or shúxí) | *Vst.* | be familiar with |
| 10. | 方式 | 方式 | fāngshì | *N.* | fashion, pattern, style, way |
| 11. | 飲食 | 饮食 | yǐnshí | *N.* | food and beverages, diet |
| | 食物 | | shíwù | *N.* | food |
| 12. | 其實 | 其实 | qíshí | *Adv.* | in fact, as a matter of fact, actually |
| 13. | 包子 | 包子 | bāozi | *N.* | steamed bun (with meat and vegetable filling) |
| 14. | 春捲 | 春卷 | chūnjuǎn | *N.* | spring roll or egg roll |
| 15. | 另外 | 另外 | lìngwài | *Adv.* | in addition, furthermore |
| 16. | 地區 | 地区 | dìqū | *N.* | local; area |
| 17. | 口味<br>味道 | 口味 | kǒuwèi<br>wèidào | *N.*<br>*N.* | flavor or taste of food; a person's taste<br>flavor or taste of food; smell |
| 18. | 比如 | 比如 | bǐrú | *V.* | for example |
| 19. | 炒米粉 | 炒米粉 | chǎo mǐfěn | *N.* | stir-fried thin rice noodles |
| 20. | 豬腳 | 猪脚 | zhūjiǎo | *N.* | pig's feet |
| 21. | 臭 | 臭 | chòu | *Vs.* | stinking, smelly |
| 22. | 遠近馳名 | 远近驰名 | yuǎnjìn chímíng | *Id.* | to be known far and near; to be widely known |
| 23. | 傳統 | 传统 | chuántǒng | *Vs.* | traditional |
| 24. | 店面 | 店面 | diànmiàn | *N.* | the size or facade of a store |
| 25. | 到處可見 | 到处可见 | dàochù kějiàn | *Id.* | can be found everywhere |
| 26. | 經濟 | 经济 | jīngjì | *Vs.* | economical; *N.* economy |
| 27. | 受歡迎 | 受欢迎 | shòu huānyíng | *Vs.* | to be popular; to be well received |
| 28. | 巷子 | 巷子 | xiàngzi | *N.* | alley, lane |
| 29. | 凳子 | 凳子 | dèngzi | *N.* | stool, bench |
| 30. | 用具<br>玩具<br>文具 | 用具 | yòngjù<br>wánjù<br>wénjù | *N.*<br>*N.*<br>*N.* | utensils and appliances<br>toys<br>stationery *(See chart in "Supplementary Materials" for this lesson)* |
| 31. | 像 | 像 | xiàng | *Vst.* | such as, like |
| 32. | 營業<br>營業時間 | 营业<br>营业时间 | yíngyè<br>yíngyè shíjiān | *N.*<br>*N.* | business<br>business hours |

| | | | | | |
|---|---|---|---|---|---|
| 33. | 供應 | 供应 | gōngyìng | *V.* | to provide, to offer |
| 34. | 消夜 | 消夜 | xiāoyè | *N.* | night snack (消 here is also written as 宵) |
| 35. | 深夜 | 深夜 | shēnyè | *N.* | late at night or early morning |

# 文法 Grammar

Each pattern below is illustrated by sample sentences. When blanks are provided, complete the sentences. When English sentences are given, give Chinese counterparts.

## 1. 隨著 suízhe + (Event) + (Event): following the (event) of, as a result of

a. 隨著夏天的到來，街上賣冷飲的攤子也多起來了。
(随着夏天的到来，街上卖冷饮的摊子也多起来了。)
With the arrival of summer, stands selling cold drinks have increased.

b. 隨著學生人數的增加，今年的宿舍已經不夠了。
(随着学生人数的增加，今年的宿舍已经不够了。)
As a result of the increase in student enrollment, there are not enough dormitory spaces this year.

c. 隨著______________________________，那家電影院已經關門了。
(随着______________________________，那家电影院已经关门了。)

d. 隨著______________________________，出國旅行的人越來越多了。
(随着______________________________，出国旅行的人越来越多了。)

e. Because of the increasing popularity of mainland jade, more and more people are visiting museums.

f. As a result of the recent economic success, people are enjoying greater political freedom.

## 2. Verb + 做 zuò: (Verb) as, to be, to be called

a. 這種小吃叫做"臭豆腐"，是這家店最有名的。
(这种小吃叫做"臭豆腐"，是这家店最有名的。)
This is called "smelly tofu." It is the best-known dish of this restaurant.

b. 他的年紀最大，他同學總是把他當做自己的哥哥。
（他的年纪最大，他同学总是把他当做自己的哥哥。）
He is the oldest, so his fellow students regard him as their big brother.

c. Ms. Ding is often mistaken for Ms. Lin.

### 3. 另外 lìngwài:
**(Adv.) furthermore, additionally (frequently occurring with 還、也、又)**
**(Adj.) additional, the other, another (with optional 外 and 的)**

a. 這碗麵你先吃，我另外又叫了一碗。
（这碗面你先吃，我另外又叫了一碗。）
You have these noodles first! I've ordered another bowl.

b. 我得去銀行提錢。另外，我還得去郵局寄一封信呢！
（我得去银行提钱。另外，我还得去邮局寄一封信呢！）
I have to go to the bank to get some cash as well as the post office to mail a letter.

c. 我們有兩個校園，一個在加州北部，另（外）一個在中部。
（我们有两个校园，一个在加州北部，另（外）一个在中部。）
We have two campuses, one in northern California and the other in central California.

d. 湯在這家叫，菜到另外的買。
（汤在这家叫，菜到另外的买。）
Let's get the soup from this restaurant and the other dishes from another one.

e. His other sister is still a college student.

f. The owner of this bookshop has a bookshop at another university.

### 4. 所 suǒ +Verb:
*This grammatical element from classical Chinese is still often used in formal writings, occurring in front of verbal elements. It is best understood as a verbal marker and not to be translated as a concrete term in English. The combinations 有所 and 所有的 are common, and 所 also occurs frequently with relative clauses.*

a. 他把所有的錢都拿去買房地產了。
（他把所有的钱都拿去买房地产了。）
He put all his money into the real estate business.

b. 現在你所看見的，只是這個學校的一部分。
（现在你所看见的，只是这个学校的一部分。）
What you see now is only a portion of this school.

c. 據我所知，________________________________________。
（据我所知，________________________________________。）

d. 我所說的都是 ____________________________________。
（我所说的都是 ____________________________________。）

e. He wrote a report on what he experienced in China last year.

f. What you heard is only half the truth（真相）.

## 5. 直到...才 zhídào ... cái: not until ... (then) ...

*(The adv 直 is optional and gives an additional sense of "without interruption.")*

a. 昨天晚上小王在公司加班，直到天亮才回家。
（昨天晚上小王在公司加班，直到天亮才回家。）
Xiao Wang worked overtime in his office last night and didn't go home until the following morning.

b. 直到上了飛機，他才想起來他忘了帶照像機。
（直到上了飞机，他才想起来他忘了带照像机。）
It didn't occur to him that he had forgotten his camera until he was already on the airplane.

c. 直到十七歲，______________________________________。
（直到十七岁，______________________________________。）

d. 直到我去了中國，__________________________________。
（直到我去了中国，__________________________________。）

e. He had never left home until he went to college.

f. Some stores in big cities stay open till 11 p.m.

## 6. 可 kě +(Verb): can be (Verb)-ed; (V.)-ful/-able

| | | | | | |
|---|---|---|---|---|---|
| 可愛 | 可爱 | lovable, lovely | 可口 | 可口 | palatable; tasty |
| 可靠 | 可靠 | reliable | 可笑 | 可笑 | laughable, ridiculous |
| 可憐 | 可怜 | pitiful, pitiable | 可見 | 可见 | visible; one can see that ...; it is apparent that ... |

a. 那道菜，一到中午就賣完了，可見多受歡迎。
（那道菜，一到中午就卖完了，可见多受欢迎。）
That dish gets sold out by noon every day, so you can see how popular it is.

b. 明天的晚會你不能來參加，實在太可惜了。
（明天的晚会你不能来参加，实在太可惜了。）
It's too bad you can't come to the party tomorrow.

c. 可靠的人______________________________________________。
（可靠的人______________________________________________。）

d. ______________________________________________的人最可憐。
（______________________________________________的人最可怜。）

### 7. 既 . . . 又 . . . jì ... yòu ...: not merely ..., but ... as well

(*Note that while* 又 . . . 又 . . . *conjoins two more or less equal states,* B *in* '既 A 又 B' *is in a more intensive state than* A.)

a. 大城市裡的人既不友善又不可靠。
（大城市里的人既不友善又不可靠。）
People in large cities are not only unfriendly but are unreliable as well.

b. 住在宿舍裡，既不經濟又不方便。
（住在宿舍里，既不经济又不方便。）
Living in the dorm is neither economical nor convenient.

c. 清早去公園運動，既可呼吸新鮮空氣又可認識不少新朋友。
（清早去公园运动，既可呼吸新鲜空气又可认识不少新朋友。）
You should exercise in the park early in the morning. You'll not only get some fresh air but a chance to meet new friends.

d. 這樣的速食店，越來越受歡迎，因為他們賣的東西，既便宜又可口。
（这样的速食店，越来越受欢迎，因为他们卖的东西，既便宜又可口。）
Fast-food restaurants like this one are getting more and more popular because what they sell is both inexpensive and tasty.

e. 在小攤上吃速食，______________________________________。
（在小摊上吃速食，______________________________________。）

f. 每天大吃大喝，________________________________________。
（每天大吃大喝，________________________________________。）

10/23/KT

# 練習 Exercises

## 1. 寫出音似異義詞 Give Near-Homophonous Words

例 EXAMPLE: yanjing → 眼鏡 眼镜 yǎnjìng: glasses
眼睛 眼睛 yǎnjīng: eyes

a. zhujiao →

b. shuijiao →

c. jingji →

d. jiandan →

e. chuantong →

## 2. 請問在什麼地方可以進行下面各個動作？

Write down a place or location where the following action usually occurs:

例 EXAMPLE: 念書 → 圖書館 （念书 → 图书馆）

a. 吃漢堡 吃汉堡 →

b. 炒米粉 炒米粉 →

c. 玩水球 玩水球 →

d. 買便宜東西 买便宜东西 →

e. 和朋友吃消夜 和朋友吃消夜 →

f. 休息 休息 →

g. 散步 散步 →

h. 換錢 换钱 →

i. 擺攤子 摆摊子 →

## 3. 填充 Fill in the blank with the most appropriate word of the given choices:

a. 動物的表演很 ______ 小朋友們的歡迎。
（动物的表演很 ______ 小朋友们的欢迎。）

1)被 （被） 2)對 （对） 3)受 （受） 4)把 （把）

b. 王老板的臭豆腐已經______夜市裡最吸引人的小吃了！
（王老板的臭豆腐已经______夜市里最吸引人的小吃了！）

1)可見 （可见） 2)成為 (成为) 3)熟悉 （熟悉） 4)叫做 （叫做）

c. 那家店星期天就只營業半天，中午就______。
（那家店星期天就只营业半天，中午就______。）

1)停業 （停业） 2)關門 （关门） 3)開張 （开张） 4)休息 （休息）

d. 這家餐廳______各種西式餐飲，漢堡、炸雞他們都有。
（这家餐厅______各种西式餐饮，汉堡、炸鸡他们都有。）

1) 應有盡有 （应有尽有） 2) 買不到 （买不到）
3) 供應 （供应） 4) 有所不同 （有所不同）

e. 台灣菜的_____比較重，常常放很多佐料，比如鹽、醬油和味精，都用得多。
（台湾菜的_____比较重，常常放很多佐料，比如盐、酱油和味精，都用得多。）

1)口味 （口味） 2)用具 （用具） 3)方式 （方式） 4)品質 （品质）

f. 杭州西湖風景的美麗是____的，就是沒去過的人一定也聽過。
（杭州西湖风景的美丽是____的，就是没去过的人一定也听过。）

1) 到處可見 （到处可见） 2) 遠近馳名 （远近驰名）
3) 人山人海 （人山人海） 4) 有名無實 （有名无实）

g. 京劇在台灣又叫平劇或國劇，是一種中國_____的音樂表演。
（京剧在台湾又叫平剧或国剧，是一种中国_____的音乐表演。）

1)特色（特色） 2)口味 （口味） 3)傳統 （传统） 4)熱鬧（热闹）

h. 小林______打算參加昨晚的舞會，後來家裡有事所以沒去。
（小林______打算参加昨晚的舞会，后来家里有事所以没去。）

1)本來 （本来） 2)另外（另外） 3)這樣 （这样） 4)往往 （往往）

i. 小吃攤上買的包子______要比大飯館裡做得好吃的多！
（小吃摊上买的包子______要比大饭馆里做得好吃的多！）

1)雖然 （虽然） 2)沒有（没有） 3)或是（或是） 4)其實 （其实）

j. ______是住在這條巷子裡的人，跟巷口賣豬腳的陳老板都很熟。
（______是住在这条巷子里的人，跟巷口卖猪脚的陈老板都很熟。）

1)隨著（随着） 2)只要（只要） 3)比如（比如） 4)不過（不过）

## 4. 閱讀及寫作練習 Reading Comprehension and Writing Exercises

**A.** Answer the following questions based on the notice below:

> **包餃子晚會**
>
> 歡迎今年新來的同學，下星期六晚五時在大學餐廳舉行一年一次的新生包餃子晚會。晚會上餐廳將供應包餃子的材料和各種飲料，各人包自己的餃子，多吃多包，少吃少包，餐廳廚房的服務人員負責煮餃子。歡迎所有的同學和老師都來參加。門票每人五元，在大學書店預售。

> **包饺子晚会**
>
> 欢迎今年新来的同学，下星期六晚五时在大学餐厅举行一年一次的新生包饺子晚会。晚会上餐厅将供应包饺子的材料和各种饮料，各人包自己的饺子，多吃多包，少吃少包，餐厅厨房的服务人员负责煮饺子。欢迎所有的同学和老师都来参加。门票每人五元，在大学书店预售。

| | | | |
|---|---|---|---|
| 舉行 | 举行 | jǔxíng | to hold (a meeting) |
| 材料 | 材料 | cáiliào | ingredients |
| 負責 | 负责 | fùzé | to be responsible for |
| 預售 | 预售 | yùshòu | to sell in advance |

a. 為什麼要舉行包餃子晚會呢？
（为什么要举行包饺子晚会呢？）

b. 誰可以去參加？
（谁可以去参加？）

c. 如果你打算去，得預備什麼東西？
（如果你打算去，得预备什么东西？）

d. 買了票去參加的人，一定得會做什麼才能吃到餃子？
（买了票去参加的人，一定得会做什么才能吃到饺子？）

**B.** 請寫一個聚餐的通知，說明時間、地點，並計畫聚餐的菜式（主菜、肉、蔬菜、麵、飯、湯、點心和水果等）及飲料，請參加聚餐的人各預備一樣。
（请写一个聚餐的通知，说明时间、地点，并计画聚餐的菜式（主菜、肉、蔬菜、面、饭、汤、点心和水果等）及饮料，请参加聚餐的人各预备一样。）
Compose a flyer to be circulated among friends regarding a potluck party. Indicate the time, place, and purpose for the gathering, and also list the dishes, desserts, and beverages to be prepared by each guest.

## 5. 食譜 Recipe

下面是一個鍋貼的食譜，可是作法的先後順序錯了，請寫出正確的順序。
（下面是一个锅贴的食谱，可是作法的先后顺序错了，请写出正确的顺序。）
You would like to make some "pot-sticker" dumplings according to the following recipe, but unfortunately, the instructions are not in the proper order. List the instructions in their proper order.

《 鍋貼 guōtiē 五十個 》

材料 Ingredients:

| | | | |
|---|---|---|---|
| | 絞肉 | 12 | 兩 |
| （1） | 麻油 | 6 | 大匙 |
| （1） | 糖 | 2 | 小匙 |
| （1） | 鹽 | 3/4 | 小匙 |
| （1） | 胡椒粉 | 1/4 | 小匙 |
| | 包心菜 | 12 | 兩 |
| | 蔥 | 4 | 兩 |
| | 水餃皮 | 50 | 張 |
| | 鹽 | 1 | 小匙 |

步驟 Steps:

a. 包餃子。
b. 蔥切碎，把所有的材料拌在一起。
c. 鍋裡放油，燒熱。
d. 絞肉加（1）料。
e. 把餃子放鍋裡，用小火煎一分鐘。
f. 加半杯水，蓋上鍋蓋，用中火煮六分鐘，拿出來。
g. 把包心菜切碎，加一小匙鹽，十五分鐘後擠水。

生詞：

| | | | |
|---|---|---|---|
| 絞肉 | 绞肉 | jiǎoròu | ground meat |
| 麻油 | 麻油 | máyóu | sesame oil |
| 胡椒粉 | 胡椒粉 | hújiāofěn | black pepper |
| 包心菜 | 包心菜 | bāoxīncài | cabbage |
| 蔥 | 葱 | cōng | green onion |
| 皮 | 皮 | pí | dumpling skin |
| 兩 | 两 | liǎng | measurement (12 兩= 1 lb.) |
| 匙 | 匙 | chí | spoon (小匙 teaspoon; 大匙 tablespoon) |
| 切 | 切 | qiē | to cut (切碎 qiēsuì; to chop) |
| 拌 | 拌 | bàn | to mix, to stir |
| 鍋 | 鍋 | guō | large pan or wok |
| 蓋 | 蓋 | gài | to cover; lid |

正確的順序是 **The proper order is:** ___/___/___/___/___/___/___

## 6. 作文 Composition

請寫一寫你吃過最奇怪最難忘的一個菜。
（请写一写你吃过最奇怪最难忘的一个菜。）
What is the most unusual and unforgettable food you have ever eaten?

## 7. 教室活動 Suggested Classroom Activities

比手畫腳遊戲 Charades

把班上學生分為兩組比賽。讓每組學生坐在一起討論，寫出幾個生詞、片語或是短句作為給對方的題目。題目準備好了先讓老師過目確定無誤後，每組輪流派出一個代表，由對方的幾個題目中抽出一個，用比手畫腳的方式把這個題目表演出來，讓同組的同學猜。記住，表演的代表不可說話或發出任何聲音來。在一定的時間內（老師可依情況定一分鐘或一分半）猜出正確答案即可得一分。然後換另一組做表演和猜題。題目不一定非得寫出，可用口述。

（把班上学生分为两组比赛。让每组学生坐在一起讨论，写出几个生词、片语或是短句作为给对方的题目。题目准备好了先让老师过目确定无误后，每组轮流派出一个代表，由对方的几个题目中抽出一个，用比手画脚的方式把这个题目表演出来，让同组的同学猜。记住，表演的代表不可说话或发出任何声音来。在一定的时间内（老师可依情况定一分钟或一分半）猜出正确答案即可得一分。然后换另一组做表演和猜题。题目不一定非得写出，可用口述。）

Divide the class into two teams. The instructor gives different words from this lesson to alternating representatives from each team. The representative then acts out the word. If his or her teammates can guess the word within a given time period, say one minute, that team gets one point. Talking, of course, is not allowed.

## 補充資料 Supplementary Materials

### 1. 早餐 Breakfast

| 早餐 zǎocān Breakfast | | |
|---|---|---|
| 豆漿 | dòujiāng | soybean milk |
| 燒餅 | shāobǐng | sesame seed pancake |
| 油條 | yóutiáo | twisted fried dough |
| 包子 | bāozi | steamed filled bun |
| 饅頭 | mántóu | steamed bun |
| 稀飯 | xīfàn | rice porridge |

Fried Dough 燒餅油條

### 2. 餐具 Tableware

| 餐具 cānjù Tableware | | |
|---|---|---|
| 刀子 | dāozi | knife （把） |
| 叉子 | chāzi | fork （把） |
| 湯匙 | tāngchí | spoon （把） |
| 盤子 | pánzi | plate （個） |
| 碗 | wǎn | bowl （個） |
| 筷子 | kuàizi | chopsticks （雙） |
| 餐巾 | cānjīn | napkin （張） |

## 3. 食物相剋 Conflicting Properties of Foods

| 食物相剋表 Foods with Conflicting Properties | | |
|---|---|---|
| 同時食用 *Combinations* | 結果 *Result* | 解法 *Remedy* |
| 蔥和蜜 scallion & honey | 中毒 poison | 綠豆 green beans |
| 菠菜和牛奶 spinach & milk | 瀉肚 diarrhea | 綠豆 green beans |
| 蝦和南瓜 shrimps & pumpkin | 瀉肚 diarrhea | 黑豆或甘草 black beans |
| 柿子和酒 persimmon & liquor | 中毒 poison | 綠豆 green beans |

## 4. 食物的冷熱 Special Properties of Foods

| 食物的冷熱 Special Properties of Foods | | |
|---|---|---|
| 潤 rùn | 保留水份 | 鳳梨，牛奶，蘋果 |
| 燥 zào | 助水份排出 | 螃蟹，蕃茄，雞肉 |
| 涼 liáng | 對身體有鎮靜清涼作用 | 西瓜，芒果，蜂蜜 |
| 溫 wēn | 使身體興奮增加活力 | 牛肉，花生，核桃 |
| 瀉 xiè | 將病毒排出 | 大蒜，梨，茶 |
| 補 bǔ | 增加體力和元氣 | 人參，蝦，鰻魚 |

## 5. 小吃分類 Chinese Snacks

民俗小吃大約可分成以下幾類：

1） 海鮮類：天婦羅，土托魚湯，虱目魚粥，蚵仔煎等。

2） 肉禽類：當歸雞，道口雞，醉雞，火雞肉飯，鴨賞，鴨頭，鹹水鴨等。

3） 畜肉類：羊肉爐，排骨酥，豬腳麵線，豬血湯，大腸湯，肉圓，貢丸，牛肉麵等。

4） 麵食類：新竹炒米粉，鱔魚意麵，擔仔麵，棺材板，肉粽，陽春麵，餛飩湯等。

5） 豆食類：臭豆腐，大溪豆乾，豆漿，豆腐乳，豆皮湯，豆瓣醬等。

6） 糕點類：花生糖，牛舌餅，太陽餅，麥芽糖，龍鬚糖，鳳梨酥，芝麻豬油恠等。

7） 飲料類：冰桔茶，木瓜牛奶，芋頭冰，酸梅冰，彎豆冰，楊桃汁等。

# 6. 傳統小吃 Traditional Snacks

大腸香腸，加上大蒜 Chinese Hot Dogs

Cold Drinks and Ices

# 第 四 課

# 茶 與 中 國 人

## 繁体課文 Traditional Text

茶是中國人傳統的日常飲料，茶葉幾乎是每個家庭都必備的。中國人講究品茶；喝茶不只是解渴，而且是一種享受，一種藝術。首先選擇茶葉就是一門學問。中國茶的種類五花八門，常見的如紅茶、清茶、香片、烏龍茶等，都各有各的味道。

近幾年來流行用茶袋泡茶，方便是方便，然而這對一般中國人來說絕不是喝好茶的方法。就好像會喝咖啡的人不喝即溶咖啡，非得用剛磨好的咖啡來煮不可。懂得喝茶的不但重視泡茶的方式、時間、次數，而且對茶具也十分講究。各式各樣的茶杯、茶壺，除了實用以外，也有非常高的藝術價值。

在現代化的中國社會，雖然不少人開始享受喝咖啡的樂趣，街頭上到處也可以看見咖啡店；但是在中國人的心目中，茶還是最佳飲料。古色古香的茶藝館也很適合一個人品茶、看書，或是和三兩好友喝茶、聊天。飲茶文化也從家庭走入街頭了。

## 简体课文 Simplified Text

茶是中国人传统的日常饮料，茶叶几乎是每个家庭都必备的。中国人讲究品茶；喝茶不只是解渴，而且是一种享受，一种艺术。首先选择茶叶就是一门学问。中国茶的种类五花八门，常见的如红茶、清茶、香片、乌龙茶等，都各有各的味道。

近几年来流行用茶袋泡茶，方便是方便，然而这对一般中国人来说绝不是喝好茶的方法。就好像会喝咖啡的人不喝速溶咖啡，非得用刚磨好的咖啡来煮不可。懂得喝茶的不但重视泡茶的方式、时间、次数，而且对茶具也十分讲究。各式各样的茶杯、茶壶，除了实用以外，也有非常高的艺术价值。

在现代化的中国社会，虽然不少人开始享受喝咖啡的乐趣，街头上到处也可以看见咖啡店；但是在中国人的心目中，茶还是最佳饮料。古色古香的茶艺馆也很适合一个人品茶、看书，或是和三两好友喝茶、聊天。饮茶文化也从家庭走入街头了。

## 生詞 Vocabulary

| | | | | | |
|---|---|---|---|---|---|
| 1. | 與 | 与 | yǔ | *Conj.* | and (usually used as a written style) |
| 2. | 茶葉 | 茶叶 | cháyè | *N.* | tea leaves |
| 3. | 幾乎 | 几乎 | jīhū | *Adv.* | almost; nearly |
| 4. | 家庭 | 家庭 | jiātíng | *N.* | family |
| 5. | 必備<br>必須<br>準備 | 必备 | bìbèi<br>bìxū<br>zhǔnbèi | *Vs-attr.*<br>*Vaux.*<br>*V.* | indispensable, essential<br>must, have to, necessarily<br>to prepare |
| 6. | 講究 | 讲究 | jiǎngjiù | *Vst.* | to be particular or meticulous (about something); expensive and exquisite |

| | | | | | |
|---|---|---|---|---|---|
| 7. | 品茶 | 品茶 | pǐnchá | *V-sep.* | to drink tea properly |
| 8. | 解渴 | 解渴 | jiěkě | *Vs.* | to quench one's thirst |
| 9. | 享受 | 享受 | xiǎngshòu | *Vst.* | to enjoy, enjoyment |
| 10. | 藝術 | 艺术 | yìshù | *N.* | art |
| 11. | 首先 | 首先 | shǒuxiān | *Adv.* | first of all |
| 12. | 選擇 | 选择 | xuǎnzé | *V.* | to choose, to select |
| 13. | 門 | 门 | mén | *M.* | measure word (for 學問、功課) |
| 14. | 學問 | 学问 | xuéwèn | *N.* | special knowledge, scholarship |
| 15. | 種類 | 种类 | zhǒnglèi | *N.* | varieties |
| 16. | 五花八門 | 五花八门 | wǔhuā bāmén | *Id.* | abundant (in many varieties) |
| 17. | 清茶 | 清茶 | qīngchá | *N.* | green tea |
| 18. | 香片茶 | 香片茶 | xiāngpiàn | *N.* | jasmine tea |
| 19. | 烏龍茶 | 乌龙茶 | wūlóngchá | *N.* | Oolong tea |
| 20. | 泡 | 泡 | pào | *V.* | to brew, to soak something in liquid |
| 21. | 茶袋 | 茶袋 | chádài | *N.* | tea bag |
| 22. | 絕不<br>絕對 | 绝不 | juébù<br>juéduì | *Adv.*<br>*Adv.* | absolutely not<br>absolutely, definitely |
| 23. | 即溶咖啡<br>速溶咖啡 | 即溶咖啡<br>速溶咖啡 | jíróng kāfēi<br>sùróng kāfēi | *N.*<br>*N.* | instant coffee (Taiwan usage)<br>instant coffee (Mainland China usage) |
| 24. | 磨 | 磨 | mó | *V.* | to grind |
| 25. | 重視 | 重视 | zhòngshì | *Vst.* | to pay attention to, consider important |
| 26. | 次數 | 次数 | cìshù | *N.* | number of times |
| 27. | 各式各樣 | 各式各样 | gèshì gèyàng | *Id.* | various kinds of |
| 28. | 壺 | 壶 | hú | *N.* | (tea) pot |
| 29. | 實用 | 实用 | shíyòng | *Vs.* | practical |
| 30. | 價值 | 价值 | jiàzhí | *N.* | value |
| 31. | 現代化<br>現代 | 现代化 | xiàndài huà<br>xiàndài | *Vs.*<br>*N.* | modernized<br>modern times; *Vp.* ...化 huà; -ized |
| 32. | 社會 | 社会 | shèhuì | *N.* | society |
| 33. | 街頭 | 街头 | jiētóu | *N.* | street corner; street |
| 34. | 心目 | 心目 | xīnmù | *N.* | mind; mind's eye; feelings |
| 35. | 最佳 | 最佳 | zuìjiā | *Vs-attr.* | the best |
| 36. | 古色古香 | 古色古香 | gǔsè gǔxiāng | *Id.* | quaint; having an antique air |
| 37. | 茶藝館 | 茶艺馆 | cháyì guǎn | *N.* | tea shop, tea house |
| 38. | 適合 | 适合 | shìhé | *Vst.* | to serve as ... nicely; suitable for |

| | | | | | |
|---|---|---|---|---|---|
| 39. | 聊天 | 聊天 | liáotiān | *V-sep.* | to chat; shoot the breeze |
| 40. | 文化 | 文化 | wénhuà | *N.* | culture |
| 41. | 入 | 入 | rù | *V.* | to enter; into (classical Chinese) |

## 文法 Grammar

Each pattern below is illustrated by sample sentences. When blanks are provided, complete the sentences. When English sentences are provided, give Chinese counterparts.

### 1. 幾乎 jīhū: (Adv.) almost, nearly

a. 她高興得幾乎說不出話來。
(她高兴得几乎说不出话来。)
She was so pleased she could hardly utter a word.

b. 我們對這件事情的看法幾乎完全一樣。
(我们对这件事情的看法几乎完全一样。)
Our views on this are almost identical.

c. 懂得喝茶的人，________________________________。
(懂得喝茶的人，________________________________。)

d. 他起得太晚，________________________________。
(他起得太晚，________________________________。)

e. Almost everyone in our class has had jasmine tea before.

f. Mary was so depressed she couldn't sleep (almost) all night.

### 2. 各 gè: (Adv.) each

*Cf.* 個個 gège: *(Adv.) each and every*
彼此 bǐcǐ: *(Adv.) each other; mutually*
"你...我，我...你" *(Adv.) "They ... each other"*

a. 逛完夜市，他們就各回各的宿舍了。
(逛完夜市，他们就各回各的宿舍了。)
After visiting the night market, each went back to his own dorm.

b. 年輕人各有各的看法，父母應該尊重他們的意見。
(年轻人各有各的看法，父母应该尊重他们的意见。)
Young people have their own ways of seeing things, and their parents ought to respect their views.

c. 懂得喝茶的人，個個都講究茶具。
（懂得喝茶的人，个个都讲究茶具。）
Of people who understand tea, each and every one is fussy about tea sets.

d. 那條街上的攤子，他個個都熟悉。
（那条街上的摊子，他个个都熟悉。）
He knows each one of the stands along that street.

e. 這是他們第一次見面，彼此還不太熟悉。
（这是他们第一次见面，彼此还不太熟悉。）
This is the first time they've met, so they don't feel familiar with each other yet.

f. 一起工作的人應該彼此信任。
（一起工作的人应该彼此信任。）
There should be mutual trust among colleagues.

g. 他們兩個人，你擠我，我擠你，誰也不肯讓。
（他们两个人，你挤我，我挤你，谁也不肯让。）
They pushed and jostled each other. Neither one wanted to yield.

h. 等公共汽車的人，你推我，我推你，每個人都想先上車。
（等公共汽车的人，你推我，我推你，每个人都想先上车。）
Those who had been waiting for the bus pushed each other; each one wanted to board first.

i. Each of our teachers has his/her own way of teaching.

j. In order to save time, let's each drive our own cars.

## 3. (Time Phrase) + 來: (Ever) since + (Time)

a. 一九八〇年來，亞洲在工業上、經濟上都有很大的改變。
（一九八〇年来，亚洲在工业上、经济上都有很大的改变。）
Asia has experienced great industrial and economic changes since 1980.

b. 這三個月來，我認識了不少新朋友。
（这三个月来，我认识了不少新朋友。）
I've made many new friends over the last three months.

c. 最近幾年來，重視生活享受的人越來越多。
（最近几年来，重视生活享受的人越来越多。）
These last few years have seen an increase in those who care about enjoying life.

d. 近幾年來，中國 ________________________________ 。
（近几年来，中国 ________________________________ 。）

e. ______________________，他的中文水準提高了許多。
（______________________，他的中文水准提高了许多。）

f. My teacher's English has improved a lot over the last nine months.

g. I've been busy writing a report these last two months.

## 4. 然而 **rán'ér: (Conj.) however; on the other hand**

*(This is a literary counterpart of* 可是 *or* 不過*.)*

a. 街道兩旁燈火通明，然而不見行人。
（街道两旁灯火通明，然而不见行人。）
Both sides of the street are brightly lit, but no pedestrians can be seen.

b. 這個古茶壺非常實用，然而藝術價值不高。
（这个古茶壶非常实用，然而艺术价值不高。）
This old teapot is very useful, but its artistic value is not high.

c. 他很努力學習，然而 ________________________________ 。
（他很努力学习，然而 ________________________________ 。）

d. ____________________________，然而茶葉的價錢還是很高。
（____________________________，然而茶叶的价钱还是很高。）

e. It's been raining every day in the north, but the water shortage in the south is still serious.

f. There are several department stores in the city, but most people still shop at the night market.

## 5. 對 . . . 來說 **duì ... láishuō: with regard to; as far as ... is concerned**

a. 對講究穿的人來說，顏色並不是最重要的。
（对讲究穿的人来说，颜色并不是最重要的。）
Color is not the most important concern of those who are particular about clothing.

b. 接到家信，對在外國念書的人來說，是最讓他們高興的事。
（接到家信，对在外国念书的人来说，是最让他们高兴的事。）
Nothing makes those studying in a foreign country happier than getting letters from home.

c. A: 我覺得用茶袋泡茶既方便又乾淨，你覺得怎麼樣？
（我觉得用茶袋泡茶既方便又乾净，你觉得怎么样？）
B: ____________________________________________ 。

d. A: 傳統的小吃店又經濟又好吃，你覺得呢？
（传统的小吃店又经济又好吃，你觉得呢？）
B: ____________________________________________ 。

e. ____________________________________________，非常不方便。
（____________________________________________，非常不方便。）

f. ____________________________________________，絕對沒有問題。
（____________________________________________，绝对没有问题。）

g. As far as Chinese people are concerned, tea is the most popular beverage.

h. As far as the students are concerned, a swimming pool is more important than a language lab.

### 6. 非...不可 fēi ... bùkě: it is imperative that ...

a. 想看藝術價值高的畫，非到法國的博物館去不可。
（想看艺术价值高的画，非到法国的博物馆去不可。）
If you want to view paintings of high artistic value, visiting museums in France is a must.

b. 享受喝好茶的樂趣非得先懂得選擇好茶葉不可。
（享受喝好茶的乐趣非得先懂得选择好茶叶不可。）
To enjoy the pleasure of drinking good tea, one must first learn how to select good tea leaves.

c. 你要是去台灣，＿＿＿＿＿＿＿＿＿＿＿＿＿＿＿＿＿＿＿＿。
（你要是去台湾，＿＿＿＿＿＿＿＿＿＿＿＿＿＿＿＿＿＿＿＿。）

d. 如果你想多了解外國文化，＿＿＿＿＿＿＿＿＿＿＿＿＿＿＿＿。
（如果你想多了解外国文化，＿＿＿＿＿＿＿＿＿＿＿＿＿＿＿＿。）

e. Since you majored in geography, a trip to mainland China is a must.

f. It's imperative that we receive your payment before the first of next month.

### 7. 在...（心目）中 zài ... (xīnmù) zhōng: in the eyes/mind of; from the perspective of ...

a. 在學生心目中，他是少有的好老師。
（在学生心目中，他是少有的好老师。）
In the eyes of the students, he is a rare example of a good teacher.

b. 沒有人能代替王小姐在他心目中的地位。
（没有人能代替王小姐在他心目中的地位。）
Nobody can take Ms. Wang's place in his heart.

c. 在藝術家眼中，廣告畫的藝術價值很低。
（在艺术家眼中，广告画的艺术价值很低。）
In the eyes of artists, commercial art has little value.

d. 在父母的眼中，兒女永遠是未成年的孩子。
（在父母的眼中，儿女永远是未成年的孩子。）
Children are always children in the eyes of their parents.

e. ＿＿＿＿＿＿＿＿＿＿＿＿＿＿＿＿是年輕人心目中的偶像 (idol)。
（＿＿＿＿＿＿＿＿＿＿＿＿＿＿＿＿是年轻人心目中的偶像 (idol)。）

f. 在美國人的心目中，日本車＿＿＿＿＿＿＿＿＿＿＿＿＿＿＿＿。
（在美国人的心目中，日本车＿＿＿＿＿＿＿＿＿＿＿＿＿＿＿＿。）

# 練習 Exercises

## 1. 生詞練習 Vocabulary Drills

相似詞 Match words of similar meaning from the following two columns:

| | | | | | |
|---|---|---|---|---|---|
| ( ) | 1. | 幾乎 | 几乎 | a. 然而 | 然而 |
| ( ) | 2. | 談話 | 谈话 | b. 傳統 | 传统 |
| ( ) | 3. | 但是 | 但是 | c. 差不多 | 差不多 |
| ( ) | 4. | 和 | 和 | d. 聊天 | 聊天 |
| ( ) | 5. | 古色古香 | 古色古香 | e. 與 | 与 |

相反詞 Match opposites from the following two columns:

| | | | | | |
|---|---|---|---|---|---|
| ( ) | 6. | 出 | 出 | a. 一個人 | 一个人 |
| ( ) | 7. | 首先 | 首先 | b. 不受歡迎 | 不受欢迎 |
| ( ) | 8. | 流行 | 流行 | c. 沒想到 | 没想到 |
| ( ) | 9. | 傳統 | 传统 | d. 入 | 入 |
| ( ) | 10. | 重視 | 重视 | e. 最後 | 最后 |
| ( ) | 11. | 一起 | 一起 | f. 現代化 | 现代化 |

## 2. 找相關詞 Related Words

Select words from the right column and put them into appropriate categories as given on the left. You can put more than one word in each category.

| | | | | | |
|---|---|---|---|---|---|
| ( ) | 1. | 茶具 | 茶具 | a. 鍋 | 锅 |
| | | | | b. 苦 | 苦 |
| | | | | c. 咖啡 | 咖啡 |
| ( ) | 2. | 廚房用具 | 厨房用具 | d. 茶盤 | 茶盘 |
| | | | | e. 烏龍 | 乌龙 |
| | | | | f. 辣 | 辣 |
| ( ) | 3. | 藝術 | 艺术 | g. 香片 | 香片 |
| | | | | h. 京劇 | 京剧 |
| | | | | i. 菜刀 | 菜刀 |
| ( ) | 4. | 飲料 | 饮料 | j. 啤酒 | 啤酒 |
| | | | | k. 酸 | 酸 |
| | | | | l. 奶茶 | 奶茶 |
| ( ) | 5. | 茶葉 | 茶叶 | m. 香 | 香 |
| | | | | n. 茶壺 | 茶壶 |
| | | | | o. 礦泉水 | 矿泉水 |
| ( ) | 6. | 味道 | 味道 | p. 品茶 | 品茶 |

## 3. 填充 Fill in the blanks with appropriate words taken from this lesson (one character per space):

a. 這壺茶____得太久了，味道很濃，喝的時候得多加一點兒水。
（这壶茶____得太久了，味道很浓，喝的时候得多加一点儿水。）

b. 喝汽水一點也不______渴，還是喝白開水最好。
（喝汽水一点也不______渴，还是喝白开水最好。）

c. 張先生雖然對住和穿都非常隨便，但是對吃卻十分____ ____。
（张先生虽然对住和穿都非常随便，但是对吃却十分____ ____。）

d. 這裡是出口，我們要進去得到______口去。
（这里是出口，我们要进去得到______口去。）

e. 小李剛到美國去，因為語言和____ ____的不同，常常鬧出笑話。
（小李刚到美国去，因为语言和____ ____的不同，常常闹出笑话。）

f. 這樣的音樂一年前很_______ ______，可是現在已經沒人聽了！
（这样的音乐一年前很_______ ______，可是现在已经没人听了！）

g. 要喝好茶，______ 得現泡不可。
（要喝好茶，______ 得现泡不可。）

h. 在中國人的______ ______中，家庭往往是最重要的。
（在中国人的______ ______ 中，家庭往往是最重要的。）

i. 他們打算去海邊過周末，_______ ______一下夏天戲水的樂趣。
（他们打算去海边过周末，_______ ______一下夏天戏水的乐趣。）

j. 沒有______ ______價值的電影，張教授是絕對不看的。
（没有______ ______价值的电影，张教授是绝对不看的。）

## 4. 閱讀練習 Reading Comprehension

請依照下面的短文，講出泡老人茶的正確步驟，可以分組進行討論，每組三到四人。各組報告時，組員輪流説明先後步驟。
（请依照下面的短文，讲出泡老人茶的正确步骤，可以分组进行讨论，每组三到四人。各组报告时，组员轮流说明先后步骤。）

After reading the following passage, the class splits up into several groups of from three to four students each. After some discussion, each group member takes a turn explaining part of the procedure involved in making traditional Chinese tea.

昨天朋友帶我去一家茶藝館喝老人茶。老人茶是台灣很流行的一種品茶方式。首先，服務小姐請我們選擇茶葉。我什麼中國茶都沒喝過，所以朋友點了很有名的烏龍茶。服務小姐拿了一個很大的茶盤，上面放了一個小茶壺、兩個極小的茶杯和一包茶葉。她先把茶壺和茶杯用熱開水燙了一遍，然後把那包茶葉打開，拿了一半放在小茶壺裡再加入熱水。她告訴我們，第一次泡的茶太淡，不要喝，倒掉再加水泡第二次。我等得口渴死了，所以茶一泡好，我就拿起小茶杯，一口氣就喝完了。哎呀！沒想到這麼燙！不過茶的味道很香很濃。我們喝了幾乎三個小時才離開。

（昨天朋友带我去一家茶艺馆喝老人茶。老人茶是台湾很流行的一种品茶方式。首先，服务小姐请我们选择茶叶。我什么中国茶都没喝过，所以朋友点了很有名的乌龙茶。服务小姐拿了一个很大的茶盘，上面放了一个小茶壶、两个极小的茶杯和一包茶叶。她先把茶壶和茶杯用热开水烫了一遍，然后把那包茶叶打开，拿了一半放在小茶壶里再加入热水。她告诉我们，第一次泡的茶太淡，不要喝，倒掉再加水泡第二次。我等得口渴死了，所以茶一泡好，我就拿起小茶杯，一口气就喝完了。哎呀！没想到这么烫！不过茶的味道很香很浓。我们喝了几乎三个小时才离开。）

| | | | |
|---|---|---|---|
| 盤 | 盘 | pán | tray |
| 淡 | 淡 | dàn | bland, tasteless |
| 燙 | 烫 | tàng | boiling hot, scalding |
| 倒掉 | 倒掉 | dàodiào | to throw away |
| 一口氣 | 一口气 | yīkǒuqì | at one gulp, in one breath |
| 濃 | 浓 | nóng | strong (tea, coffee), thick (soup, ink) |

## 5. 短劇 Skit

廣告公司給一種新的飲料作廣告：
（广告公司给一种新的饮料作广告：）
An advertising company is promoting a new beverage:

a. 請給這種新飲料想一個好聽的名字。
（请给这种新饮料想一个好听的名字。）
Please give the new product a nice-sounding name.

b. 兩人或三人一組。演一個兩分鐘的短劇，推銷這種飲料。
（两人或三人一组。演一个两分钟的短剧，推销这种饮料。）
Find one or two partners and act out a two-minute skit promoting this new beverage.

| | | | |
|---|---|---|---|
| 短劇 | 短剧 | duǎnjù | short play; skit |
| 廣告 | 广告 | guǎnggào | advertisement; to advertise |
| 推銷 | 推销 | tuīxiāo | to promote ( a product) |

## 6. 作文 Composition

在下列飲料中任意選出一種，對它做一個較深入的介紹和探討。
（在下列饮料中任意选出一种，对它做一个较深入的介绍和探讨。）
Introduce and comment on one of the following beverages. You may choose to discuss the popularity of this beverage, how it affects people's lives, or your feelings about it.

| | | | |
|---|---|---|---|
| 咖啡 | 咖啡 | 礦泉水 | 矿泉水 |
| 啤酒 | 啤酒 | 果汁 | 果汁 |
| 汽水 | 汽水 | 牛奶 | 牛奶 |
| 葡萄酒 | 葡萄酒 | | |

（參考生詞）

| | | | |
|---|---|---|---|
| 可樂 | 可乐 | kělè | cola |
| 礦泉水 | 矿泉水 | kuàngquánshuǐ | mineral water |
| 葡萄 | 葡萄 | pútáo | grape |
| 葡萄酒 | 葡萄酒 | pútáojiǔ | wine |
| 全脂牛奶 | 全脂牛奶 | quánzhī niúnǎi | whole milk |
| 脫脂牛奶 | 脱脂牛奶 | tuōzhī niúnǎi | nonfat milk |
| 不含咖啡因的 | 不含咖啡因的 | bùhán kāfēi'yīnde | decaffeinated |

## 7. 教室活動 Suggested Classroom Activity

### 拼湊句子遊戲 Sentence Matching

老師事先準備好一些句子，在紙上寫好，再把每個句子剪斷成兩半，不依次序，分給學生。每個學生都有一個斷句，要找出另一半，拼湊成一個完整的句子。（若要增加難度，也可把句子剪斷成三份。要注意剪斷句子的位置，不要出現三四個句子都可接在一起的情況。）

（老师事先准备好一些句子，在纸上写好，再把每个句子剪断成两半，不依次序，分给学生。每个学生都有一个断句，要找出另一半，拼凑成一个完整的句子。（若要增加难度，也可把句子剪断成三份。要注意剪断句子的位置，不要出现三四个句子都可接在一起的情况。）

The teacher first prepares several sentences and writes each on a separate slip of paper. The slips are then cut in half and each student is given one slip at random. The object of the game is for the student to locate the other half of his/her slip, thereby reconstructing the sentence. (To increase the difficulty, the sentences can be cut into thirds, but be careful: this increases the likelihood of there being more than one possible combination for each sentence.)

# 補充資料 Supplementary Materials

## I. 成語 Idioms with Numbers

| | | | | |
|---|---|---|---|---|
| 一 | 一見鍾情 | 一见钟情 | yíjiàn zhōngqíng | to fall in love at first sight |
| | 一舉兩得 | 一举两得 | yìjǔ liǎngdé | to kill two birds with one stone |
| 二 | 二八佳人 | 二八佳人 | èrbā jiārén | a budding beauty (2x8=16) |
| 三 | 三長兩短 | 三长两短 | sāncháng liǎngduǎn | unforeseen disasters or accidents |
| | 三思而行 | 三思而行 | sānsī érxíng | Look before you leap! |
| 四 | 四海一家 | 四海一家 | sìhǎi yìjiā | The whole world is one family. |
| | 四面八方 | 四面八方 | sìmiàn bāfāng | in all directions |
| 五 | 五花八門 | 五花八门 | wǔhuā bāmén | rich in variety |
| | 五十步笑百步 | 五十步笑百步 | wǔshíbù xiào bǎibù | the pot calling the kettle black |
| 六 | 六根清靜 | 六根清静 | liùgēn qīngjìng | free from human desires and passions |
| | 六神無主 | 六神无主 | liùshén wúzhǔ | stunned out of one's wits |
| 七 | 七上八下 | 七上八下 | qīshàng bāxià | an unsettled state of mind |
| | 七手八腳 | 七手八脚 | qīshǒu bājiǎo | with a great commotion |
| 八 | 八九不離十 | 八九不离十 | bājiǔ bùlíshí | not far from the target |
| | 八面玲瓏 | 八面玲珑 | bāmiàn línglóng | person with good connections; smooth operator |
| 九 | 九牛一毛 | 九牛一毛 | jiǔniú yīmáo | a drop in the ocean |
| | 九死一生 | 九死一生 | jiǔsǐ yìshēng | a ten percent chance to survive |
| 十 | 十之八九 | 十之八九 | shízhi bājiǔ | in eight or nine cases out of ten |
| | 十全十美 | 十全十美 | shíquán shíměi | perfect in every way |

## 2. 中國茶 Chinese Tea

| 中國茶 Chinese Tea | |
|---|---|
| 香片 Xiāngpiàn | jasmine tea |
| 龍井 Lóngjǐng | Dragon Well tea |
| 紅茶 Hóngchá | Chinese black tea |
| 綠茶 Lǜchá | green tea |
| 鐵觀音 Tiěguānyīn | Chinese green tea |
| 烏龍茶 Wūlóngchá | Oolong tea |
| 普洱茶 Pǔ'ěrchá | fermented black tea |

刻上佛語的茶壺

Teapot for Contemplating

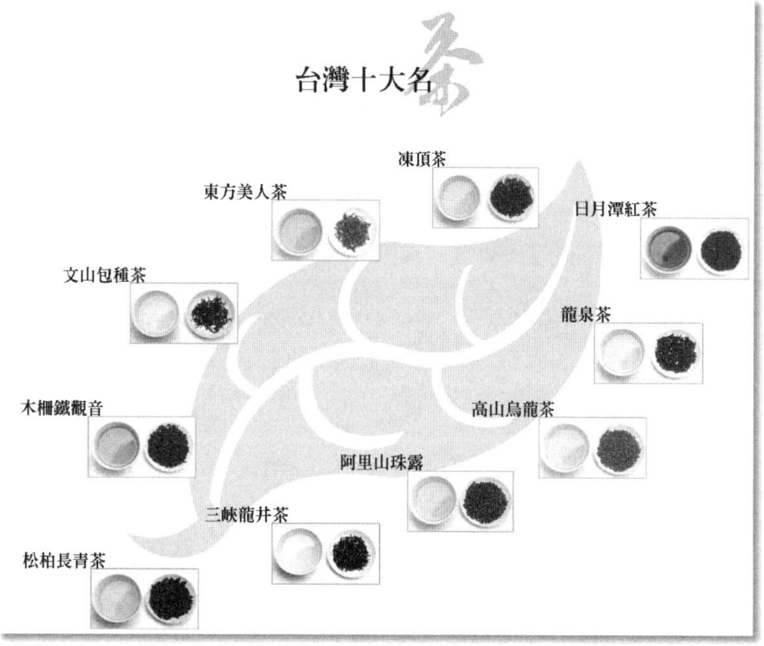


Teas from Various Regions and Climates

功夫茶、老人茶

各種茶壺

# 第 五 課

# 我 愛 紅 娘

## 繁体課文 Traditional Text

中國人的家庭觀念很重，結婚生子是一生最重要的一件事了。不論男女，只要過了三十還沒結婚，父母或親戚朋友都會積極地幫忙介紹對象。尤其是女孩子，嫁個好『老公』，在許多人心目中可能比找個好工作更要緊。在這個現代化社會裡，男女平等的口號雖然流行，然而一般人到底還是比較偏向傳統，不太能接受不打算結婚的單身女性。

在保守的舊式社會裡，因為婚姻是父母決定的，子女的意見，並不受到父母的重視。而且男女雙方往往在婚前缺少交往的機會，彼此了解不夠，造成了不少悲劇。

現在時代不同了，男女可以自由談戀愛。如果因為工作的關係，缺少認識對象的機會，介紹交友的管道也很多：可以相親，可以參加團體活動，也可以在報上徵婚。至於婚禮的方式，就因人而異了。但是不管是在教堂結婚，或是在飯館舉行婚禮，一定得請親朋好友喝一杯喜酒。去喝喜酒的，也一定會包個紅包給一對新人，祝他們『百年好合』、『早生貴子』。

## 简体课文 Simplified Text

中国人的家庭观念很重，结婚生子是一生最重要的一件事了。不论男女，只要过了三十还没结婚，父母或亲戚朋友都会积极地帮忙介绍对象。尤其是女孩子，嫁个好『老公』，在许多人心目中可能比找个好工作更要紧。在这个现代化社会里，男女平等的口号虽然流行，然而一般人到底还是比较偏向传统，不太能接受不打算结婚的单身女性。

在保守的旧式社会里，因为婚姻是父母决定的，子女的意见，并不受到父母的重视。而且男女双方往往在婚前缺少交往的机会，彼此了解不够，造成了不少悲剧。

现在时代不同了，男女可以自由谈恋爱。如果因为工作的关系，缺少认识对象的机会，介绍交友的管道也很多：可以相亲，可以参加团体活动，也可以在报上征婚。至于婚礼的方式，就因人而异了。但是不管是在教堂结婚，或是在饭馆举行婚礼，一定得请亲朋好友喝一杯喜酒。去喝喜酒的，也一定会包个红包给一对新人，祝他们『百年好合』、『早生贵子』。

# 生詞 Vocabulary

| | | | | | |
|---|---|---|---|---|---|
| 1. | 紅娘 | 红娘 | hóngniáng | *N.* | matchmaker |
| 2. | 觀念 | 观念 | guānniàn | *N.* | concept; sense of ...; view of things |
| 3. | 不論 | 不论 | búlùn | *Adv.* | no matter ... |
| 4. | 親戚 | 亲戚 | qīnqi | *N.* | relatives |
| 5. | 積極 | 积极 | jījí | *Vs.* | active; positive |
| 6. | 對象 | 对象 | duìxiàng | *N.* | prospective spouse |
| 7. | 尤其 | 尤其 | yóuqí | *Adv.* | especially |
| 8. | 嫁<br>娶 | 嫁 | jià<br>qǔ | *V.*<br>*V.* | to marry (a man)<br>to marry (a woman) |
| 9. | 老公<br>老婆 | 老公 | lǎogōng<br>lǎopó | *N.*<br>*N.* | husband. (*Coll.* This term is borrowed from the Cantonese dialect.)<br>*(Coll.)* wife |
| 10. | 要緊 | 要紧 | yàojǐn | *Vs.* | important |
| 11. | 平等 | 平等 | píngděng | *Vs.* | equal; equality |
| 12. | 口號 | 口号 | kǒuhào | *N.* | slogan |
| 13. | 到底 | 到底 | dàodǐ | *Adv.* | after all; in the long run; finally. *(Emphatic)* What on earth ...? |
| 14. | 偏向 | 偏向 | piānxiàng | *Vst.* | inclined toward; to tend to be |
| 15. | 接受 | 接受 | jiēshòu | *V.* | to accept |
| 16. | 單身 | 单身 | dānshēn | *N.* | unmarried; single |
| 17. | 女性<br>男性 | 女性 | nǚxìng<br>nánxìng | *N.*<br>*N.* | woman; female sex<br>man; male sex |
| 18. | 保守 | 保守 | bǎoshǒu | *Vs.* | conservative, old-fashioned |
| 19. | 舊式 | 旧式 | jiùshì | *Vs-attr.* | old-fashioned; outdated |
| 20. | 婚姻<br>離婚<br>訂婚<br>求婚 | 婚姻 | hūnyīn<br>líhūn<br>dìnghūn<br>qiúhūn | *N.*<br>*V-sep.*<br>*V-sep.*<br>*V-sep.* | marriage; matrimony<br>to divorce<br>to be engaged<br>to propose marriage |
| 21. | 決定 | 决定 | juédìng | *Vi.* | to decide; *N.* decision |
| 22. | 意見 | 意见 | yìjiàn | *N.* | opinion, suggestion |
| 23. | 雙方 | 双方 | shuāngfāng | *N.* | both parties; both sides |
| 24. | 缺少 | 缺少 | quēshǎo | *Vst.* | to lack; to be short of |

| | | | | | |
|---|---|---|---|---|---|
| 25. | 交往 | 交往 | jiāowǎng | *N.* | contact; *Vi.* association |
| 26. | 彼此 | 彼此 | bǐcǐ | *Adv.* | each other, one another |
| 27. | 造成 | 造成 | zàochéng | *V.* | to cause; to result in |
| 28. | 悲劇 | 悲剧 | bēijù | *N.* | tragedy; great unhappiness |
| 29. | 時代 | 时代 | shídài | *N.* | period of time; era |
| 30. | 自由 | 自由 | zìyóu | *Vs.* | free; *N.* freedom |
| 31. | 談戀愛 | 谈恋爱 | tán liàn'ài | *V-sep.* | to court; to fall in love |
| 32. | 交友 | 交友 | jiāoyǒu | *Vi.* | to make friends |
| 33. | 管道 | 管道 | guǎndào | *N.* | channel; way |
| 34. | 相親 | 相亲 | xiàngqīn | *V-sep.* | to be introduced with intent to marry |
| 35. | 團體 | 团体 | tuántǐ | *N.* | group |
| 36. | 徵婚 | 征婚 | zhēnghūn | *Vi-sep.* | to solicit prospective spouse |
| 37. | 至於 | 至于 | zhìyú | *Part.* | as for, as to |
| 38. | 婚禮 | 婚礼 | hūnlǐ | *N.* | wedding ceremony |
| 39. | 因人而異 | 因人而异 | yīnrén éryì | *Id.* | to vary in each case, according to the individual |
| 40. | 教堂 | 教堂 | jiàotáng | *N.* | church (building) |
| 41. | 舉行 | 举行 | jǔxíng | *V.* | to hold (an event or ceremony) |
| 42. | 喜酒 | 喜酒 | xǐjiǔ | *N.* | wedding banquet or reception |
| 43. | 紅包 | 红包 | hóngbāo | *N.* | red envelope or paper bag containing money as a gift *(See chart in "Supplementary Materials" for this lesson)* |
| 44. | 對 | 对 | duì | *M.* | measure for a pair or a couple |
| 45. | 百年好合 | 百年好合 | bǎinián hǎohé | *Id.* | a harmonious union lasting a hundred years *(See chart in "Supplementary Materials" for this lesson)* |

# 文法 Grammar

Each pattern below is illustrated by sample sentences. When blanks are provided, complete the sentences. When English sentences are given, give Chinese counterparts.

## 1. 不論 **búlùn: (Conj.) no matter ... ; regardless of whether or not**

(*Note that this conjunction is freely interchangeable with* 不管.)

a. 這種婚禮，不論男方、女方都不會同意。
（这种婚礼，不论男方、女方都不会同意。）
Neither the bridegroom's nor the bride's family would ever consent to this kind of wedding.

b. 不管是小吃還是大餐，那家飯館都很合適。
（不管是小吃还是大餐，那家饭馆都很合适。）
That restaurant is quite suitable for either a casual meal or a formal dinner.

c. 不論刮風、下雨，他每天都騎車上班。
（不论刮风、下雨，他每天都骑车上班。）
He rides his bicycle to work regardless of whether it is windy or rainy.

d. 不管什麼時候，夜市總是一樣擠、一樣吵。
（不管什么时候，夜市总是一样挤、一样吵。）
Night markets are always crowded and noisy, no matter what time it is.

e. 不論你以後____________________，你現在也應該存點錢。
（不论你以后____________________，你现在也应该存点钱。）

f. 不論他說什麼，你都別______________________________。
（不论他说什么，你都别______________________________。）

g. Whether they are college students or high-school students, they will find this Chinese-English dictionary very useful.

h. No matter what he paints, his paintings are always very popular.

## 2. 到底 **dàodǐ: (Adv.)**

(1) *what exactly? (indicating inquisitiveness and, frequently, impatience )*
(2) *after all, in the final analysis (indicating concession)*
(3) *finally, at the very end (referring to eventuality)*

a. 常常聽人家提到《紅包》，到底是什麼東西？
（常常听人家提到《红包》，到底是什么东西？）
"Hongbao" is often mentioned, but what exactly is it?

b. 他不喜歡提過去，到底發生了什麼事？
（他不喜欢提过去，到底发生了什么事？）
He doesn't like to talk about the past; exactly what happened?

c. 他們到底是經過相親的方式結婚的，彼此缺少認識。
（他们到底是经过相亲的方式结婚的，彼此缺少认识。）
I understand that they had an arranged marriage and didn't know each other very well.

d. 他到底年紀比較大，不能接受男女平等的想法。
（他到底年纪比较大，不能接受男女平等的想法。）
After all, he's relatively old and can't accept the concept of equality of the sexes.

e. 事情過了幾天，他的心情到底平靜下來了。
（事情过了几天，他的心情到底平静下来了。）
Several days after the incident he finally calmed down.

f. 經過介紹人的努力，他們的婚事到底成功了。
（经过介绍人的努力，他们的婚事到底成功了。）
Through the efforts of the matchmaker, their wedding finally took place.

### 3. 並 (+Neg) bìng: (Adv.) however; it is not the case that; not as expected (indicating a situation contrary to general expectations)

*(Note that* 並且"bìngqiě" *is sometimes shortened to* 並，*which should not be confused with* 並 *under discussion.)*

a. 他們是自由戀愛的，但是結果並不很理想。
（他们是自由恋爱的，但是结果并不很理想。）
They married for love, but the results were not exactly ideal.

b. 她並不是不願意結婚，而是因為家有年老的父母需要照顧。
（她并不是不愿意结婚，而是因为家有年老的父母需要照顾。）
It's not that she doesn't want to get married; it's because she has elderly parents who need looking after.

c. 學生提了很多意見，但王教授並沒全部接受。
（学生提了很多意见，但王教授并没全部接受。）
The students offered many suggestions, but not all were accepted by Professor Wang.

d. They don't get along well, but they haven't actually divorced.

e. He grew up in Germany, but that's not why he takes his vacation there every year.

## 4. 受到 shòudào ... 的 + (Verb): to be (verb)+ed by (usually occurring with 重視 "to consider important"; 影響 "to be influenced by," etc.)

a. 他在這兒工作十年了，一直沒有受到公司的重用。
（他在这儿工作十年了，一直没有受到公司的重用。）
He has worked here for ten years, but the company has never assigned him to an important position.

b. 我家人生病的時候，受到各位的關心和照顧，非常感謝。
（我家人生病的时候，受到各位的关心和照顾，非常感谢。）
I am very grateful for the concern and assistance I received from everyone when my family member was ill.

c. 大家都認為他的小說很少受到歐美文學的影響。
（大家都认为他的小说很少受到欧美文学的影响。）
Everyone agrees that his novels are little influenced by European or American literature.

d. 這裡最近經常停電停水，市政府不斷受到民眾的批評。
（这里最近经常停电停水，市政府不断受到民众的批评。）
Recently, electric and water outages have been frequent here, and the city government is under constant criticism from the residents.

e. The new cafeteria in the student center is well loved（喜愛）by the students.

f. Violinists from China are gradually attracting the regard（重視）of the western world.

## 5. Verb + 成 chéng:

*This verb-particle variously defines (1) a result, (2) a change or transformation (into, as, become), and (3) success.*

a. 這次的大車禍，造成了二死三傷。真是不幸。
（这次的大车祸，造成了二死三伤。真是不幸。）
This auto accident resulted in two deaths and three injuries. It was really very unfortunate.

b. 李老師把他班上的學生分成五個小組。
（李老师把他班上的学生分成五个小组。）
Mr. Li divided the students in his class into five groups.

c. 星期天下雨下得太大，同事的婚禮沒有去成。
（星期天下雨下得太大，同事的婚礼没有去成。）
On Sunday, it rained heavily, so we didn't attend our colleague's wedding.

d. Could you please cut the birthday cake into eight slices?

e. There was a long line at the cinema, so we didn't get to see the movie.

## 6. (因為)...的關係 (yīnwèi) ... de guānxi: due to, because of

a. 因為生病的關係，他已經很久沒有來夜市擺攤子了。
（因为生病的关系，他已经很久没有来夜市摆摊子了。）
Because of his illness, he hasn't come to the night market to set up a stand for a long time.

b. 因為眼光太高的關係，他一直找不到合適的對象。
（因为眼光太高的关系，他一直找不到合适的对象。）
He could not find a wife because he set his sights too high.

c. They are moving again because of their father's job.

d. Many people marry in August because it is an auspicious month.

## 7. 至於 zhìyú: (Prep.) regarding; as for; as far as ... is concerned (referring to a change in topic)

a. 我只知道他要去中國學中文，至於去多久，我就不清楚了。
（我只知道他要去中国学中文，至于去多久，我就不清楚了。）
I only know that he is going to China to study Chinese; as for how long, I have no idea.

b. 這是我自己的看法，至於別人能不能接受，我全不在乎。
（这是我自己的看法，至于别人能不能接受，我全不在乎。）
This is my own view; whether or not it is acceptable to others, I don't care a bit.

c. 他的收入很高，至於他為什麼到現在還欠債，我可就不知道了。
（他的收入很高，至于他为什么到现在还欠债，我可就不知道了。）
His income is very high; as to why he is still in debt, I certainly don't know.

d. I have already sent my letter to the newspaper company; as to whether or not they will publish it, that will be their decision.

e. This Chinese family has been in the United States for fifty years, but as for where they originally came from, nobody has a clear idea.

# 練習 Exercises

## 1. 造句 Make one sentence with each of the given vocabulary:

| | | | |
|---|---|---|---|
| a. 觀念 | 观念 | e. 彼此 | 彼此 |
| b. 造成 | 造成 | f. 平等 | 平等 |
| c. 偏向 | 偏向 | g. 意見 | 意见 |
| d. 積極地 | 积极地 | h. 受到...的重視 | 受到...的重视 |

## 2. 挑出同一組中和其他生詞沒有關聯的詞：

**Single out the word in the group that is least related to the others and justify your choice.**

| | 1) | 2) | 3) | 4) |
|---|---|---|---|---|
| **EXAMPLE:** 2 | 海 (ocean) | 浴 (to bathe) | 湖 (lake) | 河 (river) |
| a. ______ | 傳統 传统 | 保守 保守 | 悲劇 悲剧 | 舊式 旧式 |
| b. ______ | 對象 对象 | 家庭 家庭 | 親戚 亲戚 | 兒女 儿女 |
| c. ______ | 交友 交友 | 徵婚 徵婚 | 選擇 选择 | 單身 单身 |
| d. ______ | 丈夫 丈夫 | 新人 新人 | 老公 老公 | 愛人 爱人 |
| e. ______ | 平等 平等 | 一樣 一样 | 自由 自由 | 公平 公平 |
| f. ______ | 社會 社会 | 教堂 教堂 | 球場 球场 | 飯館 饭馆 |
| g. ______ | 想法 想法 | 看法 看法 | 觀念 观念 | 地位 地位 |
| h. ______ | 喝喜酒 喝喜酒 | 小吃 小吃 | 紅包 红包 | 婚禮 婚礼 |
| i. ______ | 娶 娶 | 祝 祝 | 愛 爱 | 嫁 嫁 |
| j. ______ | 悲劇 悲剧 | 難過 难过 | 痛苦 痛苦 | 樂趣 乐趣 |

## 3. 完成句子 Complete the Sentences

a. 他們已經訂婚了，______________________________。
（他们已经订婚了，______________________________。）

b. 李小姐三十五歲了還沒結婚，______________________________。
（李小姐三十五岁了还没结婚，______________________________。）

c. 在現代的中國社會裡，______________________________。
（在现代的中国社会里，______________________________。）

d. 王小姐說她結婚的時候________________________________________。
（王小姐说她结婚的时候________________________________________。）

e. 張老先生是舊式社會的讀書人，________________________________。
（张老先生是旧式社会的读书人，________________________________。）

f. 我父母不能接受____________________________________________。
（我父母不能接受____________________________________________。）

g. 談戀愛是________________________________________________。
（谈恋爱是________________________________________________。）

h. 他們打算用最簡單的婚禮方式，所以決定__________________________。
（他们打算用最简单的婚礼方式，所以决定__________________________。）

i. 老吳一直不要相親，________________________________________。
（老吴一直不要相亲，________________________________________。）

k. 因為缺少________________________________________________。
（因为缺少________________________________________________。）

## 4. 重組句子 Form a Sentence

請用所有格子中的字組成一句文法詞義通順的句子。依班上學生人數分成幾組比賽，每組二到四人。先找出答案的那組就得一分。
（请用所有格子中的字组成一句文法词义通顺的句子。依班上学生人数分成几组比赛，每组二到四人。先找出答案的那组就得一分。）
Use all the characters presented in the grid to form a single sentence. The class can be divided into several teams (two to four students per team) to compete with each other. The first group with the answer gets one point.

a.

| | | |
|---|---|---|
| 的 | 人 | 家 |
| 重 | 國 | 念 |
| 庭 | 觀 | 中 |

句子：______________________________________

b.

| | | |
|---|---|---|
| 愛 | 由 | 比 |
| 有 | 親 | 戀 |
| 相 | 趣 | 自 |

句子：______________________________________

c.

| | | |
|---|---|---|
| 對 | 人 | 生 |
| 早 | 貴 | 新 |
| 子 | 祝 | 那 |

句子：__________________________________

d.

| | | | |
|---|---|---|---|
| 身 | 性 | 不 | 都 |
| 許 | 單 | 婚 | 著 |
| 結 | 多 | 急 | 女 |

句子：__________________________________

e.

| | | | |
|---|---|---|---|
| 算 | 們 | 堂 | 禮 |
| 舉 | 教 | 不 | 他 |
| 在 | 打 | 行 | 婚 |

句子：__________________________________

(Now make a grid puzzle of your own for other teams to solve:)

f.

| | | |
|---|---|---|
| | | |
| | | |
| | | |

句子：__________________________________

## 5. 訪問 Interview

請根據下面的問題進行一個訪問。老師事先安排合適的人來班上接受訪問。
（请根据下面的问题进行一个访问。老师事先安排合适的人来班上接受访问。）
Use the following questions as a basis for an interview with someone who has been invited by the instructor.

1. 你和你先生（或太太）是怎麼認識的？
（你和你先生（或太太）是怎么认识的？）

2. 結婚以前，認識了多久？
（结婚以前，认识了多久？）

3. 先生求婚的時候，說了什麼？
（先生求婚的时候，说了什么？）

4. 你為什麼決定跟他結婚？
（你为什么决定跟他结婚？）

5. 你的家人對你的婚事有沒有意見？
（你的家人对你的婚事有没有意见？）

6. 談談你婚禮的準備工作。
（谈谈你婚礼的准备工作。）

7. 婚禮用什麼樣的方式？在哪裡舉行的？參加的客人有多少？
（婚礼用什么样的方式？在哪里举行的？参加的客人有多少？）

8. 酒席上有什麼讓你最難忘的事？
（酒席上有什么让你最难忘的事？）

9. 婚前和婚後的生活，最大的不同是什麼？
（婚前和婚后的生活，最大的不同是什么？）

## 6. 教室活動 Act Out Words

老師事先準備好一疊生詞（或短句），每個寫在一張小卡片或紙上。把一個生詞拿給一個學生看，請他用描寫、填充、同義字或反義字的方式，述說一下這個詞，但是不可以用到任何一個出現在這個生詞裡的字。其他的同學根據描述，來猜一猜這是什麼詞。比方說，寫在紙上的詞是<飲茶>。學生可以先告訴大家有兩個字。第一個字是動詞，『喝』的意思；第二個字是名詞，是中國人最喜歡喝的一種東西。也可以說廣東人吃點心又叫什麼。如果要猜的詞是<首先>，學生可以說是『第一』的意思，不是『最後』。述說的人不可以用手勢或動作。學生輪流述說生詞。

（老师事先准备好一叠生词（或短句），每个写在一张小卡片或纸上。把一个生词拿给一个学生看，请他用描写、填充、同义字或反义字的方式，述说一下这个词，但是不可以用到任何一个出现在这个生词里的字。其他的同学根据描述，来猜一猜这是什么词。比方说，写在纸上的词是<饮茶>。学生可以先告诉大家有两个字。第一个字是动词，『喝』的意思；第二个字是名词，是中国人最喜欢喝的一种东西。也可以说广东人吃点心又叫什么。如果要猜的词是<首先>，学生可以说是『第一』的意思，不是『最后』。述说的人不可以用手势或动作。学生轮流述说生词。）

The teacher prepares several cards, each containing a word or phrase from this lesson. Each student in turn receives a card and then elicits the word or phrase from his/her fellow students using description, synonyms, antonyms, or other methods. No part of the word or phrase may be used directly, and no hand or body movements are allowed. The other students try to guess the word or phrase.

If, for instance, the phrase was "drink tea," the student might say that there were two words involved, that the first was a verb meaning "to imbibe," and that the second was a noun and is the favorite beverage of Chinese people. The student might also point out that the phrase is synonymous with the term that Cantonese use when referring to eating *dim sum.*

| 中國臉 |
| --- |
| 嘴巴變薄 |
| 眉毛變濃 |
| 頭型變圓 |
| 髮質變細 |
| 下巴變單 |

The Ideal Face for a Chinese Bride

# 補充資料 Supplementary Materials

## 1. 送紅包 Presenting Red Envelopes

| 送紅包 Presenting Red Envelopes | |
|---|---|
| 婚礼 hūnlǐ | wedding reception 喝喜酒 |
| 過年 guònián | Chinese New Year |
| 生日 shēngrì | birthday |
| 滿月 mǎnyuè | a child is one month old |
| 送禮 sònglǐ | gift on auspicious occasions |
| 送白包 Presenting White Envelopes | |
| 喪事 sāngshì | funeral |

Select Your Date; Leave the Rest to Us

## 2. 賀辭 Felicitous Phrases

| 賀辭 hècí Felicitous Phrases | | |
|---|---|---|
| 新年 | 恭喜發財 Gōngxǐ fācái | May fortune come your way! |
| 結婚 | 新婚快樂 Xīnhūn kuàilè | Happy wedding! |
| | 白頭偕老 Báitóu xiélǎo | Till death do you part! |
| | 百年好合 Bǎinián hǎohé | Harmony for a hundred years! |
| | 愛河永浴 Àihé yǒngyù | Bathe forever in the River of Love! |
| | 早生貴子 Zǎoshēng guìzǐ | May you have a male child soon! |
| 生日 | 生日快樂 Shēngrì kuàilè | Happy birthday! |
| | 福如東海，壽比南山 Fúrú Dōnghǎi, shòubǐ Nánshān | Fortune as (great as) the Eastern Sea, longevity as (great as) South Mountain |

《情人節活動報導》

## 民俗公園　男士上台拋繡球

【記者賴佩如・台中報導】「老是等著接女孩子的繡球，機率太少了！」台中市民俗公園昨天舉辦拋繡球活動，首度有男士上台拋繡球，打破只有女孩子上台的「習慣」。第一位拋繡球的郭原宏，已是第四度參加，前三次都「槓龜」，今年決定自己上台，終於不再落空。

這項名爲「情拋繡球緣」的活動，由民俗公園和忠貞國際同濟會主辦，有八十六位男士，四十三位女士參加，約比去年少了五十人。主辦單位表示，去年參加人數爆滿，「繡球拋都拋不完」，所以今年嚴格控制人數，以一百五十人爲上限，所以參加的人少了。

參加人數減少，活動一樣熱鬧。除了重頭戲－拋繡球以外，主辦單位還安排了愛的小天使、分組聯誼、團康、牽線遊戲、禮服秀和抬新娘轎等活動，參加者不僅在拋繡球前可以先彼此認識，在拋完繡球後也可以進一步聯誼。

Catch the Auspicious Silk, Boys!

未婚

本週活動預告

**4/15 男大專女高專聯誼**

本週六晚 7:00辦「我的溫柔未婚聯誼會，歡迎男大專27-34歲，女高上22-30歲人士參加

**4/16 高專大哥大姊聯誼**

本週日下午3：30辦未婚大哥大姊聯誼會，男35-45歲，女30-40歲高上人士可參加，二春人士亦可報名

※參加活動者請先電話報名，並需檢驗有關證件，利人利己，敬請合作※

台中市愛禮青年協會主辦

中市五權路2-30號11F電話:3723100

Parties for Singles

朋友，您忙碌與追求理想的心，我們深深地了解。我們不是上帝，更不是神，不會造人，但我們卻擁有數萬名您所想要的理想對象，在此誠摯地希望您給自己一次機會，讓我們能爲您服務。因爲，同樣地也有很多人想認識您。

Ad for a Dating Service

## 4. 結婚 Getting Married

| 十五年間台灣男女結婚年齡平均數 | | | |
|---|---|---|---|
| 年 | 新郎 | 新娘 | 結婚率 |
| 民國69年 | 27歲 | 24歲 | 9.68% |
| 民國74年 | 29歲 | 25.5歲 | 8.02% |
| 民國79年 | 29.8歲 | 26.6歲 | 7.10% |
| 民國84年 | 32歲 | 29歲 | 6.05% |
| 資料來源：台灣地區人口統計表 | | | |

Age When Married

謹詹於中華民國（ ）國曆八十八年元月十七日 星期日
農曆八十八年十二月初一

為 次女津華 長男錫教 **舉行結婚典禮並敬備喜筵** **恭請**

闔第光臨

**鄧漢光 鞠躬**
**鄭有生**

恕邀

******

席設：全國大飯店九龍十鳳廳
台中市中港路九十號

時間：電話：二六三一七五九
中午十二時入席

Wedding Invitation

Shop Specializing in Wedding Ware

Wedding Boulevard

## 5. 離婚 Getting Divorced

### 兩性狂想曲

### 如果婚姻有三部曲

記者・廖和敏

訂婚、結婚，有時包括離婚，是婚姻三「步」曲，如果婚姻有三「部」曲，更棒！

二十來歲時社會經驗有限，最好找大上個十歲二十歲的好對象，如此，對方豐富的人生歷練正好是年輕另一半的生活導師，節省其在各方面的摸索時間。三四十歲時，已經經歷了一些人生的起承轉合，對事情的判斷和看法都有了自己的觀點，和伴侶之間的關係最好是平起平坐，能彼此互相震盪，相互激勵，讓雙方更確定他（她）的人生定位。過了中壯年，進入前老年的五六十歲，如果再結一次婚，最好是比自己小上三十歲的青年人。對方的年輕活力正可補足自己在遲暮之年對不再年輕的追悼！而這時自己的人生經歷也可成為另一半徬徨人生上的最佳指導。

現實人生中，如此結三次婚幾乎是不可能的，但正因此，讓「狂想」有了更大的空間。

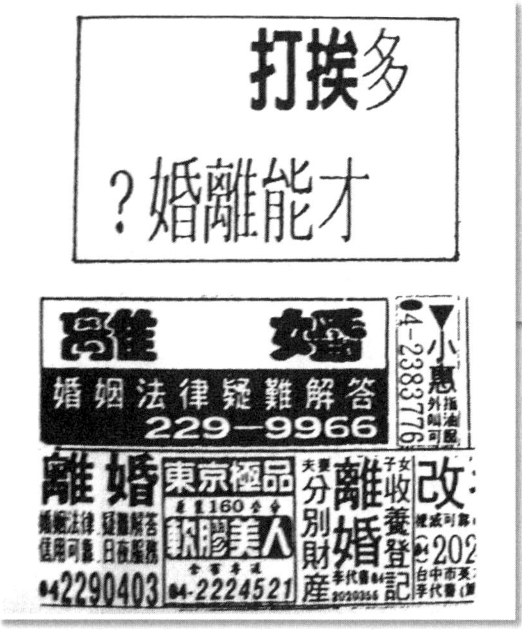

# 第六課

# 台北怎麼那麼擠？

## 繁体課文 Traditional Text

到過台北的觀光客一定都記得故宮博物院裡看不完的藝術品。但是他們一定也不會忘記台北讓人頭痛的交通。想知道這個國際大都市的交通到底擠到什麼程度嗎？隨便選一天站在一個大街路口吧！首先看到的是一條條汽車長龍，不少機車蛇行其中。路兩旁是一群群的人潮，在騎樓下停放的機車和做生意的攤販中間步步慢行。要是碰到早晚上下班時間，主要的道路總是塞車。想在市區內找個地方停車真是不容易。那麼改坐公車吧！不過，非得很有耐心，才能等到一班沒有客滿的巴士。有時甚至連計程車也不見得叫得到。

台北交通的擠和亂主要是因為人口和車輛增加得太快了。再加上有許多不遵守交通規則的駕駛和行人，於是路上的情況越來越糟糕！用『馬路如虎口』來形容台北街頭的危險，絕不過分。如何改善交通，以及減少車禍的發生是每個台北市民都很關心的問題。希望地下鐵的建立能根本解決台北的交通問題。

# 简体课文 Simplified Text

到过台北的观光客一定都记得故宫博物院里看不完的艺术品。但是他们一定也不会忘记台北让人头痛的交通。想知道这个国际大都市的交通到底挤到什么程度吗？随便选一天站在一个大街路口吧！首先看到的是一条条汽车长龙，不少机车蛇行其中。路两旁是一群群的人潮，在骑楼下停放的机车和做生意的摊贩中间步步慢行。要是碰到早晚上下班时间，主要的道路总是塞车。想在市区内找个地方停车真是不容易。那么改坐公车吧！不过，非得很有耐心，才能等到一班没有客满的巴士。有时甚至连出租车不见得叫得到。

台北交通的挤和乱主要是因为人口和车辆增加得太快了。再加上有许多不遵守交通规则的驾驶和行人，于是路上的情况越来越糟糕！用『马路如虎口』来形容台北街头的危险，绝不过分。如何改善交通，以及减少车祸的发生是每个台北市民都很关心的问题。希望地下铁的建立能根本解决台北的交通问题。

## 生詞 Vocabulary

| | | | | | |
|---|---|---|---|---|---|
| 1. | 觀光<br>觀光客 | 观光 | guānguāng<br>guānguāngkè | *Vi.*<br>*N.* | to do sightseeing<br>tourist |
| 2. | 故宮<br>博物院<br>博物館 | 故宫<br>博物院 | gùgōng<br>bówùyuàn<br>bówùguǎn | *N.*<br>*N.*<br>*N.* | the National Palace Museum<br>museum<br>museum |
| 3. | 頭痛 | 头痛 | tóutòng | *Vs.* | to have a headache (痛=疼 téng) |
| 4. | 國際 | 国际 | guójì | *Vs-attr.* | international |
| 5. | 都市 | 都市 | dūshì | *N.* | city |
| 6. | 程度 | 程度 | chéngdù | *N.* | extent; degree; level |
| 7. | 龍<br>長龍 | 龙<br>长龙 | lóng<br>chánglóng | *N.*<br>*N.* | dragon<br>long line |
| 8. | 機車 | 机车 | jīchē | *N.* | motorcycle |
| 9. | 蛇<br>蛇行 | 蛇<br>蛇行 | shé<br>shéxíng | *N.*<br>*N.* | snake<br>to move like a snake |
| 10. | 潮<br>人潮 | 潮<br>人潮 | cháo<br>rénchāo | *N.*<br>*N.* | tide; damp, moist<br>a tide (crowd) of people |
| 11. | 停<br>停車場 | 停 | tíng<br>tíngchēchǎng | *V., Vi.*<br>*N.* | to park; to stop<br>parking lot |
| 12. | 騎樓 | 骑楼 | qílóu | *N.* | covered sidewalk |
| 13. | 碰到 | 碰到 | pèngdào | *Vpt.* | to be caught in, to run into |
| 14. | 上下班 | 上下班 | shàngxiàbān | *N.* | going to work and leaving work |
| 15. | 主要 | 主要 | zhǔyào | *Vs-attr.* | major |
| 16. | 道路 | 道路 | dàolù | *N.* | road |
| 17. | 塞車 | 塞车 | sāichē | *Vs.* | traffic jam (or 堵車 dǔchē) |
| 18. | 改 | 改 | gǎi | *V.* | to switch over to (something else); to correct; to alter; to change |
| 19. | 班 | 班 | bān | *M.* | measure for a scheduled bus, train, flight or other forms of transportation |
| 20. | 客滿 | 客满 | kèmǎn | *Vp.* | full of passengers |
| 21. | 巴士 | 巴士 | bāshì | *N.* | bus (transliteration from English) |
| 22. | 甚至 | 甚至 | shènzhì | *Adv.* | even, (go) as far as to |

| | | | | | |
|---|---|---|---|---|---|
| 23. | 計程車<br>出租(汽)車<br>的士 | 计程车<br>出租(汽)车 | jìchéngchē<br>chūzū(qì)chē<br>díshì | *N.*<br>*N.*<br>*N.* | taxi (Taiwan usage)<br>rental cars, taxi (Mainland China usage)<br>taxi (esp. in Hong Kong) |
| 24. | 不見得 | 不见得 | bújiànde | *Adv.* | not necessarily; not likely |
| 25. | 增加 | 增加 | zēngjiā | *V.* | to increase |
| 26. | 再加上 | 再加上 | zài jiāshàng | *Adv.* | in addition; also; furthermore |
| 27. | 遵守 | 遵守 | zūnshǒu | *V.* | to obey or comply with (rules, regulations, laws, etc.) |
| 28. | 規則 | 规则 | guīzé | *N.* | regulations, rules |
| 29. | 駕駛<br>司機 | 驾驶 | jiàshǐ<br>sījī | *N.*<br>*N.* | driver; *V.* to drive<br>driver |
| 30. | 於是 | 于是 | yúshì | *Conj.* | thereupon; hence; consequently |
| 31. | 情況 | 情况 | qíngkuàng | *N.* | situation; conditions |
| 32. | 如 | 如 | rú | *Vst.* | like; as; as if |
| 33. | 形容 | 形容 | xíngróng | *V.* | to describe |
| 34. | 危險 | 危险 | wéixiǎn | *N.* | danger; *Vs.* dangerous |
| 35. | 過分 | 过分 | guòfèn | *Vs.* | excessive, undue |
| 36. | 如何 | 如何 | rúhé | *Adv.* | how, what |
| 37. | 改善 | 改善 | gǎishàn | *V.* | to improve; *N.* improvement |
| 38. | 以及 | 以及 | yǐjí | *Conj.* | as well as; along with; and |
| 39. | 減少 | 减少 | jiǎnshǎo | *V.* | to decrease; reduce |
| 40. | 車禍 | 车祸 | chēhuò | *N.* | auto accident |
| 41. | 發生 | 发生 | fāshēng | *Vp.* | to occur; to happen |
| 42. | 關心 | 关心 | guānxīn | *Vst.* | to care or be concerned about; *N.* concern |
| 43. | 將來<br>未來<br>不久的將來 | 将来<br><br>不久的将来 | jiānglái<br>wèilái<br>bùjiǔde jiānglái | *N.*<br>*N.*<br>*N.* | in the future<br>in the future<br>in the near future |
| 44. | 地下鐵 | 地下铁 | dìxiàtiě | *N.* | subway (system) = 地鐵 |
| 45. | 建立 | 建立 | jiànlì | *V.* | to establish; to found; to set up |
| 46. | 根本 | 根本 | gēnběn | *Adv.* | fundamentally; essentially; at the root |
| 47. | 解決 | 解决 | jiějué | *V.* | to solve (a problem) |

# 文法 Grammar

Each pattern below is illustrated by sample sentences. When blanks are provided, complete the sentences. When English sentences are provided, give Chinese counterparts.

## 1. 讓 **ràng: (V.) to yield to; to let; allow; to make/cause; (Prep.) passive marker**

a. 到歐洲去觀光這件事，讓我再研究研究吧。
（到欧洲去观光这件事，让我再研究研究吧。）
As to the matter of a sightseeing trip to Europe, let me think it over.

b. 在大街路口，車輛應該讓行人先走。
（在大街路口，车辆应该让行人先走。）
Automobiles ought to yield to pedestrians at intersections.

c. 都已經夜裡十一點了，他還沒回來，真讓人著急。
（都已经夜里十一点了，他还没回来，真让人着急。）
It's already 11 p.m. and he's not back yet; it really makes one worry.

d. 很抱歉，我的車讓兒子給開走了，不能借給你。
（很抱歉，我的车让儿子给开走了，不能借给你。）
Sorry, I let my son borrow my car. I can't lend it to you.

e. 停下來！你怎麼能讓行人 ______________________________ ?
（停下来！你怎么能让行人 ______________________________ ?）

f. 我今天開車不小心，讓警察給 ______________________________ 。
（我今天开车不小心，让警察给 ______________________________ 。）

g. He waited two hours for the bus, but it didn't come, which made him really angry.

## 2. 甚至（於） **shènzhì(yú): (Adv./Conj.) even; to the point of (usually occurring with the prepositions 於 and 連)**

a. 這輛車碰得太厲害了，甚至連他都修不好。
（这辆车碰得太厉害了，甚至连他都修不好。）
This car had such a serious collision, even he cannot repair it.

b. 甚至紐約人都會受不了台北的交通的。
（甚至纽约人都会受不了台北的交通的。）
Even New Yorkers find Taipei traffic intolerable.

c. 七月四日，城里舉行慶祝活動。路的兩旁，甚至路口都擠滿了人。
（七月四日，城里举行庆祝活动。路的两旁，甚至路口都挤满了人。）
When the town celebrated July 4th, both sides of the street were crowded with people, even at intersections.

d. 在亞洲，機車不但是男士，甚至也是女士的主要交通工具。
（在亚洲，机车不但是男士，甚至也是女士的主要交通工具。）
In Asia, men and even women depend on motorcycles as a major means of transportation.

e. 上下班時間，不但等不到公車，甚至 ______________________。
（上下班时间，不但等不到公车，甚至 ______________________。）

f. 路的兩旁停滿了車，甚至於連 ______________________。
（路的两旁停满了车，甚至于连 ______________________。）

g. Cars are parked on both sides of the street, even on the sidewalks.

h. My motorcycle, and even my bicycle, were stolen last night.

## 3. 於是 yúshì: (Conj.) hence; thereupon; as a result

a. 市長很關心交通問題，於是決定開會討論解決的方法。
（市长很关心交通问题，于是决定开会讨论解决的方法。）
The mayor was concerned about traffic problems, so he decided to hold a meeting to discuss methods for solving them.

b. 因為市區內停車不容易，於是許多人改搭公車。
（因为市区内停车不容易，于是许多人改搭公车。）
Since parking in the city is a serious problem, many people have taken to riding buses.

c. 有能力出國觀光的人多了，於是旅行社的生意越來越好了。
（有能力出国观光的人多了，于是旅行社的生意越来越好了。）
As more people are able to travel abroad, travel agencies' business is getting better and better.

d. 亞洲的經濟地位越來越重要，______________________。
（亚洲的经济地位越来越重要，______________________。）

e. 車站太遠又得換好幾次車，______________________。
（车站太远又得换好几次车，______________________。）

f. ______________________，於是 ______________________。
（______________________，于是 ______________________。）

g. All the flights were full, so he cancelled his travel plans.

h. Recently the mayor's office raised the traffic fines. As a result, the city's traffic situation has improved a great deal.

### 4. 如何 rúhé:

A. *(Adv.) how (to); in what manner?*
B. *(V.) How is ...? What is ...?*
C. *(Idiomatic) How about it? What do you think?*

a. 如何改善兩國的關係，是這一次開會所討論的主要題目。
（如何改善两国的关系，是这一次开会所讨论的主要题目。）
How to improve the relationship between the two countries is a major topic for discussion at this meeting.

b. 他如何辦理這件事，每個人都很關心。
（他如何办理这件事，每个人都很关心。）
Everyone is concerned about how he deals with this matter.

c. 對增加交通警察來改善交通，你的看法如何？
（对增加交通警察来改善交通，你的看法如何？）
What is your view on increasing highway patrols in order to improve traffic?

d. 周末到夜市走走，如何？
（周末到夜市走走，如何？）
How about going to the night market this weekend?

e. 停車的地方不容易找，走路去上班如何？
（停车的地方不容易找，走路去上班如何？）
A parking space is so hard to find; how about going to work on foot?

f. 如何 ______________________ 是本校今年最重要的工作。
（如何 ______________________ 是本校今年最重要的工作。）

g. 下學期我們一起 ______________________ 如何？
（下学期我们一起 ______________________ 如何？）

h. In the future, how do you want me to contact you?

i. How shall we simplify our cumbersome traffic regulations?

### 5. 根本 gēnběn:

(Adj.) *fundamental, essential*
(Adv.) *(positive) radically; (negative) simply; not at all; none whatsoever*

a. 解決同事之間的問題，最根本的法子就是彼此多溝通。
（解决同事之间的问题，最根本的法子就是彼此多沟通。）
The most fundamental way of resolving conflicts among colleagues is to open lines of communication.

b. 近十年來，人民的生活有了根本的變化。
（近十年来，人民的生活有了根本的变化。）
There have been fundamental changes in people's lives over the last ten years.

c. 他開車向來很遵守規則，我根本就沒想到他會發生車禍。
（他开车向来很遵守规则，我根本就没想到他会发生车祸。）
He has always been a very law-abiding driver. I simply can't imagine him being involved in an accident.

d. 我根本就不能同意你所提出的要求。
（我根本就不能同意你所提出的要求。）
I just cannot agree to your demands.

e. 要根本解決 ____________________，還需要______________________。
（要根本解决 ____________________，还需要______________________。）

f. 只有建立地下鐵才能根本 _________________________________。
（只有建立地下铁才能根本 _________________________________。）

g. Sometimes pedestrians in Taipei simply can't make their way to the other side of the street.

h. I don't know how this accident happened; I didn't see the other car coming.

## 練習 Exercises

**I. 造句 Construct grammatically and logically correct sentences, using both words of the given pairs.**

例：多，擠 → 洛杉磯的車子特別多，所以交通很擠。
（多，挤 → 洛杉矶的车子特别多，所以交通很挤。）

| | | | | |
|---|---|---|---|---|
| a. | 藝術品， | 頭痛 | 艺术品， | 头痛 |
| b. | 規則， | 亂 | 规则， | 乱 |
| c. | 婚禮， | 塞車 | 婚礼， | 塞车 |
| d. | 觀光客， | 增加 | 观光客， | 增加 |
| e. | 糟糕， | 改善 | 糟糕， | 改善 |
| f. | 車禍， | 關心 | 车祸， | 关心 |
| g. | 情況， | 解決 | 情况， | 解决 |
| h. | 危險， | 改 | 危险， | 改 |

## 2. 填入合適的動詞 Supply appropriate verbs for these sentences.

a. 在市區內 ______ 車不易又貴，於是許多本來開車上班的人都改 ______ 公車。
（在市区内 ______ 车不易又贵，于是许多本来开车上班的人都改 ______ 公车。）

b. 下午四點到六點下班時間最好別出門，因為主要的道路往往_____車。
（下午四点到六点下班时间最好别出门，因为主要的道路往往_____车。）

c. 這輛機車老是有毛病，千萬不要______得太快，更不可以載人， 很危險的！
（这辆机车老是有毛病，千万不要______得太快，更不可以载人，很危险的！）

d. 隨著經濟能力的改善，許多人都有錢出國 ______，於是旅行社的生意也越來越好。
（随着经济能力的改善，许多人都有钱出国 ______，于是旅行社的生意也越来越好。）

e. 若是要根本______這個問題，非得用一兩年的時間不可。
（若是要根本______这个问题，非得用一两年的时间不可。）

f. 上山的路窄，又缺少路燈的設備，所以常常______車禍。
（上山的路窄，又缺少路灯的设备，所以常常______车祸。）

g. 因為司機不夠，公車的班次也隨著_______，造成許多市民的不便。
（因为司机不够，公车的班次也随着_______，造成许多市民的不便。）

h. 要_____夜市的衛生情況，首先得從餐具的清洗以及冷凍設備兩方面談起。
（要_____夜市的卫生情况，首先得从餐具的清洗以及冷冻设备两方面谈起。）

i. 亞洲的經濟在國際市場上越來越重要，來這裡______生意的西方商人也一年比一年______。
（亚洲的经济在国际市场上越来越重要，来这里______生意的西方商人也一年比一年______。）

## 3. 路考 Test Your Driving

選出合適的答案填入空格中，答案可能不只一個。
（选出合适的答案填入空格中，答案可能不只一个。）

Fill in the blanks using the given words. There may be more than one answer to each question.

| | | | |
|---|---|---|---|
| 加速 | 加速 | jiāsù | speed up |
| 速限 | 速限 | sùxiàn | speed limit |
| 公里 | 公里 | gōnglǐ | kilometer (km.) |
| 救護車 | 救护车 | jiùhùchē | ambulance |
| 超車 | 超车 | chāochē | to overtake or pass a car |

a. 黃燈的時候，你應該 ______________。
（黄灯的时候，你应该 ______________。）

1) 停下來（停下来）　2) 加速（加速）　3) 慢下來（慢下来）　4) 以上都可以（以上都可以）

b. 在速限一百公里的路上，你會開 ______________ 公里。
（在速限一百公里的路上，你会开 ______________ 公里。）

1) 99-101　2) 95-110　3) 80-95　4) 以上都有可能

c. 要是你有急事，得找一個地方停車，可是附近已經沒有停車位了。這時候，你會怎麼辦呢？
（要是你有急事，得找一个地方停车，可是附近已经没有停车位了。这时候，你会怎么办呢？）

1) 停在站牌旁邊（停在站牌旁边）　2) 停在塞車的車輛中（停在塞车的车辆中）
3) 停在十字路口（停在十字路口）　4) 以上都不對（以上都不对）

d. 在下面哪種情形下不可以開車？
（在下面哪种情形下不可以开车？）

1) 未滿十八歲（未满十八岁）　2) 剛跟朋友喝了兩罐啤酒（刚跟朋友喝了两罐啤酒）
3) 剛跟太太吵了一架（刚跟太太吵了一架）　4) 前一天晚上一夜沒睡（前一天晚上一夜没睡）

e. 如果你是駕駛，下面哪些事情你認為是可以做的？
（如果你是驾驶，下面哪些事情你认为是可以做的？）

1) 跟著救護車走，因為又快又安全。（跟着救护车走，因为又快又安全。）
2) 趕時間在塞車的長龍裡蛇行。（赶时间在塞车的长龙里蛇行。）
3) 只要有行人要過街，就讓他們先走。（只要有行人要过街，就让他们先走。）
4) 從左邊超車。（从左边超车。）

## 4. 說故事 Storytelling

根據下面的生詞，編出一個故事。
（根据下面的生词，编出一个故事。）
Use the following key words to compose a short story.

下班 → 著急 → 客滿 → 塞車 → 紅燈 → 走路 → 快樂
（下班 → 着急 → 客满 → 塞车 → 红灯 → 走路 → 快乐）

## 5. 情況對話 Role-Play

兩位同學一組，扮演下面的角色。
（两位同学一组，扮演下面的角色。）
Choose a partner and act out the following roles:

**Role A**:
一位警察，在路上攔下一位超速的駕駛，開罰單。
（一位警察，在路上拦下一位超速的驾驶，开罚单。）
A policeman is writing a traffic ticket to a speeder.

**Role B**:
因為上班遲到，所以開快車。自己的車子壞了送去修理，開著一輛租來的紅跑車。
（因为上班迟到，所以开快车。自己的车子坏了送去修理，开着一辆租来的红跑车。）
A driver who sped because he/she is late for work. The red sportscar he/she is driving was rented; his/her own car was sent to the garage for repairs.

| | | | |
|---|---|---|---|
| 警察 | 警察 | jǐngchá | police |
| 超速 | 超速 | chāosù | to speed; to exceed the speed limit |
| 罰單 | 罚单 | fádān | traffic ticket |
| 修理 | 修理 | xiūlǐ | to repair; repairs |
| 修車廠 | 修车厂 | xiūchēchǎng | (mechanic's) garage; auto repair shop |
| 租 | 租 | zū | to rent |

## 6. 閱讀練習 Reading Comprehension

從三個句子中選出一句和原句意思相同的。
（从三个句子中选出一句和原句意思相同的。）
From the choices given, select one sentence that agrees with the original statement.

**A.** 一想到台北的交通，我馬上想到一句老生常談的話：
《問題人人會談，就是沒有人設法解決。》
（一想到台北的交通，我马上想到一句老生常谈的话：
《问题人人会谈，就是没有人设法解决。》）

(1) 台北的交通是一個除了老年人以外人人都談的問題，可是沒人能解決。
（台北的交通是一个除了老年人以外人人都谈的问题，可是没人能解决。）
(2) 大家都十分關心交通問題，不過只說不做。
（大家都十分关心交通问题，不过只说不做。）
(3) 要解決交通問題非得先談一談才有辦法。
（要解决交通问题非得先谈一谈才有办法。）

**B.** 如果可能的話，過馬路時應走天橋或地下道，比較沒有危險。
（如果可能的话，过马路时应走天桥或地下道，比较没有危险。）

(1) 走天橋或地下道危險是危險，可是方便。
（走天桥或地下道危险是危险，可是方便。）
(2) 過馬路沒有走天橋或地下道那麼危險。
（过马路没有走天桥或地下道那么危险。）
(3)『馬路如虎口』，行人還是走天橋或地下道的好。
（『马路如虎口』，行人还是走天桥或地下道的好。）

**C.** 中國人脾氣好，人們眼見車輛超車、蛇行、闖紅燈，也很少發火。
（中国人脾气好，人们眼见车辆超车、蛇行、闯红灯，也很少发火。）

(1) 超車、蛇行等都是讓人頭痛的問題。
（超车、蛇行等都是让人头痛的问题。）
(2) 脾氣好的中國人是絕對不會不遵守交通規則的。
（脾气好的中国人是绝对不会不遵守交通规则的。）
(3) 街上的交通情況亂是亂，可是一般中國人看了不太生氣。
（街上的交通情况乱是乱，可是一般中国人看了不太生气。）

**D.** 計程車搭載的對象往往是自己沒有機車、汽車，而又不想擠公車，不肯走路，沒有被同行載走的那種人。
（计程车搭载的对象往往是自己没有机车、汽车，而又不想挤公车，不肯走路，没有被同行载走的那种人。）

(1) 常坐計程車的人多半自己沒有交通工具，覺得搭公車太擠，走路又太累。
（常坐计程车的人多半自己没有交通工具，觉得搭公车太挤，走路又太累。）
(2) 計程車司機因為不肯擠公車，也不愛走路，所以決定做駕駛這一行。
（计程车司机因为不肯挤公车，也不爱走路，所以决定做驾驶这一行。）
(3) 許多不肯走路去車站搭車的人，常常就搭計程車去，一路上可認識不少同行。
（许多不肯走路去车站搭车的人，常常就搭计程车去，一路上可认识不少同行。）

## 7. 作文 Composition

談談你經歷過或看過聽過的一個車禍事件。
（谈谈你经历过或看过听过的一个车祸事件。）
Have you ever been involved in a car accident? If yes, describe it. If no, write about an accident you have witnessed or heard of.

# 補充資料 Supplementary Materials

## 1. 交通工具 Means of Transportation

| 交通工具 Means of Transportation | | |
|---|---|---|
| 貨車 | huòchē | truck; van; trailer |
| 救護車 | jiùhùchè | ambulance |
| 救火車 | jiùhuǒchē | fire engine |
| 地下鐵 | dìxiàtiê | subway ＝地鐵 |
| 警車 | jǐngchè | police car |

## 2. Chaos over the Tomb-Sweeping Holiday

### 購票返鄉・大排長龍

【本報記者 小宇・台北報導】

一年一度的清明節快到了，台北火車站又見購買長龍！昨天鐵路局開始預售四月一日的全線車票，售票開始不到二小時，全線各級對號列車車票，全部銷售一空。許多買不到票的旅客抱怨連連，悻悻然地離開車站。

每年逢清明掃墓祭祖的節日，火車票就一位難求。幸好今年的假期遇上周休二日，疏散了返鄉的人潮。

台灣鐵路局呼籲民眾，可多利用網路及語音訂位系統，若欲現場購票，也應先準備好心目中理想的車次及相關資料，方便票務人員儘速處理，亦能有效減少排隊等候的時間。

## 3. Desperate Figures & Scenes

Towing Scooters

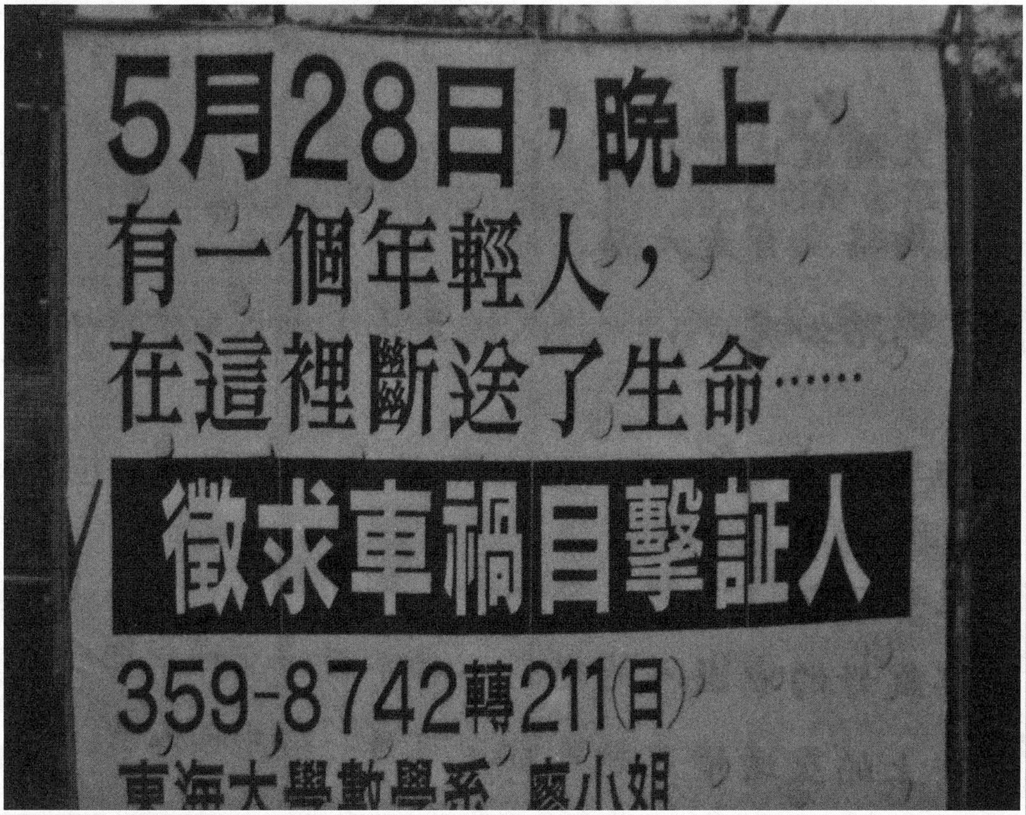

# 第七課

# 熱鍋上的「烤」生

## 繁体課文 Traditional Text

高中、大學的入學考試雖然是公平的競爭，但由於過分重視一次考試的結果，帶來了不少問題。有人因為聯考失敗而自殺；很多學生在填鴨式的教學下只會考試，缺乏思考的能力。因此，許多人要求廢除聯考制度，進行教育改革—從推薦入學，申請入學到現在採用的多元入學方式。舉行五十幾年的『聯考』終於成為歷史名詞了。

在這種多元入學的制度下，大學各校系所採用的入學標準不盡相同，學生可以依據自己的專長及興趣，選擇不同的指定科目，應考有興趣的科系。學生不再只是為考試成績而努力，各項特殊才能可以因此被發掘、重視。

改革教育制度的出發點正確，然而家長及學生觀念沒有隨著改變，仍受到升學主義影響，還是對明星學校有迷思。因此，多元入學不但沒有減輕學生的考試壓力，學生為了在大大小小的科目、考試中都取得好成績，壓力反而更重。不過，跟過去聯考制度比起來，多元入學帶來的正面意義及優點，是過去聯考無法取代的。

## 简体课文 Simplified Text

高中、大学的入学考试虽然是公平的竞争，但由于过分重视一次考试的结果，带来了不少问题。有人因为联考失败而自杀；很多学生在填鸭式的教学下只会考试，缺乏思考的能力。因此，许多人要求废除联考制度，进行教育改革—从推荐入学、申请入学到现在采用的多元入学方式。举行五十几年的『联考』终于成为历史名词了。

在这种多元入学的制度下，大学各校系所采用的入学标准不尽相同，学生可以依据自己的专长及兴趣，选择不同的指定科目，应考有兴趣的科系。学生不再只是为考试成绩而努力，各项特殊才能可以因此被发掘、重视。

改革教育制度的出发点正确，然而家长及学生观念没有随着改变，仍受到升学主义影响，还是对明星学校有迷思。因此，多元入学不但没有减轻学生的考试压力，学生为了在大大小小的科目、考试中都取得好成绩，压力反而更重。不过，跟过去联考制度比起来，多元入学带来的正面意义及优点，是过去联考无法取代的。

# 生詞 Vocabulary

| | | | | | |
|---|---|---|---|---|---|
| 1. | 入學考試 | 入学考试 | rùxué kǎoshì | *N.* | school entrance examination |
| 2. | 公平 | 公平 | gōngpíng | *Vs.* | fair |
| 3. | 競爭<br>比賽 | 竞争 | jìngzhēng<br>bǐsài | *N., Vs.*<br>*N.* | competition; to compete<br>race; game; match |
| 4. | 由於 | 由于 | yóuyú | *Conj.* | due to, because of |
| 5. | 結果 | 结果 | jiéguǒ | *N.* | result, outcome; as a result |
| 6. | 聯考 | 联考 | liánkǎo | *N.* | standardized school-placement exam |
| 7. | 帶來 | 带来 | dàilái | *Vpt.* | to bring; to bring along |
| 8. | 自殺 | 自杀 | zìshā | *Vi.* | to commit suicide; suicide |
| 9. | 填鴨式 | 填鸭式 | tiányāshì | *N.* | cramming (lit. stuffing a duck) |
| 10. | 缺乏 | 缺乏 | quēfá | *Vs-pred.* | to lack, to be short of |
| 11. | 思考 | 思考 | sīkǎo | *V.* | to think deeply, to reflect on |
| 12. | 因此 | 因此 | yīncǐ | *Conj.* | therefore, because of this |
| 13. | 失敗 | 失败 | shībài | *N.* | failure |
| 14. | 要求 | 要求 | yāoqiú | *V.* | to ask; to request; to demand |
| 15. | 廢除 | 废除 | fèichú | *V.* | to abolish; to abrogate; to cancel |
| 16. | 制度 | 制度 | zhìdù | *N.* | system |
| 17. | 進行 | 进行 | jìnxíng | *V.* | to proceed |
| 18. | 教育改革 | 教育改革 | jiàoyùgǎigé | *N.* | education innovation |
| 19. | 推薦 | 推荐 | tuījiàn | *V.* | to recommend; to commend |
| 20. | 申請 | 申请 | shēnqǐng | *V., N.* | to apply for; application |
| 21. | 採用 | 采用 | cǎiyòng | *V.* | to adopt, to use |
| 22. | 多元入學 | 多元入学 | duōyuánrùxué | *N.* | the Multiroute Promotion Program (MRPP) for College-bound Seniors |
| 23. | 舉行 | 举行 | jǔxíng | *V.* | to hold (a meeting, conference, etc.); to come off |
| 24. | 系所<br>科系<br>研究所 | 系所 | xìsuǒ<br>kēxì<br>yánjiùsuǒ | *N.*<br>*N.*<br>*N.* | (academic) subjects, departments, and institute<br>subjects and departments<br>institute |

| | | | | | |
|---|---|---|---|---|---|
| 25. | 標準 | 标准 | biāozhǔn | *N.* | standard |
| 26. | 不盡相同 | 不尽相同 | bújìnxiāngtóng | *Vs.* | not all the same |
| 27. | 依據 | 依据 | yījù | *Prep.* | in accordance with |
| 28. | 專長 | 专长 | zhuāncháng | *N.* | specialty; a special skill |
| 29. | 指定科目 | 指定科目 | zhǐdìngkēmù | *N.* | College Testing of Proficiency for Selected Subjects |
| 30. | 成績 | 成绩 | chéngjì | *N.* | scholastic record in school, grades, achievement |
| 31. | 特殊才能 | 特殊才能 | tèshūcáinéng | *N.* | a special skill |
| 32. | 發掘 | 发掘 | fājué | *V.* | to discover |
| 33. | 出發點 | 出发点 | chūfādiǎn | *N.* | a starting point |
| 34. | 正確 | 正确 | zhèngquè | *Vs.* | correct; right; proper |
| 35. | 家長 | 家长 | jiāzhǎng | *N.* | the parent or guardian of a child |
| 36. | 改變 | 改变 | gǎibiàn | *N.* | change; *V.* to change |
| 37. | 升學主義 | 升学主义 | shēngxuézhǔyì | *N.* | persistent pursuit of higher education |
| 38. | 影響 | 影响 | yǐngxiǎng | *N.* | to affect, influence |
| 39. | 明星學校 | 明星学校 | míngxīng xuéxiào | *N.* | famous school |
| 40. | 迷思 | 迷思 | mísī | *N.* | misconception |
| 41. | 減輕 | 减轻 | jiǎnqīng | *V.* | to lighten, to ease, to alleviate |
| 42. | 壓力 | 压力 | yālì | *N.* | pressure |
| 43. | 為了 | 为了 | wèile | *Prep.* | in order to, for the sake of, for (a particular reason) |
| 44. | 取得 | 取得 | qǔdé | *V.* | to obtain; to acquire |
| 45. | 反而 | 反而 | fǎnér | *Conj.* | on the contrary; instead |
| 46. | 正面意義 | 正面意义 | zhèngmiàn yìyì | *N.* | positive meaning |
| 47. | 優點 | 优点 | yōudiǎn | *N.* | an advantage |
| 48. | 取代 | 取代 | qǔdài | *V.* | to replace; to substitute for; to supersede; to take the place of |

# 文法 Grammar

Each pattern below is illustrated by sample sentences. When blanks are provided, complete the sentences. When English sentences are provided, give Chinese counterparts.

## 1. 由於 yóuyú: (Prep/Conj.) due to, as a result of

(*Unlike* 因為，由於 *cannot occur in the second clause, but can co-occur with other conj.'s such as* 因此 *and* 因而).

a. 由於工作的關係，他在香港停留了幾天。
（由于工作的关系，他在香港停留了几天。）
He stayed in Hong Kong for a few days because of business.

b. 由於醫科競爭激烈，我想改讀理科。
（由于医科竞争激烈，我想改读理科。）
Since competition to get into medical schools is rather keen, I am thinking of majoring in the sciences instead.

c. 車禍的發生往往是由於司機開快車的結果。
（车祸的发生往往是由于司机开快车的结果。）
Auto accidents usually happen as a result of speeding.

d. 由於每個人的觀點不同，因而意見也不能完全一致。
（由于每个人的观点不同，因而意见也不能完全一致。）
Views cannot be identical since perspectives vary.

e. 由於 ________________________________，我準備休學一年。
（由于 ________________________________，我准备休学一年。）

f. 由於 ______________________，他一直到現在都還沒有對象。
（由于 ______________________，他一直到现在都还没有对象。）

g. Mike Mei had to change his travel plans because of his family.

h. Lucy Li is not going to a graduate school as she has already found a job that pays quite well.

## 2. 對...有+ (Noun):

(*This is a high-frequency pattern in literary texts. The nouns that are usually associated with this structure include* 影響、興趣、 經驗、 *and* 研究.)

a. 從他的小說，可以看得出來西洋文學對他有很大的影響。
（从他的小说，可以看得出来西洋文学对他有很大的影响。）
His novels show that he has been strongly influenced by Western literature.

b. 由於對近代日本歷史很有興趣，他決定畢業以後到日本去留學。
（由于对近代日本历史很有兴趣，他决定毕业以后到日本去留学。）
He decided to pursue further studies in Japan after graduation because of his keen interest in modern Japanese history.

c. 陳教授對中國文學很有研究。你如果這方面有問題，可以請教他。
（陈教授对中国文学很有研究。你如果这方面有问题，可以请教他。）
Prof. Chen is well-versed in Chinese literature. You can consult with him if you have any questions.

d. Prof. Wang is a veteran instructor of Chinese.

e. Germany has had an enormous impact on the development of modern Japan.

## 3. 為了 wèile: (Prep.) for the sake of, because of, in order to (defining the cause of the second clause)

a. 為了解決市內停車問題，政府希望市民多坐公車。
（为了解决市内停车问题，政府希望市民多坐公车。）
In order to improve parking in the city, the authorities urge residents to take advantage of bus service.

b. 為了將來的工作，一般男學生不肯念文學院。
（为了将来的工作，一般男学生不肯念文学院。）
Most male students do not want to major in the humanities because of (the lack of) future job prospects.

c. 為了停車方便，____________________________________。
（为了停车方便，____________________________________。）

d. 為了明天的考試，____________________________________。
（为了明天的考试，____________________________________。）

e. In order to better understand Chinese culture, Mr. White spent several years in a remote Chinese village.

f. Old Zhang is quite happy to do anything for his students, as long as it can help them get into a good college.

## 4. Properties of 而 ér: (Conj.)

### a. It conjoins items of opposing meanings, similar to 然而，但是 and 卻。

1. 七月對考生是緊張而又重要的日子。
（七月对考生是紧张而又重要的日子。）
July is a tense yet important month for students who are taking exams.

2. 地攤上買的東西，價錢便宜而品質並不見得低。
（地摊上买的东西，价钱便宜而品质并不见得低。）
Goods at roadside stands are inexpensive but not necessarily poor in quality.

3. 幾乎所有的學生都在開夜車，而他還在開開心心地玩。
（几乎所有的学生都在开夜车，而他还在开开心心地玩。）
Almost all the students have been working hard into the night, but he has been having a lot of fun doing other things.

**b. It conjoins items of complementary meanings.**

1. 梅同學聰明而（又）努力，很得老師們的喜愛。
（梅同学聪明而（又）努力，很得老师们的喜爱。）
Ms. Mei is not only bright but is industrious as well, and is thus well liked by her teachers.

2. 一些現代作家的小說寫得生動而有趣。
（一些现代作家的小说写得生动而有趣。）
Some modern writers' works are both vivid and interesting.

3. 這並不是一個個人的問題，而是關係到整個社會的大問題。
（这并不是一个个人的问题，而是关系到整个社会的大问题。）
This is not a personal issue but a concern of the whole society.

**c. When 而 pairs with monosyllabic prepositions in the first clause, what follows it is usually also monosyllabic.**

1. 工作不能完全隨個人的興趣而定。
（工作不能完全随个人的兴趣而定。）
A job description cannot be defined entirely on the basis of an individual's interests.

2. 而且工作要求也不能因人而異。
（而且工作要求也不能因人而异。）
At the same time, what's expected at the job should not vary from person to person.

3. 薪水難道能依需要而定嗎？
（薪水难道能依需要而定吗？）
Is it really possible to set the salary on the basis of needs?

4. 就我們系而言，男同事跟女同事的比例是一樣的。
（就我们系而言，男同事跟女同事的比例是一样的。）
As to our department, the ratio between male and female colleagues is 1:1.

5. 學費的調整，對一般學生而言是不利的。
（学费的调整，对一般学生而言是不利的。）
The tuition has been adjusted against the interests of most students.

**d. When it pairs with disyllabic prepositions, 而 conjoins clauses.**

1. 他因為科系不理想而決定重考。
（他因为科系不理想而决定重考。）
He decided to try again since he didn't get into a department he wanted.

2. 由於競爭過分激烈而帶來許多社會問題。
（由于竞争过分激烈而带来许多社会问题。）
Overly stiff competition brought about many social problems.

3. 大部分的學生為了得到好成績而日夜捧著書。
（大部分的学生为了得到好成绩而日夜捧着书。）
Most students bury themselves in books in order to secure good grades.

4. In order to get a good job easily after graduation, he chose to major in engineering.

5. Our trip today has been postponed until next week, as the weather is not good enough.

6. Their marriage did not work out since their parents would not agree to it.

## 5. 在 . . . 的 + (Noun) + 下：

(*This is a high-frequency structure, which sets the stage, i.e. defining the pre-condition, for the implementation of what is defined in the second clause. The nouns occurring before* 下 *may include* 指導，影響，鼓勵， *and* 壓力.)

a. 在目前考試制度的壓力下，多數學校只能重視考試方法。
（在目前考试制度的压力下，多数学校只能重视考试方法。）
Under the pressure of the present examination system, most schools cannot afford not to coach their students in how to tackle (standardized) examinations.

b. 在朋友的鼓勵下，李先生到底參加了一次交友的團體活動。
（在朋友的鼓励下，李先生到底参加了一次交友的团体活动。）
Urged by his friends, Mr. Li finally took part in a special 'get-acquainted event' (an event for people looking for prospective marriage partners).

c. 在老師耐心地指導下，我們班得到合唱比賽的第一名。
（在老师耐心地指导下，我们班得到合唱比赛的第一名。）
Under our teacher's patient instruction, our class took first place in the chorus competition.

d. 在一些不良少年的影響下，他的生活起了很大的變化。
（在一些不良少年的影响下，他的生活起了很大的变化。）
Influenced by some juvenile delinquents, his life underwent serious changes.

e. Under the instruction of a famous teacher, she has made great progress.

## 6. 終於 zhōngyú: (Adv.) eventually, has finally ...

*(This is a pure temporal adverb while* 到底 *has an added element of "realization after repeated attempts.")*

a. 見到離別四十年的家人，他終於忍不住流下淚來。
（见到离别四十年的家人，他终于忍不住流下泪来。）
Seeing the family members he'd been separated from for forty years, he finally broke down in tears.

b. 由於長時間不斷地運動，他的身體終於健康起來了。
（由于长时间不断地运动，他的身体终于健康起来了。）
With regular exercises over a long period of time, his health eventually returned.

c. 警方經過一番努力，終於把那群非法偷渡的人抓到了。
（警方经过一番努力，终于把那群非法偷渡的人抓到了。）
After some effort, the police eventually apprehended the illegal immigrants.

d. 經過多次談判，雙方終於達成妥協，准許非官方往來。
（经过多次谈判，双方终于达成妥协，准许非官方往来。）
After much negotiation, the two parties eventually reached a compromise allowing unofficial contact.

e. 那個不合理的法律終於________________________________。
（那个不合理的法律终于________________________________。）

f. 政府終於改變了________________________________。
（政府终于改变了________________________________。）

g. Two years ago they finally mentioned the unpleasant trip to their native village.

h. After her repeated appeals, both her parents eventually agreed to the divorce.

# 練習 Exercises

## 1. 填充 Fill in the blanks with the adjective compounds given below:

| | | | | |
|---|---|---|---|---|
| 成敗 | 成败 | chéngbài | *(success/failure)* | success or failure |
| 好壞 | 好坏 | hǎohuài | *(good/bad)* | quality |
| 大小 | 大小 | dàxiǎo | *(big/small)* | size |
| 長短 | 长短 | chángduǎn | *(long/short)* | length |
| 高低 | 高低 | gāodī | *(tall/low)* | height; relative superiority or inferiority |

| | | | | |
|---|---|---|---|---|
| 高矮 | 高矮 | gāo'ǎi | *(tall/short)* | height (often referring to a person's height) |
| 深淺 | 深浅 | shēnqiǎn | *(deep/shallow)* | depth; relative difficulty or ease |
| 濃淡 | 浓淡 | nóngdàn | *(strong/light)* | consistency; thickness; taste (of soup, coffee) |
| 難易 | 难易 | nányì | *(difficult/easy)* | relative difficulty or ease |
| 快慢 | 快慢 | kuàimàn | *(fast/slow)* | speed |
| 輕重 | 轻重 | qīngzhòng | *(light/heavy)* | weight; relative importance or seriousness; propriety |

a. 若是你不知道這個湖的________，最好不要下去游泳。
（若是你不知道这个湖的________，最好不要下去游泳。）

b. 兩隊競爭十分激烈，難分__________。
（两队竞争十分激烈，难分__________。）

c. 這個人說話不知 __________，常常說錯話。
（这个人说话不知 __________，常常说错话。）

d. 老陳太高了，所以很難買到__________ 合適的長褲。
（老陈太高了，所以很难买到__________ 合适的长裤。）

e. 這雙球鞋的__________不太合適，換一雙吧！
（这双球鞋的__________不太合适，换一双吧！）

f. 貨品品質的__________不一定能從價錢上決定。
（貨品品質的__________不一定能从价钱上决定。）

g. 在這條路上開車，行車的__________是沒有限制的。
（在这条路上开车，行车的__________ 是没有限制的。）

h. 湯好喝極了，__________正好，不需要再放鹽了。
（汤好喝极了，__________ 正好，不需要再放盐了。）

i. 這科考試的______只要看看考生臉上的表情就知道了。
（这科考试的______ 只要看看考生脸上的表情就知道了。）

j. 子女在學校成績的______往往是父母最關心的一件事。
（子女在学校成绩的______ 往往是父母最关心的一件事。）

k. 他的前途完全就看這件事情的____________了。
（他的前途完全就看这件事情的____________了。）

l. 這張書桌特別低，得找一張__________合適的椅子來坐。
（这张书桌特别低，得找一张__________合适的椅子来坐。）

## 2. 填字遊戲 Crossword Puzzle

橫 Horizontal:

a. 朋友結婚時，祝他們很快有小孩的話。（朋友结婚时，祝他们很快有小孩的话。）

b. 每天這個時候，路上交通最糟糕。（每天这个时候，路上交通最糟糕。）

c. 考試的分數。（考试的分数。）

d. 排了許多的人或車。（排了许多的人或车。）

e. 若是今年考不上的話，只好明年______。
（若是今年考不上的话，只好明年______。）

直 Vertical:

1. 清早開出的公車。（清早开出的公车。）
2. 參加考試的學生。（参加考试的学生。）
3. 父母都要子女成功，前途光明。（父母都要子女成功，前途光明。）
4. 學校夏天的時候不上課。（学校夏天的时候不上课。）
5. 現代人都很 ______ 身體的健康。（现代人都很 ______ 身体的健康。）
6. 因為進大學不能申請，得通過______，帶給年輕人很大的壓力。
（因为进大学不能申请，得通过______，带给年轻人很大的压力。）

## 3. 加標點 Add Punctuation Marks

下面是一封沒有標點符號的信，請你加上標點符號。
（下面是一封没有标点符号的信，请你加上标点符号。）
The following letter is not punctuated; please add correct punctuation.

親愛的小平
　你的信我早就收到了我因為七月參加了大學聯考每天都猛K書現在考完了我才有時間寫信給你真對不起我不知道考得上考不上我的爸媽雖然沒有給我什麼壓力但是你知道所有的中國父母都是望子成龍的他們當然希望我能進一所好大學尤其是我的兩個哥哥都是國立大學畢業的我若是考不上或是考得不理想就打算進補習班明年重考我覺得你在美國念書真好不必參加聯考有空請再寫信給我告訴我你在美國的生活

祝順利
小英上
民國八十四年八月一日

亲爱的小平
　你的信我早就收到了我因为七月参加了大学联考每天都猛K书现在考完了我才有时间写信给你真对不起我不知道考得上考不上我的爸妈虽然没有给我什么压力但是你知道所有的中国父母都是望子成龙的他们当然希望我能进一所好大学尤其是我的两个哥哥都是国立大学毕业的我若是考不上或是考得不理想就打算进补习班明年重考我觉得你在美国念书真好不必参加联考有空请再写信给我告诉我你在美国的生活

祝顺利
小英上
民国八十四年八月一日

## 4. 讀日記 Reading a Diary

這是一位國中生李小龍的日記，請先讀一次然後在課堂上討論下面的問題。
（这是一位国中生李小龙的日记，请先读一次然后在课堂上讨论下面的问题。）
This is a diary of a junior high school student, Li Xiaolong. Read it first and then discuss the questions that follow in class.

七月九日　　　　　　　　　天氣晴　很熱

今天是高中聯考的第一天。早上我五點就起來了。我把英文課本拿出來可是看了半天也看不下去。心裡太緊張了！若是考不上一所理想的高中，以後我就不能上很好的大學，也找不到有前途的工作了。爸媽都要去陪考，但是我覺得陪「烤」太累了，而且給我很大的壓力。所以我要他們都留在家裡，就叫姐姐陪我去。姐姐是東海大學數學系的學生。她告訴我上了大學以後，沒有聯考的壓力，功課輕鬆多了！還可以自己選擇喜歡的課上，真好！

今天考國文、歷史、地理和英文。前面三科我覺得都考得不錯，但是英文考差了！很多生字我都不知道，而且時間不夠，沒寫完。明天考數學、物理、化學和生物，我一定得好好考！念了一個晚上的數學真痛苦。不知道「臨時抱佛腳」有沒有用。數學最可怕了！我的數學成績一直很差。真希望明天要考試的人是姐姐，不是我。

七月九日　　　　　　　　　天气晴　很热

今天是高中联考的第一天。早上我五点就起来了。我把英文课本拿出来可是看了半天也看不下去。心里太紧张了！若是考不上一所理想的高中，以后我就不能上很好的大学，也找不到有前途的工作了。爸妈都要去陪考，但是我觉得陪『烤』太累了，而且给我很大的压力。所以我要他们都留在家里，就叫姐姐陪我去。姐姐是东海大学数学系的学生。她告诉我上了大学以后，没有联考的压力，功课轻松多了！还可以自己选择喜欢的课上，真好！

今天考国文、历史、地理和英文。前面三科我觉得都考得不错，但是英文考差了！很多生字我都不知道，而且时间不够，没写完。明天考数学、物理、化学和生物，我一定得好好考！念了一个晚上的数学真痛苦。不知道『临时抱佛脚』有没有用。数学最可怕了！我的数学成绩一直很差。真希望明天要考试的人是姐姐，不是我。

| | | | |
|---|---|---|---|
| 陪考 | 陪考 | péikǎo | to accompany someone to attend an exam (usually refers to the School Entrance Exams, which may take several days) |
| 留 | 留 | liú | to stay |
| 物理 | 物理 | wùlǐ | physics |
| 化學 | 化学 | huàxué | chemistry |

| | | | |
|---|---|---|---|
| 生物 | 生物 | shēngwù | biology |
| 痛苦 | 痛苦 | tòngkǔ | painful |
| 臨時抱佛腳 | 临时抱佛脚 | línshí bào fójiǎo | make a frantic last-minute effort (Lit. embrace Buddha's feet in one's hour of need) |

a. 今天李小龍去做什麼了？
（今天李小龙去做什么了？）

b. 為什麼李小龍不要他的父母陪考？
（为什么李小龙不要他的父母陪考？）

c. 為什麼李小龍希望明天參加聯考的是他姐姐？
（为什么李小龙希望明天参加联考的是他姐姐？）

d. 為什麼李小龍想上大學以後真好？
（为什么李小龙想上大学以后真好？）

e. 小龍想如果考不上理想的高中，就不能進好的大學，也找不到有前途的工作？你覺得他的看法對不對？為什麼？
（小龙想如果考不上理想的高中，就不能进好的大学，也找不到有前途的工作？你觉得他的看法对不对？为什么？）

f. 你有沒有臨時抱佛腳過？什麼時候？有用嗎？
（你有没有临时抱佛脚过？什么时候？有用吗？）

## 5. 情況對話 Role Play

下面有四則短短的留言，刊登在報紙上一個特別的廣告欄。請任選一個，根據留話的內容，編演一段對話或獨白。
（下面有四则短短的留言，刊登在报纸上一个特别的广告栏。请任选一个，根据留话的内容，编演一段对话或独白。）

Four messages are given as follows. Choose any one of them as a basis for a dialogue or monologue to be presented to the class.

a.
失望 shīwàng: to disappoint, disappointed
加油 jiāyóu: to pep up, an expression used to cheer somebody on

佳玉：
今年別再讓爸媽
失望好嗎？
加油！
三姐 留

國中老師：　<武X翁>
經過一連串的“烤”試
我終于進入了理想的學
校，但是你一周五天國
文課考六天試的教學方
式，真是烤過頭了吧！
國中生

b.
一連串 yìliánchuàn: a series of
過頭 guòtóu: overdo, go beyond the limit

賀！
城北扶輪社社長
林凡琦千金林靖宜
金榜題名
有其父必有其女，硬是要的！
SuSon

c.
賀 hè: to congratulate (=祝)
扶輪社 fúlúnshè: Rotary Club
千金 qiānjīn: daughter (Lit. thousand pieces of gold)
榜 bǎng: list of successful candidates

給三度落榜的女兒：
不要說這是“刺激”，
媽媽受到的“打擊”實在太大了。
就算沒好好念書，同樣的課本聽
老師講，總也有三遍了嗎？252
分比去年還少8分，說得過去嗎？
失望的媽媽

d.
度 dù: times (=次)
落 luò: to fall, to drop
落榜 luòbǎng: to fail the Entrance Exam, to fail to be admitted
刺激 cìjī: shock
打擊 dǎjí: impact, shock, hit, attack

## 6. 作文 Composition

請談談你進入大學的經過，是如何做的選擇？怎麼樣申請的？
（请谈谈你进入大学的经过，是如何做的选择？怎么样申请的？）
How did you apply to your university? What was the application process like? How did you select your university?

| | | | |
|---|---|---|---|
| 學費 | 学费 | xuéfèi | tuition |
| 獎學金 | 奖学金 | jiǎngxuéjīn | scholarship |
| 推薦信 | 推荐信 | tuījiànxìn | letter of recommendation |
| 成績單 | 成绩单 | chéngjīdān | transcript |
| 面試 | 面试 | miànshì | interview (as part of an exam) |
| 入學許可 | 入学许可 | rùxué xǔkě | (school) admission |

## 7. 找理想的補習班 Looking for an Ideal School

以下有四家補習班的廣告，小龍今年沒考上大學，想補習一年，明年再參加一次聯考。請依照他的條件，為他找一家補習班。

（以下有四家补习班的广告，小龙今年没考上大学，想补习一年，明年再参加一次联考。请依照他的条件，为他找一家补习班。）

Xiao Long did not get into a college this year and would like to spend a year in a prep school before he tries again next year. On the basis of his requirements, choose the best school for Xiao Long from the four advertised below.

| | |
|---|---|
| 1. 幫助升大學 | 帮助升大学 |
| 2. 交通方便，要位於南陽街 | 交通方便，要位于南阳街 |
| 3. 九月中旬才開課 | 九月中旬才开课 |

# 補充資料 Supplementary Materials

## 1. 中國的假日 Chinese Holidays

| 中國的假日 jiàrì Chinese Holidays | | | |
|---|---|---|---|
| 元旦 | Yuándàn | 一月一日 | New Year's Day |
| 青年節 | Qīngniánjié | 三月二十九日 | Youth Day |
| 兒童節 | Értóngjié | 四月四日 | Children's Day |
| 清明節 | Qīngmíngjié | 四月五日 | Tomb-Sweeping Day |
| 勞動節 | Láodòngjié | 五月五日 | Labor Day |
| 母親節 | Mǔqīnjié | 五月第二個星期日 | Mother's Day |
| 父親節 | Fùqīnjié | 八月八日 | Father's Day |
| 教師節 | Jiàoshījié | 九月二十八日 | Teacher's Day |
| 雙十節 | Shuāngshíjié | 十月十日 | National Day |

## 2. 中文裡的英文 English in Chinese

| 中文裏的英文 English in Chinese | | |
|---|---|---|
| K書 | kēishū | to study for exams |
| T恤 | tīxù | T-Shirt |
| 很Q | hěn kiū | nice chewy consistency, as of rice |
| 很酷 | hěn kù | Cool! |
| 小Case | xiǎo kēisi | No big deal! |
| MTV | | small movie lounge |
| KTV | | MTV & karaoke combined |
| 卡拉OK | kǎlā OK | sing-along bar, nightclub |

English Words Mixed with Chinese

## 3. 大學科系 Academic Departments

| 大學科系 Academic Departments | | | | |
|---|---|---|---|---|
| 文學院<br>wénxuéyuàn | 語言、<br>yǔyán | 文學、<br>wénxué | 歷史、<br>lìshǐ | 哲學<br>zhéxué |
| 理學院<br>lǐxuéyuàn | 物理、<br>wùlǐ | 化學、<br>huàxué | 數學<br>shùxué | |
| 法學院<br>fǎxuéyuàn | 法律、<br>fǎlǜ | 政治、<br>zhèngzhì | 社會<br>shèhuì | |
| 商學院<br>shāngxuéyuàn | 國貿、<br>guómào | 經濟、<br>jīngjì | 企管、<br>qìguǎn | 會計<br>kuàijì |
| 農學院<br>nóngxuéyuàn | 植物、<br>zhíwù | 動物、<br>dòngwù | 生物、<br>shēngwù | 畜牧<br>xùmù |
| 工學院<br>gōngxuéyuàn | 電機、<br>diànjī | 機械、<br>jīxiè | 土木、<br>tǔmù | 資訊<br>zīxùn |
| 醫學院<br>yīxuéyuàn | 醫學、<br>yīxué | 護理、<br>hùlǐ | 牙科<br>yákē | |
| 教育學院<br>jiàoyù xuéyuàn | 教育<br>jiàoyù | | | |

# 大學窄門 越來越寬

**錄取率世界第一？**
**現今大學的定位應重新思考！**

編輯/小宇/綜合整理

針對2004年大學入學指定考試錄取率突破87%，教育部長杜正勝語重心長地指出，將近九成的錄取率，不僅顯示臺灣已進入大學生的社會，並且有九成的高中職學生可順利進入大學院校就讀。他希望提醒各界，大學教育的定位需要改變，包括大學教育的意義爲何？大學教育應該做些什麼？

杜正勝也提到，雖然學生想念大學就可以念，的確代表著大學教育不再是少數的菁英教育，但是各界也應該思考，如何提升大學的教育品質？否則將產生「大學高中職化、研究所大學化」等不良的現象，要盡力避免讓「大學生」只成爲一個虛無的代名詞！

## 大學放榜：錄取率87.05%
### 教育部長杜正勝：避免大學高中化

【記者/怡靜/台北報導】 2004.08.01

九十三學年度大學考試分發入學昨天放榜，聯分會表示，今年考試分發繳交志願卡人數十萬二千一百三十二人，錄取八萬八千九百三十九人，錄取率八七・〇五%，比去年的八三・二二%又提升將近四個百分點。

校系錄取門檻則創新低，最低的是眞理大學數學系，英、數甲及物理三科（不加權）六十八・五分就上榜，平均每科不到廿三分。

### 大學三冠王出爐：全部落在台大！

【記者/Jimmy.Xiufen/台北訊】

2004年大學入學指定考試今天放榜！各類組最高原始總分（不含加權），仍由台灣大學各系囊括。第一類組部份，台大法律學系法學組376.94分拿下第一，第二類組由台大電機工程學系420.73分奪魁，第三類組一如往例，仍然是台大醫學系（自費生）540.3分獨佔鰲頭。

## 5. ...But Not Wide Enough

落榜學生的去處

最後一分鐘的準備

## 何時了？教改後補習風氣更盛！

九十二學年起，英語增加為二堂，並且從語文領域撥出節數上課，看到部份學生連國語注音符號都還有問題，又要他們去學、去記不同發音的英語，很難想像二種語言都能學得好。

英語教學的推行，造成更嚴重的補習現象，程度好的學生，社經地位高的家長，更形成高傲的心態，相對於無能力額外學習的學生，在校的表現不比他人好，久而久之，形成自卑心態，是一大隱憂。

若老師受到部份家長的壓力，只因某些程度好的學生不耐煩，就忽略其他未學過的學生，則造成教育機會不均等。一般家長的心態是重要關鍵，千萬別忽略了其他的孩子，這是有關單位必須去提倡及宣導的。

## 補習補習　越補越難自己學習！

補習班最初的功能，在廣面的解釋上，是指「正規課業以外的學習」或「課餘的學習」。補習本質上是良性，能使學生另外再尋得一學習機會，而且更為專精和整體。

補習學生的心態是，特別注重「分數」，想謀求捷徑的不良心態。另外，有部分上進的學生，無法克服某些困難，例如：學校老師教學方式不甚理想，或不適合自己，無法達到學習目的，或老師空有學識不懂教學，造成學生學習十分吃力，而且某些課程並非學生自行研讀便可獲得極大的效果。因此不僅造成自身成績無法突破，連達成了解課程的基本條件都發生困難，最後在無可奈何的情形下，加入補習一途。

為了爭取學生的青睞及提升學生的分數，總是把教材的一切打點妥貼。從講義、補充資料，到作業、習題解答，甚至讀書進度，完全抹殺學生尋找答案時的學習過程，造成學生面臨困難時，坐以待弊。研讀已整理精簡的講義，更促使學生失去統合、思考的能力。

# 第八課

# 大拜拜

## 繁体課文 Traditional Text

許多剛來台灣的外國朋友，夜晚走在街道上看見路旁住家或商店裡的紅燈，常常嚇了一跳，以為到了什麼風化區了。其實這是住家擺在屋內神位上的紅燈。一般祭拜的神包羅萬象，其中拜的也可能是祖先。但是不管是什麼神，人們每天一定按時燒香。從這裡可以看出台灣宗教的普遍。信仰是生活中相當重要的一部份。

隨著中西文化的交流，西方宗教也漸漸為人民所接受。比如天主教在山地就有廣大的信徒；基督教會更是深入社會各個角落。佛教徒的人數在台灣極多，估計至少有上百萬的信徒。還有一些地方性的民間宗教，融合了佛教、道教及儒家思想；因為最能配合當地居民的需要與想法，相當流行。台灣的大拜拜非常有趣，可算是民間宗教活動的高潮。各地寺廟裡燒香的信徒，擠得人山人海。有的還擺下數百桌酒席，雞鴨魚肉，大吃大喝，極為熱鬧。民間信仰的另一點特色則是一些特別的習俗：結婚要合八字；買房子要看風水；遇到困難要找算命先生。有人說這些是迷信，但是這樣的信仰在某些方面的確帶給人們許多精神上的安慰。

## 简体课文 Simplified Text

许多刚来台湾的外国朋友，夜晚走在街道上看见路旁住家或商店里的红灯，常常吓了一跳，以为到了什么风化区了。其实这是住家摆在屋内神位上的红灯。一般祭拜的神包罗万象，其中拜的也可能是祖先。但是不管是什么神，人们每天一定按时烧香。从这里可以看出台湾宗教的普遍。信仰是生活中相当重要的一部份。

随着中西文化的交流，西方宗教也渐渐为人民所接受。比如天主教在山地就有广大的信徒；基督教会更是深入社会各个角落。佛教徒的人数在台湾極多，估计至少有上百万的信徒。还有一些地方性的民间宗教，融合了佛教、道教及儒家思想；因为最能配合当地居民的需要与想法，相当流行。台湾的大拜拜非常有趣，可算是民间宗教活动的高潮。各地寺庙里烧香的信徒，挤得人山人海。有的还摆下数百桌酒席，鸡鸭鱼肉，大吃大喝，极为热闹。民间信仰的另一点特色则是一些特别的习俗：结婚要合八字；买房子要看风水；遇到困难要找算命先生。有人说这些是迷信，但是这样的信仰在某些方面的确带给人们许多精神上的安慰。

# 生詞 Vocabulary

| | | | | | |
|---|---|---|---|---|---|
| 1. | 嚇了一跳 | 吓了一跳 | xiàle yítiào | *Id.* | startled, scared |
| 2. | 風化區 | 风化区 | fēnghuà qū | *N.* | red light districts, morally undesirable places |
| 3. | 神位<br>神 | 神位 | shénwèi<br>shén | *N.*<br>*N.* | altar (*See chart in "Supplementary Materials" for this lesson*)<br>gods, spirits, immortals, deities |
| 4. | 祭拜 | 祭拜 | jìbài | *V.* | to worship |
| 5. | 包羅萬象 | 包罗万象 | bāoluó wànxiàng | *Id.* | to abound in varieties |
| 6. | 祖先 | 祖先 | zǔxiān | *N.* | ancestors |
| 7. | 按時 | 按时 | ànshí | *Adv.* | regularly; according to the time specified |
| 8. | 燒香<br>香 | 烧香 | shāoxiāng<br>xiāng | *V-sep.*<br>*N.* | to burn incense<br>incense |
| 9. | 宗教 | 宗教 | zōngjiào | *N.* | religion (*See chart in "Supplementary Materials" for this lesson*) |
| 10. | 普遍 | 普遍 | pǔbiàn | *Vs.* | commonplace, widespread |
| 11. | 信仰 | 信仰 | xìnyǎng | *N.* | (religious/political) belief |
| 12. | 相當 | 相当 | xiāngdāng | *Adv.* | quite, fairly |
| 13. | 交流 | 交流 | jiāoliú | *N.* | exchange, interchange |
| 14. | 漸漸 | 渐渐 | jiànjiàn | *Adv.* | gradually |
| 15. | 天主<br>天主教 | 天主 | tiānzhǔ<br>tiānzhǔjiào | *N.*<br>*N.* | the Lord, God<br>Catholicism |
| 16. | 廣大 | 广大 | guǎngdà | *Vs-attr.* | numerous; vast |
| 17. | 信徒 | 信徒 | xìntú | *N.* | believers, disciples |
| 18. | 基督<br>基督教 | 基督 | jīdū<br>jīdūjiào | *N.*<br>*N.* | (transliteration of) Jesus<br>Protestantism |
| 19. | 教會 | 教会 | jiàohuì | *N.* | the church |
| 20. | 角落 | 角落 | jiǎoluò | *N.* | corner, remote place |
| 21. | 佛<br>佛教 | 佛 | fó<br>fójiào | *N.*<br>*N.* | Buddha<br>Buddhism |
| 22. | 估計 | 估计 | gūjì | *V.* | to estimate |
| 23. | 至少 | 至少 | zhìshǎo | *Adv.* | at least |

| | | | | | |
|---|---|---|---|---|---|
| 24. | 上...<br>上百萬 | 上... | shàng ...<br>shàngbǎiwàn | *(prefix)*<br>*Vs-attr.* | up to ..., as many as ...<br>up to one million |
| 25. | ...性<br><br>地方性<br>世界性 | ...性 | ... xìng<br><br>dìfāngxìng<br>shìjièxìng | *(suffix)*<br><br>*Vs-attr.*<br>*Vs-attr.* | with ... characteristics (性 is added to certain nouns to create adjectives)<br>local, provincial<br>global, international |
| 26. | 民間 | 民间 | mínjiān | *N.* | folk, popular; of the common people |
| 27. | 融合 | 融合 | rónghé | *Vpt.* | to integrate, to mix |
| 28. | 道教 | 道教 | dàojiào | *N.* | the Tao religion (道 = the Way) |
| 29. | 儒家 | 儒家 | rújiā | *N.* | the Confucian school of philosophy |
| 30. | 思想 | 思想 | sīxiǎng | *N.* | thoughts, ideology, -ism |
| 31. | 配合 | 配合 | pèihé | *V.* | to cooperate, to support, to accommodate |
| 32. | 當地 | 当地 | dāngdì | *Vs-attr.* | in the locality, at the place in question |
| 33. | 居民 | 居民 | jūmín | *N.* | residents |
| 34. | 拜拜 | 拜拜 | bàibài | *N.* | (religious) festivals |
| 35. | 高潮 | 高潮 | gāocháo | *N.* | climax |
| 36. | 寺廟 | 寺庙 | sìmiào | *N.* | temples, shrines, monasteries *(See chart in "Supplementary Materials" for this lesson)* |
| 37. | 極為 | 极为 | jíwéi | *Adv.* | extremely |
| 38. | 則 | 则 | zé | *Prep.* | on the other hand |
| 39. | 八字<br><br>合八字 | 八字 | bāzì<br><br>hé bāzì | *N.* | the Eight Characters of the Chinese horoscope that are related to the Heavenly Stems and Earthly Branches, denoting the time, date, month, and year of a person's birth<br>to match and compare the Eight Cyclical Characters |
| 40. | 風水 | 风水 | fēngshuǐ | *N.* | system of geomancy that coordinates the principles of Yin and Yang and the five "elements" (metal, water, wood, fire and earth) to determine favorable locations and directions (of houses, tombs, etc.) |
| 41. | 困難 | 困难 | kùnnán | *N.* | difficulty; *Vs.* difficult |

| | | | | | |
|---|---|---|---|---|---|
| 42. | 算命<br><br>算命先生 | 算命 | suànmìng<br><br>suànmìng xiānshēng | *V-sep.*<br><br>*N.* | to tell one's fortune; fortune telling; divination<br>fortuneteller |
| 43. | 迷信 | 迷信 | míxìn | *Vs.* | superstitious; *N.* superstition |
| 44. | 某 | 某 | mǒu | *Det.* | a certain ... |
| 45. | 的確 | 的确 | díquè | *Adv.* | indeed |
| 46. | 精神 | 精神 | jīngshén | *N.* | spirit |
| 47. | 安慰 | 安慰 | ānwèi | *N.* | consolation; *V.* to console |

# 文法 Grammar

Each pattern below is illustrated by sample sentences. When blanks are provided, complete the sentences. When English sentences are provided, give Chinese counterparts.

## 1. Verbs with Cognate Objects

説了一聲　说了一声　to mention, utter
嚇了一跳　吓了一跳　be taken aback
打了一拳　打了一拳　to give a blow of the fist
看了一眼　看了一眼　to take a look
踢了一腳　踢了一脚　to give a kick
咬了一口　咬了一口　to take a bite

a. 顧客隻看了一眼，沒說話，就走了。
（顾客只看了一眼，没说话，就走了。）
The customer took a look and walked away without saying anything.

b. 小孩拿起蘋果，咬了一口，突然大叫一聲。
（小孩拿起苹果，咬了一口，突然大叫一声。）
The child held up the apple, took a bite and suddenly screamed.

c. 明天就搬家！你打個電話跟房東說一聲！
（明天就搬家！你打个电话跟房东说一声！）
Let's move to a new house tomorrow! Give our landlord a call and tell him that!

d. 他突然從背後打了我一下，把我 ______________________ 。
（他突然从背后打了我一下，把我 ______________________ 。）

e. 老陳的小兒子被鄰居的大狗________________，還好不太嚴重。
（老陈的小儿子被邻居的大狗________________，还好不太严重。）

## 2. 為 wèi: (Prep.)

*(Passive marker, often associated with* 所 *before the verb. Note that this is less colloquial and less commonly used than* 被*-passive.)*

a. 他才明白自己的意見不能為其他人所接受。
（他才明白自己的意见不能为其他人所接受。）
Only then did he realize that his opinions could not be accepted by others.

b. 經過這次表現，他的能力已經為大家所肯定。
（经过这次表现，他的能力已经为大家所肯定。）
Based on the way he dealt with things this time, everyone is now convinced of his abilities.

c. 傳統小吃最為________________________所________________________。
（传统小吃最为________________________所________________________。）

d. ________________________________的老師是最不為學生所歡迎的。
（________________________________的老师是最不为学生所欢迎的。）

e. In many villages, marriage for love is still not accepted by most people.

f. Some religious activities are often criticized by scholars.

## 3. 則 zé: (Adv.) however, on the other hand

a. 以前賽球，我們總是輸，今年則完全不同。
（以前赛球，我们总是输，今年则完全不同。）
We used to lose every game. However, things have been really different this year.

b. 西方思想受到宗教的影響很大；影響中國人最深的則是儒家思想。
（西方思想受到宗教的影响很大；影响中国人最深的则是儒家思想。）
Western thought has been heavily influenced by religion; Chinese people, on the other hand, have been strongly guided by Confucianism.

c. 那座廟平時非常安靜，每次大拜拜時則人山人海，熱鬧非常。
（那座庙平时非常安静，每次大拜拜时则人山人海，热闹非常。）
Ordinarily it's very quiet in that temple, but every time a festival is observed, it's crowded with noisy people.

d. 結婚的費用很高，對某些人來說不難；對一般人來說則是很大的負擔。
（结婚的费用很高，对某些人来说不难；对一般人来说则是很大的负担。）
Weddings are costly. To some people, such an expense can be borne with ease, but to others, it is a great financial strain.

e. 中國的傳統，紅顏色代表吉祥，白顏色則__________________。
（中国的传统，红颜色代表吉祥，白颜色则__________________。）

f. 道教是一種宗教，而儒家則____________________________。
（道教是一种宗教，而儒家则____________________________。）

g. Most people in England are Protestants; on the other hand, most people in Ireland are Catholics.

h. Buddhists do not worship gods, but most Taoist temples are crowded with deities.

## 4. 某 mǒu + (noun): (Det.) a certain ...

a. 我們都以為老張也是某年某月生的。
（我们都以为老张也是某年某月生的。）
We thought all along that old Mr. Zhang was also born on such and such a date.

b. 無論多好的政策總是會有某些人反對的。
（无论多好的政策总是会有某些人反对的。）
No matter how sound the policy, there are always those who oppose it.

c. 就是再好的朋友也會在某些事情上有不同的看法。
（就是再好的朋友也会在某些事情上有不同的看法。）
Even best friends do not see eye to eye on certain matters.

d. 我只知道這件事是在歐洲某國發生的。
（我只知道这件事是在欧洲某国发生的。）
I only know that it happened in a certain country in Europe.

e. I heard that he is now working with a certain Christian church in the South.

## 5. (Noun) + 上

*(In addition to locative references, e.g. in, at, by,* 上 *can also occur with abstract nouns, which can best be learned as idiomatic expressions.)*

a. 他在會議上表示支持大家的行動。
（他在会议上表示支持大家的行动。）
At the meeting, he indicated his support of the group's planned actions.

b. 現代年輕人精神上的壓力實在很大。
（现代年轻人精神上的压力实在很大。）
The young people of today are under great pressure.

c. 孔子跟老子都是中國思想史上重要的人物。
（孔子跟老子都是中国思想史上重要的人物。）
Confucius and Lao Tse are important figures in Chinese intellectual history.

d. 巴哈在音樂上下了很大的工夫，也有很偉大的成就。
（巴哈在音乐上下了很大的工夫，也有很伟大的成就。）
Bach devoted much of his time and energy to music and achieved great things.

e. 有些人無論到哪裡，生活上都會遇到許多困難。
（有些人无论到哪里，生活上都会遇到许多困难。）
Some people encounter hardship wherever they go.

f. 南非這幾年在政治上____________________。
（南非这几年在政治上____________________。）

g. 日本天皇在社會上____________________。
（日本天皇在社会上____________________。）

h. I am too embarrassed to talk about my financial difficulties.

i. Have you been happy over the last few days as far as your work is concerned?

## 練習 Exercises

### 1. 寫出合適的動詞 Supply an Appropriate Verb

例 EXAMPLE:（ 擺 ）攤子　　（ 摆 ）摊子

a. ________ 香　　________ 香

b. ________ 困難　　________ 困难

c. ________ 基督教　　________ 基督教

d. 找人 ________ 命　　找人 ________ 命

e. ________ 祖先　　________ 祖先

f. 請人來 ________ 風水　　请人来 ________ 风水

g. _____ 教堂 ______ 禮拜　　_____ 教堂 ______ 礼拜

### 2. 造句 Form Sentences

Construct grammatically and logically correct sentences, using both words provided.

a. 人山人海...估計　　人山人海...估计

b. 習俗...嚇了一跳　　习俗...吓了一跳

c. 信仰...按時　　　　信仰...按时

d. 需要...包羅萬象　　需要...包罗万象

e. 困難...安慰　　　　困难...安慰

f. 迷信...接受　　　　迷信...接受

## 3. 閱讀練習 Reading Comprehension

從三個句子中選出一句和原句意思相同的

（从三个句子中选出一句和原句意思相同的）

Select one sentence from the given choices that agrees most with the original statement:

__ A. 隨著時代的改變和文化的進步，一些不合科學觀念的迷信習俗，可能漸漸看不到了。

（随着时代的改变和文化的进步，一些不合科学观念的迷信习俗，可能渐渐看不到了。）

(1) 跟不上時代的腳步和科學的進步，許多習俗可能成為歷史名詞。

（跟不上时代的脚步和科学的进步，许多习俗可能成为历史名词。）

(2) 某些習俗在人們的心目中相當重要，就算是迷信也絕不會改變。

（某些习俗在人们的心目中相当重要，就算是迷信也绝不会改变。）

(3) 要能配合現代社會的需要及改變，傳統的習慣才能繼續下去。

（要能配合现代社会的需要及改变，传统的习惯才能继续下去。）

__ B. 風水觀念，不但深入鄉下教育程度較低的地方，其實都市中許多受過高等教育的人也非常相信。

（风水观念，不但深入乡下教育程度较低的地方，其实都市中许多受过高等教育的人也非常相信。）

(1) 不管是都市人還是鄉下人，都相信風水的重要性。

（不管是都市人还是乡下人，都相信风水的重要性。）

(2) 接不接受『看風水』這種事，其實和教育程度的高低沒有關係。

（接不接受『看风水』这种事，其实和教育程度的高低没有关系。）

(3) 風水的觀念在鄉下沒有都市裡那麼流行。

（风水的观念在乡下没有都市里那么流行。）

__ C. 許多陪祖母到廟裡燒香的小孩，看著老人家虔誠地上香拜佛，就是心裡萬分念著桌上擺的糕餅水果，也不敢吵鬧。

（许多陪祖母到庙里烧香的小孩，看着老人家虔诚地上香拜佛，就是心里万分念着桌上摆的糕饼水果，也不敢吵闹。）

(1) 廟裡往往吵鬧，主要是因為去上香的祖母不許孩子吃點心。
(庙里往往吵闹，主要是因为去上香的祖母不许孩子吃点心。)

(2) 小孩雖然不懂事，然而也知道到了廟裡要聽話，讓大人安靜拜佛。
(小孩虽然不懂事，然而也知道到了庙里要听话，让大人安静拜佛。)

(3) 廟內神像前擺放的食物是給神吃的，可是在小孩的眼中，真希望能放在自己肚子裡。
(庙内神像前摆放的食物是给神吃的，可是在小孩的眼中，真希望能放在自己肚子里。)

## 4. 翻譯 Translation

請把下面三則從報章雜誌上節錄出來的文字翻譯成中文。
(请把下面三则从报章杂志上节录出来的文字翻译成中文。)
Translate the following paragraphs into Chinese:

a. Many foreigners come to Taiwan in search of Chinese culture and are surprised to find an urban landscape reminiscent of New York. Some wonder where to look for Chinese culture—at the National Palace Museum? But culture is not a concrete thing that can be put some place for people to come and find it.

| | | | |
|---|---|---|---|
| in search of | xúnzhǎo | 尋找 | 寻找 |
| concrete | jùtǐ | 具體 | 具体 |

b. Do hills in back and water in front mean good feng-shui? Chinese people often go to great lengths in seeking an auspicious site for a building.

c. Chinese religion has been influenced by three great streams of human thought: Taoism, Confucianism, and Buddhism. Actually, each is more a philosophy than a religion.

| | | | |
|---|---|---|---|
| philosophy | zhéxué | 哲學 | 哲学 |

## 5. 動腦時間 Brainstorming Session

你住的村子有一間土地公廟，年代久了，破舊不堪，今年你們村裡的收成不錯，所以你們決定蓋一間大廟，感謝土地公的保佑。
(你住的村子有一间土地公庙，年代久了，破旧不堪，今年你们村里的收成不错，所以你们决定盖一间大庙，感谢土地公的保佑。)

You have had a good harvest in your village this year. In order to express your gratitude to the Tudi Gong, the Earth God, all of you in the village have decided to rebuild the Tudi Gong shrine, which is too small and shabby.

問題是： 你們如何募得足夠的錢來蓋廟？
（你们如何募得足够的钱来盖庙？）
請於十分鐘內討論出五個可行的辦法。
（请于十分钟内讨论出五个可行的办法。）

Use ten minutes to come up with five feasible ways to raise enough money for the reconstruction of the shrine.

## 6. 情況對話 Role Play

兩位同學一組，扮演下面的角色
（两位同学一组，扮演下面的角色）
Choose a partner and act out the following roles:

**Role A:**
一位十六歲的少女，發現自己懷孕了。男朋友已經和她分手，她不希望留下孩子，又不敢告訴家人，不知道該怎麼辦。因為父親是一位牧師，常常在教會裡叫別人不要墮胎，如果知道這件事，一定把她趕出家門。所以她來找「張老師」，希望能幫助她解決問題。
（一位十六岁的少女，发现自己怀孕了。男朋友已经和她分手，她不希望留下孩子，又不敢告诉家人，不知道该怎么办。因为父亲是一位牧师，常常在教会里叫别人不要堕胎，如果知道这件事，一定把她赶出家门。所以她来找「张老师」，希望能帮助她解决问题。）
A sixteen-year-old girl just found out that she is pregnant. She had already broken up with her boyfriend and does not want to have the child. She wants to get an abortion but does not dare tell her parents, since her father is the pastor of a church that is actively pro-life. And, if her parents found out, they'd almost certainly throw her out. Not knowing what to do, she seeks out Teacher Zhang.

**Role B:**
一位做社工服務的「張老師」，專門幫助少女解決問題。
（一位做社工服务的「张老师」，专门帮助少女解决问题。）
A social worker, Teacher Zhang, tries to help the girl to solve her problem.

| | | | |
|---|---|---|---|
| 懷孕 | 怀孕 | huáiyùn | to be pregnant |
| 墮胎 | 堕胎 | duòtāi | to have an abortion, abortion |
| 留下 | 留下 | liúxià | to keep |
| 贊成 | 赞成 | zànchéng | to agree with, to approve of |
| 寶貴 | 宝贵 | bǎoguì | precious |
| 騙 | 骗 | piàn | to cheat or lie to (someone) |
| 責任 | 责任 | zérèn | responsibility |

## 7. 作文 Composition

請你談一談你參加過的一次宗教活動或宗教儀式。
（请你谈一谈你参加过的一次宗教活动或宗教仪式。）
Write about one of the religious ceremonies or activities you have attended or participated in.

# 補充資料 Supplementary Materials

## 1. 台灣常見的神 Common Deities

| 台灣常見的神 Common Deities | | |
|---|---|---|
| 媽祖 | Māzǔ | Goddess of the Sea |
| 觀音 | Guānyīn | Goddess of Mercy |
| 關公 | Guāngōng | God of War |
| 土地公 | Tǔdìgōng | God of Earth |
| 城隍爺 | Chénghuángyé | City God |
| 財神爺 | Cáishényé | God of Wealth |
| 彌勒佛 | Mílèfó | Maitreya Buddha |

神位上祭拜的神包羅萬象

## 2. 中國的宗教 Religions in China

| 中國的宗教 zōngjiào Religions in China | | | |
|---|---|---|---|
| *Religion* | *Belief* | *Practitioner* | *Place* |
| 道教<br>dàojiào<br>Taoism | developed from a mixture of popular beliefs and Buddhism, concerned with obtaining a long life and good fortune, often by magical means | 道士 dàoshì | 廟 miào<br>觀 guàn<br>宮 gōng |
| 佛教<br>fójiào<br>Buddhism | from east and central Asia, it grows out of Gautama Buddha that pureness of spirit is the answer to suffering | 和尚 héshàng<br>尼姑 nígū | 廟 miào<br>寺 sì |
| 喇嘛教<br>lǎmājiào<br>Lamaism | a sect of Buddhism observed in Tibet and Mongolia | 喇嘛 lǎmā | 喇嘛廟 lǎmāmiào |
| 回教<br>huíjiào<br>Islam | the Muslim religion, founded by Muhammed | | 清真寺 qīngzhēnsì |

笑口常開的彌勒佛

唐玄奘

## 3. 寺廟的種類 **Places of Worship**

<table>
<tr><th colspan="4">寺廟的種類 Places of Worship</th></tr>
<tr><td rowspan="4">廟 miào</td><td rowspan="4">for worshipping ancestors, gods, Buddha, or canonized historical figures</td><td>宗廟</td><td>zōngmiào</td></tr>
<tr><td>孔廟</td><td>Kǒngmiào</td></tr>
<tr><td>媽祖廟</td><td>Māzǔmiào</td></tr>
<tr><td>城隍廟</td><td>Chénghuángmiào</td></tr>
<tr><td rowspan="3">寺 sì</td><td rowspan="3">used to refer to a Buddhist monastery, but in Taiwan it may also refer to a Buddhist-Taoist temple</td><td>少林寺</td><td>Shàolínsì</td></tr>
<tr><td>開元寺</td><td>Kāiyuánsì</td></tr>
<tr><td>龍山寺</td><td>Lóngshānsì</td></tr>
<tr><td rowspan="2">宮 gōng</td><td rowspan="2">a Taoist temple</td><td>天后宮</td><td>Tiānhòugōng</td></tr>
<tr><td>指南宮</td><td>Zhǐnángōng</td></tr>
<tr><td>觀 guàn</td><td>Taoist monastery with resident priests</td><td>白雲觀</td><td>Báiyúnguàn</td></tr>
<tr><td rowspan="3">祠 cí</td><td rowspan="3">for worshipping ancesters or for honoring soldiers or historical figures of achievement</td><td>祠堂</td><td>cítáng</td></tr>
<tr><td>忠烈祠</td><td>Zhōngliècí</td></tr>
<tr><td>延平郡王祠</td><td>Yánpíng Jùnwáng Cí</td></tr>
</table>

龍山寺

## 4. 燒香祭拜 Making Offerings

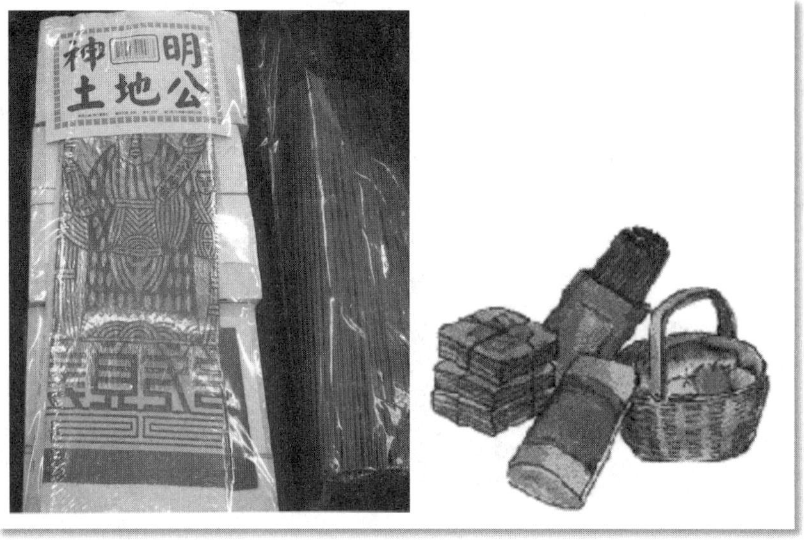


祭拜不同的神要燒不同的錢

各種祭品和香

Offerings to Deities or Ancestors

## 5. 傳統禁忌 Traditional Taboos

| 傳統禁忌 Traditional Taboos | |
|---|---|
| 住家不可以住四樓 | 四與死同音 |
| 送禮不可以送傘或扇子 | 傘，扇，與散同音 |
| 送禮不可以送鐘 | 鐘與終同音 |
| 跟打魚的人吃飯，魚不可以翻邊 | 怕會翻船 |
| 不可以跟相愛的人分吃一個梨子 | 怕會分離 |
| 懷孕時不可以釘釘子或用剪刀 | 會傷胎 |
| 鬼月不可以結婚、游泳、搬家 | 不吉利 |
| 不可以用紅色墨水簽名 | 會短命 |
| 過年的時候不可以把魚吃光 | 求年年有<餘> |

算算自己的命

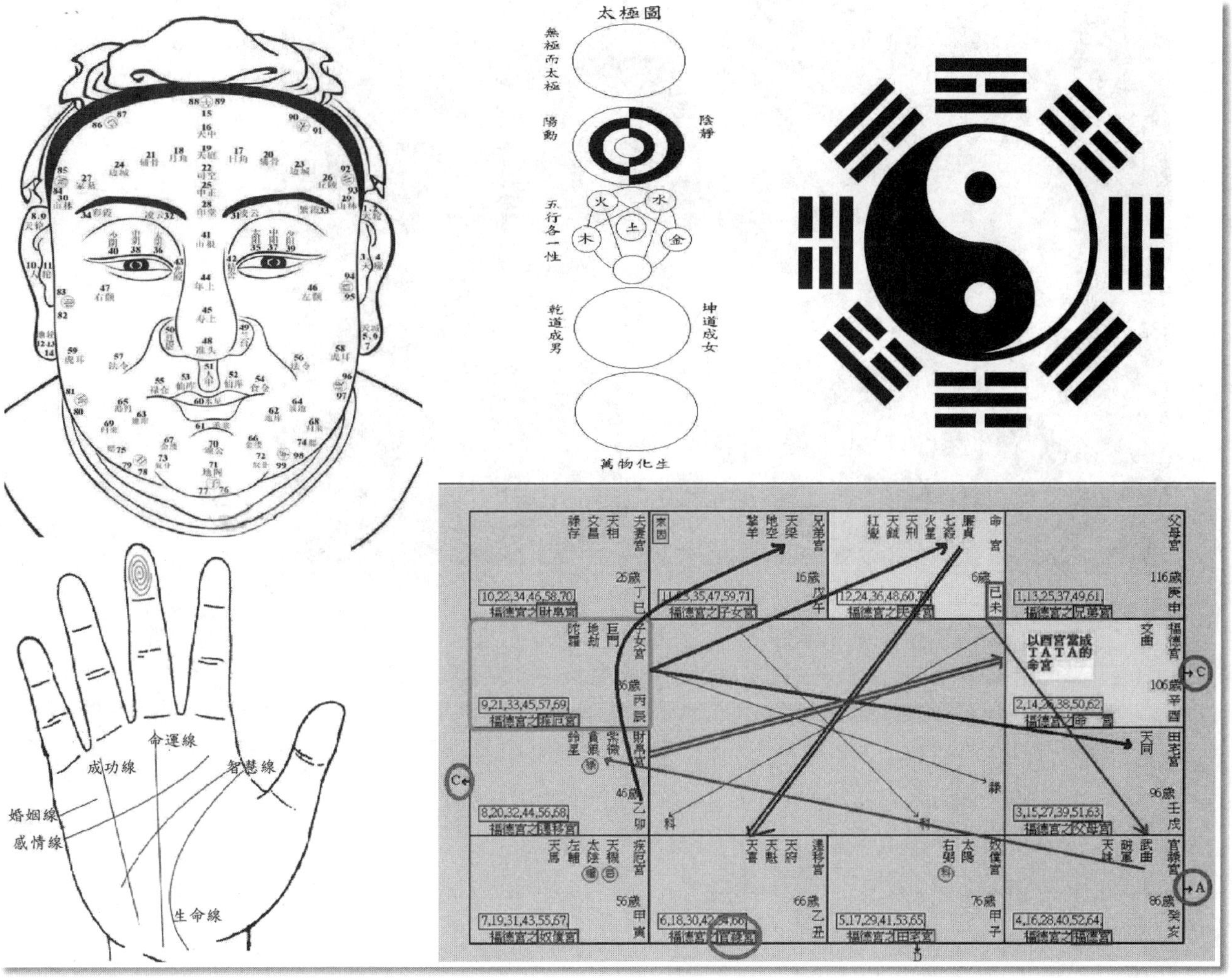

## 6. 紙錢 Money for the Other World

Money in Various Denominations

燒紙錢除了可以花錢消災，還有驅鬼的作用。

# 第九課

# 鹽水的蜂炮

## 繁体課文 Traditional Text

傳統的節慶在現代的中國社會仍然扮演了重要的角色。每逢春節、清明、端午和中秋等節日，不論在什麼地方的中國人都一定不會忘記好好慶祝一下。但是同樣的節日，常常因為每個地方風俗習慣不同，而有不一樣的慶祝方式。

在台灣，最具地方色彩的節慶可算是台南鹽水鎮慶祝元宵節的『蜂炮』了！在鹽水，慶祝元宵既沒有花燈也沒有遊行，而是瘋狂地點蜂炮。蜂炮是用無數枝沖天炮做成的。只要點燃一枝，其他數萬枝也就跟著射出，造成驚人的效果。因為射出的速度和數量就好像蜜蜂出 巢一樣嚇人，所以叫做『蜂炮』。有些蜂炮做成像動物、城門甚至於汽車和坦克的形狀。

蜂炮的起源非常傳奇。傳說在清朝時，因為鹽水鎮發生了一場大瘟疫，死了無數鎮民。鹽水人認為一定有惡鬼作怪。所以在一個元宵節，鎮民去廟裡求神幫助他們，並且大放煙火、鞭炮，希望能把惡鬼趕走。結果鹽水的瘟疫真的就消失了。從此以後，每年元宵鹽水人都舉行類似的慶祝活動。你如果有機會去參加，千萬記住戴上耳塞和安全帽；否則蜂炮才響你可能就被炮聲嚇跑了！

## 简体课文 Simplified Text

传统的节庆在现代的中国社会仍然扮演了重要的角色。每逢春节、清明、端午和中秋等节日，不论在什么地方的中国人都一定不会忘记好好庆祝一下。但是同样的节日，常常因为每个地方风俗习惯不同，而有不一样的庆祝方式。

在台湾，最具地方色彩的节庆可算是台南盐水镇庆祝元宵节的『蜂炮』了！在盐水，庆祝元宵既没有花灯也没有游行，而是疯狂地点蜂炮。蜂炮是用无数枝冲天炮做成的。只要点燃一枝，其它数万枝也就跟着射出，造成惊人的效果。因为射出的速度和数量就好像蜜蜂出巢一样吓人，所以叫做『蜂炮』。有些蜂炮做成像动物、城门甚至于汽车和坦克的形状。

蜂炮的起源非常传奇。传说在清朝时，因为盐水镇发生了一场大瘟疫，死了无数镇民。盐水人认为一定有恶鬼作怪。所以在一个元宵节，镇民去庙里求神帮助他们，并且大放烟火、鞭炮，希望能把恶鬼赶走。结果盐水的瘟疫真的就消失了。从此以后，每年元宵盐水人都举行类似的庆祝活动。你如果有机会去参加，千万记住戴上耳塞和安全帽；否则蜂炮才响你可能就被炮声吓跑了！

# 生詞 Vocabulary

| | | | | | |
|---|---|---|---|---|---|
| 1. | 鹽水 | 盐水 | yánshuǐ | *N.* | Yanshui (name of a town in Southern Taiwan) |
| 2. | 蜂炮 | 蜂炮 | fēngpào | *N.* | beehive-like platforms lifted with fire-crackers |
| 3. | 節慶 | 节庆 | jiéqìng | *N.* | festivities |
| 4. | 仍然 | 仍然 | réngrán | *Adv.* | still |
| 5. | 扮演 | 扮演 | bànyǎn | *V.* | to play the part of, to act |
| 6. | 角色 | 角色 | jiǎosè, juésè | *N.* | role, part |
| 7. | 逢<br>每逢 | 逢 | féng<br>měiféng | *V.*<br>*V.* | to meet, to come upon<br>every time or whenever (a season, festival or some specific occasion comes) |
| 8. | 春節 | 春节 | chūnjié | *N.* | Spring Festival, the lunar new year holidays |
| 9. | 清明 | 清明 | qīngmíng | *N.* | Tomb-Sweeping Day (April 5), when people visit their ancestral tombs |
| 10. | 端午 | 端午 | duānwǔ | *N.* | Dragon Boat Festival (the fifth day of the fifth lunar month) |
| 11. | 中秋 | 中秋 | zhōngqiū | *N.* | Mid-Autumn Festival (the fifteenth day of the eighth lunar month) |
| 12. | 節日 | 节日 | jiérì | *N.* | festival, holiday |
| 13. | 慶祝 | 庆祝 | qìngzhù | *V.* | to celebrate; *N.* celebration |
| 14. | 風俗 | 风俗 | fēngsú | *N.* | custom |
| 15. | 具 | 具 | jù | *V.* | to possess, to have |
| 16. | 元宵 | 元宵 | yuánxiāo | *N.* | Lantern Festival (the night of the fifteenth day of the first lunar month) |
| 17. | 花燈 | 花灯 | huādēng | *N.* | festive lantern (as displayed during the Lantern Festival) |
| 18. | 遊行 | 游行 | yóuxíng | *N.* | parade, rally, demonstration; *Vi.* to march, to rally |
| 19. | 瘋狂 | 疯狂 | fēngkuáng | *Vs.* | frantic, crazy, mad, insane |
| 20. | 點 | 点 | diǎn | *V.* | to light (a fire) |
| 21. | 無數 | 无数 | wúshù | *Vs-attr.* | numerous, countless |
| 22. | 沖天 | 冲天 | chōngtiān | *Vi.* | to shoot up to the sky |
| 23. | 點燃 | 点燃 | diǎnrán | *V.* | to light up, to ignite |

| | | | | | |
|---|---|---|---|---|---|
| 24. | 射出 | 射出 | shèchū | *V.* | to shoot, to fire |
| 25. | 造成 | 造成 | zàochéng | *V.* | to create, to cause, to bring |
| 26. | 驚人 | 惊人 | jīngrén | *Vs.* | astonishing, amazing |
| 27. | 效果 | 效果 | xiàoguǒ | *N.* | effect, result |
| 28. | 速度 | 速度 | sùdù | *N.* | speed |
| 29. | 數量 | 数量 | shùliàng | *N.* | quantity, amount |
| 30. | 巢 | 巢 | cháo | *N.* | nest, hive |
| 31. | 坦克 | 坦克 | tǎnkè | *N.* | armored tank |
| 32. | 形狀 | 形状 | xíngzhuàng | *N.* | form, shape, appearance |
| 33. | 傳奇 | 传奇 | chuánqí | *N.* | a legend |
| 34. | 傳說 | 传说 | chuánshuō | *Adv.* | it is said, people say; *N.* hearsay |
| 35. | 清朝 | 清朝 | qīngcháo | *N.* | Qing Dynasty |
| 36. | 瘟疫 | 瘟疫 | wēnyì | *N.* | plague, epidemic, pestilence |
| 37. | 惡鬼<br>鬼 | 恶鬼 | èguǐ<br>guǐ | *N.*<br>*N.* | ferocious devil<br>ghost, spirit |
| 38. | 作怪 | 作怪 | zuòguài | *Vi.* | to do mischief, to act mischievously |
| 39. | 煙火 | 烟火 | yānhuǒ | *N.* | fireworks, firecrackers |
| 40. | 鞭炮 | 鞭炮 | biānpào | *N.* | firecrackers |
| 41. | 趕走 | 赶走 | gǎnzǒu | *V.* | to drive away, to expel |
| 42. | 消失 | 消失 | xiāoshī | *Vp.* | to disappear, to vanish |
| 43. | 從此 | 从此 | cóngcǐ | *Conj.* | from then on |
| 44. | 類似 | 类似 | lèisì | *Vst.* | similar |
| 45. | 千萬 | 千万 | qiānwàn | *Adv.* | by all means |
| 46. | 耳塞 | 耳塞 | ěrsāi | *N.* | earplug |
| 47. | 否則 | 否则 | fǒuzé | *Conj.* | otherwise, if not, or else |
| 48. | 響 | 响 | xiǎng | *Vs.* | to make a sound; noisy, loud |

# 文法 Grammar

Each pattern below is illustrated by sample sentences. When blanks are provided, complete the sentences. When English sentences are provided, give Chinese counterparts.

## 1. 等 děng: (Nominal Particle)

*(Concludes exhaustive or non-exhaustive listings. When reduplicated, it always stands alone.)*

a. 這學期我選了政治、經濟、西方文學、西洋文化史、哲學史等五門課。
（这学期我选了政治、经济、西方文学、西洋文化史、哲学史等五门课。）
This semester I am taking five courses: political science, economics, Western literature, Western civilization, and the history of philosophy.

b. 想要上大學的學生都得通過高中，大學等兩次入學考試。
（想要上大学的学生都得通过高中，大学等两次入学考试。）
Students who want to attend college must pass two entrance exams: one before high school and one before college.

c. 本班車開往廣州，一路上經過北京、上海、南京等地。
（本班车开往广州，一路上经过北京、上海、南京等地。）
This train goes to Guangzhou; along the way, it stops at such places as Beijing, Shanghai, and Nanjing.

d. 那家店到現在還沒有開張是因為水、電...等都還沒有裝好。
（那家店到现在还没有开张是因为水、电...等都还没有装好。）
That store has not opened yet due to work still being done on the water, electrical, and other systems.

e. 大學商店有日用品、文具、衣服...等等。品質跟價錢都還算合理。
（大学商店有日用品、文具、衣服...等等。品质跟价钱都还算合理。）
The university store carries such items as daily necessities, stationery, and clothing. Their quality and prices are quite reasonable.

f. 這次夏季運動會比賽的項目有游泳、體操、划船...等等。
（这次夏季运动会比赛的项目有游泳、体操、划船...等等。）
The summer games this year include swimming, gymnastics, rowing, etc.

g. ____________________等地都是很受____________________歡迎的城市。
（____________________等地都是很受____________________欢迎的城市。）

h. ____________________等人都是世界上____________________的人物。
（____________________等人都是世界上____________________的人物。）

## 2. 既...也 vs. 既...又 jì ... yě jì ... yòu: (Adv.) not only ... but also ...

*(These are literary counterparts of* 不但...還..., 也...也..., *and* 又...又... *The former merely intensifies a situation, and the latter carries additional elements such as surprise, complaint, etc. Compare the two possible situations given below.)*

a. 學習一種外語，既要練習聽說，也 (or 又) 要練習讀寫。
（学习一种外语，既要练习听说，也 (or 又) 要练习读写。）
When learning a foreign language, one must practice not only listening and speaking, but also reading and writing.
(i) 也: Two equally important things
(ii) 又: Too much hard work involved

b 他平時既不注意飲食，也 (or 又) 不作健身運動，可是身體居然驚人地健康。
（他平时既不注意饮食，也 (or 又) 不作健身运动，可是身体居然惊人地健康。）
He doesn't usually pay much attention to what he eats, nor does he exercise, but he is surprisingly healthy. (又 *is more appropriate in this case*)

c. 她在戲里扮演白蛇的角色，演得既生動又活潑。
（她在戏里扮演白蛇的角色，演得既生动又活泼。）
She played the role of the White Snake. Her acting was both lively and spirited.

d. 顏太太抱怨她這次旅行既________________又________________。
（颜太太抱怨她这次旅行既________________又________________。）

e. 半工半讀________________________________。
（半工半读________________________________。）

## 3. 不是...而是... búshì ... érshì ...: (Conj.) not merely ... but actually ...

a. 鎮民相信這次大火不是人為的，而是惡鬼作怪所引起的。
（镇民相信这次大火不是人为的，而是恶鬼作怪所引起的。）
The villagers believe the fire was not caused by man but by an evil spirit.

b. 人口問題不是某個國家的問題而是整個世界的問題。
（人口问题不是某个国家的问题而是整个世界的问题。）
Overpopulation is not merely the problem of certain countries; it is actually a global concern.

c. 真正講究喝咖啡的人不用即溶咖啡而是____________________。
（真正讲究喝咖啡的人不用即溶咖啡而是____________________。）

d. 他們並不是自由戀愛認識的而是____________________。
（他们并不是自由恋爱认识的而是____________________。）

e. A university president does not represent just the professors, but should represent the whole campus.

f. Mr. White did not travel to China just for pleasure, but rather to seek friends of forty years ago.

## 4. 好像...一樣... hǎoxiàng ... yíyàng ...: look like, as if

*(In the subjunctive mood, 一樣 can be replaced or followed by 似的.)*

a. 那個紙做的汽車做得好像真的一樣。
（那个纸做的汽车做得好像真的一样。）(似的 would be inappropriate in this case)
That model car (made of paper) looks so real!

b. 他說得那麼生動，好像事情就發生在眼前一樣。
（他说得那么生动，好像事情就发生在眼前一样。）(or 似的)
His description of it was so vivid, it was as if it were happening right in front of our eyes.

c. 他跳舞跳得那麼高興好像忽然年輕了二十歲似的。
（他跳舞跳得那么高兴好像忽然年轻了二十岁似的。）
He danced so energetically, as if he were suddenly twenty years younger.

d. 他看到老高就好像看到鬼一樣那麼怕。
（他看到老高就好像看到鬼一样那么怕。）(or 似的)
He was terrified at seeing Lao Gao, it was as if he had seen a ghost.

e. 那塊石頭的形狀好像____________________一樣。
（那块石头的形状好像____________________一样。）

f. 他吃了一塊月餅就好像____________________似的。
（他吃了一块月饼就好像____________________似的。）

g. John likes to dress like a Catholic priest.

h. Steve sings folk songs so solemnly, it is as if he were singing a national anthem.

## 5. 否則 fǒuzé: (Conj.) otherwise, if not, then ...

*(This is a literary counterpart of both 不然 and 要不然 and is freely interchangeable with them.)*

a. 他一定有要緊的事找你，否則不會一再打電話來。
（他一定有要紧的事找你，否则不会一再打电话来。）
He must have something urgent to talk to you about; otherwise he would not have telephoned you repeatedly.

b. 好像他已經離開那個地方了，否則為什麼沒有他的消息？
（好像他已经离开那个地方了，否则为什么没有他的消息？）
He may have left that place; otherwise, why haven't we heard from him?

c. 除非有特別情況，否則他不可能改變原來的旅行計劃。
（除非有特别情况，否则他不可能改变原来的旅行计划。）
Unless something urgent turns up, (otherwise) he will not alter his original travel plans.

d. 你快去航空公司跟他解釋一下，否則____________________。
（你快去航空公司跟他解释一下，否则____________________。）

e. 明天的活動你一定要來參加，否則____________________。
（明天的活动你一定要来参加，否则____________________。）

f. Perhaps he was not feeling well; otherwise, he would definitely have accepted the invitation.

g. Unless the typhoon arrives tomorrow, it is going to be a bright sunny day.

### 6. 才 cái ... 就 jiù ...: (Adv.) only just ...and already ...

*(Referring to immediate occurrence of one thing after another resulting in something unexpected.)*

a. 他怎麼才吃了藥就睡著了呢？
（他怎么才吃了药就睡着了呢？）
How come he's fast asleep already when he just took the medicine a minute ago?

b. 辦公室的電腦才買沒幾天就讓人給偷走了。
（办公室的电脑才买没几天就让人给偷走了。）
It was only a couple of days ago that we bought a computer for the office, and it was already stolen.

c. 才告訴你畢業舞會在哪裡舉行，你就忘得一乾二淨！
（才告诉你毕业舞会在哪里举行，你就忘得一干二净！）
We just told you where the graduation dance is being held, and now you can't remember anything!

d. 怎麼才過了聖誕節就______________________________？
（怎么才过了圣诞节就______________________________？）

e. 老王跟小李才舉行了婚禮就__________________________。
（老王跟小李才举行了婚礼就__________________________。）

f. You just came back from a tour of China and now you are planning a trip to Japan?!

g. You've only been in the calligraphy class for two weeks and you want to drop it already?

# 練習 Exercises

## 1. 寫出對等的詞 Related Words

Fill in the blank with an appropriate answer so as to make the second or third pair of words parallel with the first one:

例子 EXAMPLE → 丈夫:妻子 ＝ ______:新娘
答案 ANSWER → 丈夫:妻子 ＝ 新郎:新娘

a. 戴（戴）: 安全帽（安全帽）＝ ______: 鞭炮（鞭炮）

b. 相同（相同）: 類似（类似）＝ 不然（不然）: ______

c. 春節（春节）: 拜年（拜年）
 ＝ ______: 吃月餅（吃月饼）
 ＝ ______: 提花燈（提花灯）

d. 扮演（扮演）: 角色（角色）
 ＝ ______: 節日（节日）
 ＝ ______: 活動（活动）

e. 失敗（失败）: 成功（成功）＝ ______: 出現（出现）

f. 蜜蜂（蜜蜂）: 蟲（蟲）
 ＝ ______: 病（病）
 ＝ ______: 朝(朝)

g. 多少（多少）: 數量（数量）＝ 快慢（快慢）: ______

h. 記得（记得）: 記住（记住）＝ 樣子（样子）: ______

## 2. 完成句子 Complete the Sentences

a. 在______，最具地方色彩的______。
（在______，最具地方色彩的______。）

b. ______在______扮演了重要的角色。
（______在______扮演了重要的角色。）

c. ______可算是他做過最瘋狂的事了。
（______可算是他做过最疯狂的事了。）

d. ______，讓我們______好好慶祝一下。
（______，让我们______好好庆祝一下。）

e. 如果 ______________________，千萬 ______________________。
（如果 ______________________，千万 ______________________。）

f. 傳說在月圓的那天晚上，____________________________。
（传说在月圆的那天晚上，____________________________。）

g. ______________________ 和 ______________________ 一樣嚇人。
（______________________ 和 ______________________ 一样吓人。）

## 3. 填字遊戲 Crossword Puzzle

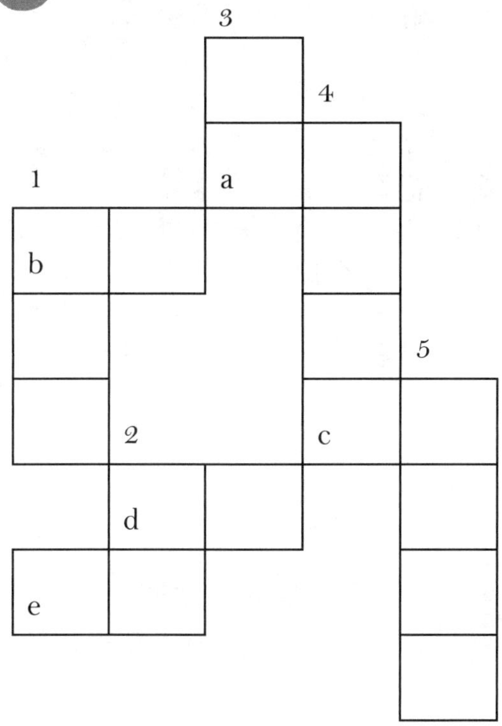


橫 Across

a. 走在路上的人。
（走在路上的人。）

b. 傳說鹽水鎮在這時發生了一場瘟疫。
（传说盐水镇在这时发生了一场瘟疫。）

c. 站在港口，一陣陣____吹來，覺得十分舒服。
（站在港口，一阵阵_____吹来，觉得十分舒服。）

d. _____ 時得請大家喝喜酒。
（_____ 时得请大家喝喜酒。）

e. 念書時一定要專心，不然_____不好念了也是白念。
（念书时一定要专心，不然_____不好念了也是白念。）

直 Down

1. 每年四月五日，要去掃墓。
（每年四月五日，要去扫墓。）
2. 這樣亂吵下去不會有什麼______。
（这样乱吵下去不会有什么______。）
3. 在美國，每逢七月四日許多城市都會在街上舉行這種活動。
（在美国，每逢七月四日许多城市都会在街上举行这种活动。）
4. 人多，擠得要死。
（人多，挤得要死。）
5. 因為每個地方的 _____ 都不一樣，所以去外地時應該先了解一下，否則常會發生一些讓人不好意思的事。
（因为每个地方的 _____ 都不一样，所以去外地时应该先了解一下，否则常会发生一些让人不好意思的事。）

## 4. 代表討論會 Panel Discussion

A. 請先閱讀以下短文：（请先阅读以下短文：）
First read the following paragraph:

鹽水鎮元宵節的蜂炮慶典年年舉行，每年都吸引了大批看熱鬧的觀光客；因此也給這個小鎮帶來了季節性的繁榮。然而，由於點燃蜂炮的花費很高，鹽水鎮的居民每家平均每年要花掉幾萬元台幣。這對收入不多的家庭來說，的確是一個很大的負擔。同時，每年在蜂炮節的時候往往會發生一些不幸的事。不但每年總有十幾個人被炮火燒傷，而且慶典之後的髒亂，更是讓人頭痛。於是，有的人建議停止這個慶典，有的人卻認為應該保持這個很有特色的民俗活動。到底鹽水該不該舉行蜂炮慶呢？

（盐水镇元宵节的蜂炮庆典年年举行，每年都吸引了大批看热闹的观光客；因此也给这个小镇带来了季节性的繁荣。然而，由於点燃蜂炮的花费很高，盐水镇的居民每家平均每年要花掉几万元台币。这对收入不多的家庭来说，的确是一个很大的负担。同时，每年在蜂炮节的时候往往会发生一些不幸的事。不但每年总有十几个人被炮火烧伤，而且庆典之后的脏乱，更是让人头痛。於是，有的人建议停止这个庆典，有的人却认为应该保持这个很有特色的民俗活动。到底盐水该不该举行蜂炮庆呢？）

| | | | |
|---|---|---|---|
| 繁榮 | 繁荣 | fánróng | prosperity, prosperous |
| 平均 | 平均 | píngjūn | average |
| 收入 | 收入 | shōurù | income |
| 負擔 | 负担 | fùdān | burden, encumbrance |
| 不幸 | 不幸 | búxìng | unfortunate, tragic |
| 建議 | 建议 | jiànyì | to suggest, suggestion |
| 保持 | 保持 | bǎochí | to maintain, to keep |

B. 對於上面所提出的問題，鹽水鎮特別舉行了一次公開討論會，由下面五個人參加。請分成五組，每組各扮演其中一位。各組成員請先自行討論立場，準備一下好所說的要點。然後由老師主持，進行討論。

（对于上面所提出的问题，盐水镇特别举行了一次公开讨论会，由下面五个人参加。请分成五组，每组各扮演其中一位。各组成员请先自行讨论立场，准备一下好所说的要点。然后由老师主持，进行讨论。）

The town of Yanshui decided to hold a panel discussion, consisting of five members and a moderator, to discuss the above mentioned problem. The class divides into five groups, each representing one of the five members mentioned below. The groups prepare statements and arguments before the discussion. The teacher acts as the moderator.

a. 觀光客
（观光客）

b. 鹽水小吃店老板
（盐水小吃店老板）

c. 鹽水居民，放蜂炮的地點在他家門前的街上
（盐水居民，放蜂炮的地点在他家门前的街上）

d. 鹽水的警察
（盐水的警察）

e. 大學人類學系教授
（大学人类学系教授）

## 5. 動腦時間 Brainstorming Session

你要組織一個旅行團，去參加某地的一個民俗活動、節慶或展覽。請出一張海報，做個簡介，並註明時間、行程、交通工具的安排，費用及報名的方法。
（你要组织一个旅行团，去参加某地的一个民俗活动、节庆或展览。请出一张海报，做个简介，并注明时间、行程、交通工具的安排，费用及报名的方法。）
You are organizing a field trip to a folk festival, fair, or exhibition. Make a poster with a brief introduction and specifying the schedule, transportation, fees, and persons to contact.

## 6. 作文 Composition

請敘述聖誕節或感恩節的起源。
（请叙述圣诞节或感恩节的起源。）
Describe the origin of Christmas or Thanksgiving.

# 補充資料 Supplementary Materials

## 1. 西方節慶 Festivities in the West

| 西方節慶 Festivities in the West | | |
|---|---|---|
| 聖誕節 | Shèngdànjié | Christmas |
| 復活節 | Fùhuójié | Easter |
| 萬聖節 | Wànshèngjié | Halloween |
| 感恩節 | Gǎn'ēnjié | Thanksgiving |

## 2. 中國的節慶 Chinese Festivals

| 中國的節慶 jiéqìng Chinese Festivals | | | |
|---|---|---|---|
| 節日 | 日期 | 活動 | 食物 |
| 新年 Xīnnián | 農曆一月一日 | 拜年，舞龍，舞獅 | 年糕 niángāo |
| 元宵節 Yuánxiāo jié | 農曆一月十五日 | 賞花燈 | 湯圓 tāngyuán |
| 清明節 Qīngmíng jié | 四月五日 | 掃墓 | 春捲 chūnjuǎn |
| 端午節 Duānwǔ jié | 農曆五月五日 | 划龍船 | 粽子 zòngzi |
| 中秋節 Zhōngqiū jié | 農曆八月十五日 | 賞月 | 月餅 yuèbǐng |

* 農曆 nónglì: Lunar Calendar 陽曆 yánglì: Solar Calendar

端午節龍舟賽 Dragon-Boat Race

新年舞獅 Lion Dance at New Year

## 3. 民俗技藝 Chinese Folk Art

| 民俗技藝 jìyì Folk Art | | |
|---|---|---|
| 剪紙 | jiǎnzhǐ | paper-cutting |
| 捏麵人 | niē miànrén | dough sculpture |
| 中國結 | Zhōngguó jié | Chinese macramé |
| 抽陀螺 | chōutuóluó | whipping the top |
| 踢毽子 | tī jiànzi | kicking the shuttlecock |
| 皮影戲 | píyǐngxì | shadow puppet |
| 布袋戲 | bùdàixì | hand-held puppet show |

a. Hand-Held Puppets
b. 大陀螺 Dà tuóluó
c. 捏麵人 Niēmiànrén
d. 如意結 Rúyì Jié

a.

b.

c.

d.

# 第十課

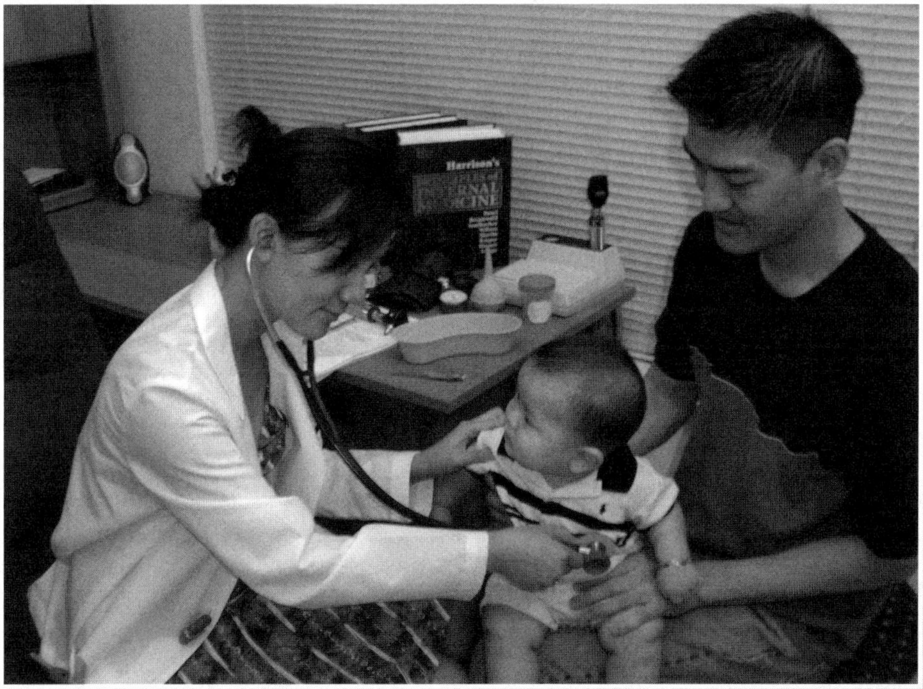

# 女強人

## 繁体課文 Traditional Text

現代的台灣社會中，由於女性教育程度的提高，許多婦女都走出廚房，到社會上和男人一爭長短。常常在報章雜誌上或人們口中出現的『女強人』一詞，指的就是各行各業中極有成就的女性。她們可能是醫生、記者、律師、學者、企業家、工程師或是政府官員。這些行業向來是男人的天下。『女強人』這個詞顯然是向『男主外，女主內』的傳統觀念挑戰。

儘管職業婦女成功的例子越來越多，男女平等的主張表面上似乎也普遍被一般人接受，但是，社會上某些角落依然有著明顯的性別歧視。比方說婦女找工作時，常會受到一些限制；較高的職位多半還是由男性擔任；結婚和生產也可能對女性工作人員有不利的影響。另外，一般人對男女關係比如外遇問題的看法也是對男性比較寬，對女性比較嚴。

『靠丈夫吃飯』不如『獨立自主』，再加上經濟上的需要，所以現在的新女性和男人一樣多半是早出晚歸的上班族。但是這並不代表婦女在家中的責任減輕了；因為下班後，不但要照顧孩子，同時洗衣燒飯等家事還是落到了作妻子的頭上。要作個標準的現代婦女，真不容易。現代台灣婦女和西方女性比較起來，恐怕還有一段路要走，不過和中國傳統裹小腳的女性比起來，她們的確已經向前進了一大步了！

## 简体课文 Simplified Text

现代的台湾社会中，由于女性教育程度的提高，许多妇女都走出厨房，到社会上和男人一争长短。常常在报章杂志上或人们口中出现的『女强人』一词，指的就是各行各业中有成就的女性。她们可能是医生、记者、律师、学者、企业家、工程师或是政府官员。这些行业向来是男人的天下。『女强人』这个词显然是向『男主外，女主内』的传统观念挑战。

尽管职业妇女成功的例子越来越多，男女平等的主张表面上似乎也普遍被一般人接受，但是，社会上某些角落依然有着明显的性别歧视。比方说妇女找工作时，常会受到一些限制；较高的职位多半还是由男性担任；结婚和生产也可能对女性工作人员有不利的影响。另外，一般人对男女关系比如外遇问题的看法也是对男性比较宽，对女性比较严。

『靠丈夫吃饭』不如『独立自主』，再加上经济上的需要，所以现在的新女性和男人一样多半是早出晚归的上班族。但是这并不代表妇女在家中的责任减轻了；因为下班后，不但要照顾孩子，同时洗衣烧饭等家事还是落到了作妻子的头上。要作个标准的现代妇女，真不容易。现代台湾妇女和西方女性比较起来，恐怕还有一段路要走，不过和中国传统裹小脚的女性比起来，她们的确已经向前进了一大步了！

# 生詞 Vocabulary

| | | | | | |
|---|---|---|---|---|---|
| 1. | 強<br>女強人 | 强 | qiáng<br>nǚqiángrén | *Vs.*<br>*N.* | strong<br>(Lit. female strong person); career women who have made noteworthy achievements |
| 2. | 提高 | 提高 | tígāo | *V.* | enhancement, improvement; to raise, to improve |
| 3. | 一爭長短 | 一争长短 | yìzhēng chángduǎn | *Id.* | to compete with (someone) |
| 4. | 報章 | 报章 | bàozhāng | *N.* | newspapers |
| 5. | 出現 | 出现 | chūxiàn | *Vp.* | to appear, to arise, to emerge |
| 6. | 指 | 指 | zhǐ | *V.* | referring to; to point to |
| 7. | 各行各業<br>行業 | 各行各业 | gèháng gèyè<br>hángyè | *Id.*<br>*N.* | all walks of life, all trades and professions<br>lines of business |
| 8. | 成就 | 成就 | chéngjiù | *N.* | achievement |
| 9. | 醫生 | 医生 | yīshēng | *N.* | medical doctor |
| 10. | 記者 | 记者 | jìzhě | *N.* | journalist, reporter |
| 11. | 律師 | 律师 | lǜshī | *N.* | lawyer |
| 12. | 學者 | 学者 | xuézhě | *N.* | scholar, learned man |
| 13. | 企業家 | 企业家 | qìyèjiā | *N.* | entrepreneur, enterpriser |
| 14. | 工程師 | 工程师 | gōngchéngshī | *N.* | engineer |
| 15. | 官員 | 官员 | guānyuán | *N.* | official |
| 16. | 向來 | 向来 | xiànglái | *Adv.* | always, all along |
| 17. | 天下 | 天下 | tiānxià | *N.* | the world (lit. land under heaven) |
| 18. | 顯然 | 显然 | xiǎnrán | *Adv.* | obvious, clear; obviously, clearly |
| 19. | 挑戰 | 挑战 | tiǎozhàn | *V.* | to challenge; *N.* challenge |
| 20. | 儘管 | 尽管 | jǐnguǎn | *Adv.* | despite, even though |
| 21. | 職業<br>職業婦女 | 职业 | zhíyè<br>zhíyè fùnǚ | *N.*<br>*N.* | profession<br>career women |
| 22. | 例子 | 例子 | lìzi | *N.* | example, case |
| 23. | 主張 | 主张 | zhǔzhāng | *N.* | view, proposition, position; *V.* to advocate |

| | | | | | |
|---|---|---|---|---|---|
| 24. | 表面<br>表面上 | 表面 | biǎomiàn<br>biǎomiàn shàng | *N.*<br>*Adv.* | surface, outside<br>on the surface, superficially |
| 25. | 似乎 | 似乎 | sìhū | *Adv.* | it seems or appears that, looks as though |
| 26. | 依然 | 依然 | yīrán | *Adv.* | still, as before |
| 27. | 明顯 | 明显 | míngxiǎn | *Vs.* | obvious, distinct |
| 28. | 性別 | 性别 | xìngbié | *N.* | gender |
| 29. | 歧視<br>性別歧視<br>種族歧視 | 歧视 | qíshì<br>xìngbié qíshì<br>zhǒngzú qíshì | *V.*<br>*N.*<br>*N.* | to discriminate against<br>sex discrimination<br>racial discrimination |
| 30. | 限制 | 限制 | xiànzhì | *N.* | restriction |
| 31. | 職位 | 职位 | zhíweì | *N.* | position, post |
| 32. | 擔任 | 担任 | dānrèn | *V.* | to assume the office of, hold the post of |
| 33. | 生產 | 生产 | shēngchǎn | *N.* | childbirth; *V.* to manufacture, to produce |
| 34. | 不利 | 不利 | búlì | *Vs.* | disadvantageous, unfavorable |
| 35. | 外遇 | 外遇 | wàiyù | *N.* | extra-marital affairs = 婚外情 *N.* hūnwàiqíng |
| 36. | 嚴 | 严 | yán | *Vs.* | strict, stern, severe |
| 37. | 靠 | 靠 | kào | *V.* | to rely on |
| 38. | 不如 | 不如 | bùrú | *Adv.* | not as good as, not equal to |
| 39. | 獨立 | 独立 | dúlì | *Vs.* | independent |
| 40. | 自主 | 自主 | zìzhǔ | *Vs.* | to act on one's own; to decide |
| 41. | 早出晚歸 | 早出晚归 | zǎochū wǎnguī | *Id.* | to go out early and return late (often said of a busy person) |
| 42. | 上班族<br>族 | 上班族 | shàngbānzú<br>zú | *N.* | nine-to-fivers<br>(suffix) a class or group of things with common features; race, nationality |
| 43. | 代表 | 代表 | dàibiǎo | *V.* | to indicate, to represent |
| 44. | 責任 | 责任 | zérèn | *N.* | responsibility |
| 45. | 照顧 | 照顾 | zhàogù | *V.* | to look after, to take care |
| 46. | 家事 | 家事 | jiāshì | *N.* | chores |
| 47. | 落 | 落 | luò | *Vp.* | to fall on |
| 48. | 段 | 段 | duàn | *N.* | section, part, paragraph |
| 49. | 裹 | 裹 | guǒ | *V.* | to bind, to wrap |
| 50. | 小腳 | 小脚 | xiǎojiǎo | *N.* | bound feet |
| 51. | 進步 | 进步 | jìnbù | *Vs.* | to make progress, to advance |

# 文法 Grammar

Each pattern below is illustrated by sample sentences. When blanks are provided, complete the sentences. When English sentences are provided, give Chinese counterparts.

## 1. 向來 xiànglái vs. 一向 yíxiàng vs. 一直 yìzhí: (Adv.) all along, has always

A. *Both* 向來 *and* 一向 *indicate "it has always been the case that" referring to habits or routines, but whereas they are generally interchangeable,* 一向 *is more compatible with sentences with positive connotations.*

(Note: *– ungrammatical; ??– questionable; OK– acceptable)

a. 家裡的事，她先生向來不過問。（一向 OK）
（家里的事，她先生向来不过问。）
Her husband has never cared about household matters.

b. 政府官員向來不會贊成學者的主張。（一向 OK）
（政府官员向来不会赞成学者的主张。）
Government officials never agree with what academics propose.

c. 有些工作在性別上一向有限制。（向來 ??）
（有些工作在性别上一向有限制。）
Some jobs have always been restricted to a certain gender.

d. 每個社會一向都有雙重標準。（向來 OK）
（每个社会一向都有双重标准。）
Every society has had some kind of double standards.

e. The responsibilities of government officials have always been greater than those of ordinary people.

f. He would never accept gifts from others. What made him change his mind this time?

B. *Though in many instances interchangeable,* 向來 *and* 一向 *focus on one reference time (i.e. up to the present) and* 一直 *two (i.e. within a time frame from X to Y).*

a. 他們結婚以後，家事一直由兩個人一塊負責。（一向、向來 OK）
（他们结婚以后，家事一直由两个人一块负责。）
They have shared house-keeping chores since their marriage.

b. 昨天開會的時候，他一直不肯接受其他人的意見。（*向來 *一向）
（昨天开会的时候，他一直不肯接受其他人的意见。）
Throughout the meeting yesterday, he just would not listen to others' suggestions.

c. 這個小孩離家出走以後，一直沒跟他的家人聯繫。(*向來 *一向)
（这个小孩离家出走以后，一直没跟他的家人联系。）
This child has never contacted his family since leaving home.

d. Ms. Chiang's（蔣）job performance has always been first-rate.

e. Mr. Yan（顏）did not smoke all day today.

## 2. 向 xiàng: (Prep.) towards (a direction), from (a source)

a. 他向記者搖搖頭，表示不接受他的意見。
（他向记者摇摇头，表示不接受他的意见。）
He shook his head at the reporter, indicating that he could not accept his idea.

b. 他的夫人在政府擔任很重要的職位，有不少人向她報告工作情形。
（他的夫人在政府担任很重要的职位，有不少人向她报告工作情形。）
His wife holds an important position in the government. Many people present status reports to her.

c. 你工作上需要什麼，隨時向公司要求好了。
（你工作上需要什么，随时向公司要求好了。）
Feel free to request whatever you need for your work at any time.

d. 你剛開始工作，應該常向同事學習。
（你刚开始工作，应该常向同事学习。）
Since you've just started working, you should consult other colleagues often.

e. 我們計劃把女同事組織起來，向不平等的待遇挑戰。
（我们计划把女同事组织起来，向不平等的待遇挑战。）
We plan to organize our female workers and challenge the unfair treatment.

f. 你的未婚妻剛才向你 ______________________________ 了嗎？
（你的未婚妻刚才向你 ______________________________ 了吗？）

g. 他為了 ____________________________________ 向大家道歉。
（他为了 ____________________________________ 向大家道歉。）

h. The reporter asked the official some very important questions.

i. The publisher of the magazine gave them a presentation on the organization of her company.

## 3. 儘管 jǐnguǎn:

A. (Adv.) *feel free to; not hesitate to; follow one's own inclination in spite of other's objection*

a. 把孩子托給他照顧，你就儘管放心吧。
（把孩子托给他照顾，你就尽管放心吧。）
Simply place the child under his care and do not worry about it.

b. 想吃什麼就儘管拿，你可千萬別客氣。
（想吃什么就尽管拿，你可千万别客气。）
Make yourself at home and eat what you'd like.

c. 有什麼意見，請儘管向負責人提出。
（有什么意见，请尽管向负责人提出。）
If you have any suggestions, please feel free to present them to the person in charge.

B. (Conj.) *though, even though, in spite of*

a. 他跳得那麼高興。儘管時候已經不早了，可是他還不肯離開。
（他跳得那么高兴。尽管时候已经不早了，可是他还不肯离开。）
He was enjoying himself at the dance and did not want to leave, even though it was getting late.

b. 儘管遇到了許多困難，我們還是要堅持下去。
（尽管遇到了许多困难，我们还是要坚持下去。）
We intend to try to hold on in spite of the difficulties.

c. 儘管受到了很多歧視，他一直對自己充滿了信心。
（尽管受到了很多歧视，他一直对自己充满了信心。）
Despite the discrimination he encountered, he never lost confidence.

d. 儘管人民的生活水準一天比一天提高了，____________________。
（尽管人民的生活水准一天比一天提高了，____________________。）

e. 儘管在一般人心目中她不是一個標準的傳統女性，________________。
（尽管在一般人心目中她不是一个标准的传统女性，________________。）

f. If you have any questions after business hours, please feel free to call me at home.

g. Even though he was informed of a more desirable position, he did not feel that he should apply for it.

## 4. 由 yóu:

A. (Verb) *to be decided by, be up to*

a. 信不信全由你。
（信不信全由你。）
Believe it or not.

b. 這麼重要的事由不得你。
（这么重要的事由不得你。）
We cannot afford to let you decide on such an important thing.

B. (Prep.) *introducing an agent*

a. 車子的牌子由他挑選，顏色就由你來決定吧。
（车子的牌子由他挑选，颜色就由你来决定吧。）
He will select the brand of the car, and it is up to you to decide on its color.

b. 昨天從日本來的觀光客是由他陪著參觀博物館的。
（昨天从日本来的观光客是由他陪着参观博物馆的。）
It was he who accompanied the Japanese tourist to the museum yesterday.

c. 一般公司裡較高薪的工作多半由男性擔任。
（一般公司里较高薪的工作多半由男性担任。）
Higher paid positions in most companies are held by men.

d. 如何教育孩子應該由______________________________。
（如何教育孩子应该由______________________________。）

e. 自從她做了職業婦女以後，孩子只好由____________________。
（自从她做了职业妇女以后，孩子只好由____________________。）

g. Dr. Wang will now give a report on the difficulties we encountered.

C. 由 vs 被

*Even though both* 由 *and* 被 *precede syntactic subjects, they rarely occur in similar situations. The former occurs strictly with agents (i.e. subject of action verbs); the latter occurs with subjects of various kinds of verbs (i.e. action, state etc.).*

| | | | |
|---|---|---|---|
| 秘密～人發現了 | 秘密～人发现了 | 被 | *由 |
| ～老張介紹 | ～老张介绍 | *被 | 由 |
| 建議～他拒絕了 | 建议～他拒绝了 | 被 | *由 |
| 客人～你陪同 | 客人～你陪同 | *被 | 由 |
| 好意～人家誤會 | 好意～人家误会 | 被 | *由 |

[* indicates incorrect grammar]

# 練習 Exercises

## 1. 請用中文解釋或說明下面的詞彙：

Define the following words in Chinese:

| | |
|---|---|
| a. 職業婦女 | 职业妇女 |
| b. 記者 | 记者 |
| c. 外遇 | 外遇 |
| d. 靠丈夫吃飯 | 靠丈夫吃饭 |
| e. 男主外、女主內 | 男主外、女主内 |
| f. 歧視 | 歧视 |
| g. 獨立 | 独立 |

## 2. 完成句子 Complete the Sentences

a. 由於＿＿＿＿＿＿＿＿＿＿的提高，＿＿＿＿＿＿＿＿＿＿。
（由于＿＿＿＿＿＿＿＿＿＿的提高，＿＿＿＿＿＿＿＿＿＿。）

b. ＿＿＿＿＿＿＿＿＿＿＿＿＿＿顯然是向傳統的習俗挑戰。
（＿＿＿＿＿＿＿＿＿＿＿＿＿＿显然是向传统的习俗挑战。）

c. ＿＿＿＿＿＿＿＿＿＿＿似乎代表＿＿＿＿＿＿＿＿＿＿＿。
（＿＿＿＿＿＿＿＿＿＿＿似乎代表＿＿＿＿＿＿＿＿＿＿＿。）

d. 傳統女性和＿＿＿＿＿＿＿＿比較起來，＿＿＿＿＿＿＿＿＿＿。
（传统女性和＿＿＿＿＿＿＿＿比较起来，＿＿＿＿＿＿＿＿＿＿。）

e. 那個政府官員＿＿＿＿＿＿＿＿，可是表面上＿＿＿＿＿＿＿＿。
（那个政府官员＿＿＿＿＿＿＿＿，可是表面上＿＿＿＿＿＿＿＿。）

f. A: 為什麼照顧父母的責任總是落到我們的頭上？
（为什么照顾父母的责任总是落到我们的头上？）
B: 因為我是長子，在中國社會裡＿＿＿＿＿＿應該由＿＿＿＿＿＿。
（因为我是长子，在中国社会里＿＿＿＿＿＿应该由＿＿＿＿＿＿。）

g. A: 真想不通，現在單身女性怎麼越來越多？
（真想不通，现在单身女性怎么越来越多？）
B: 因為＿＿＿＿＿＿＿＿＿＿，再加上＿＿＿＿＿＿＿＿＿＿。
（因为＿＿＿＿＿＿＿＿＿＿，再加上＿＿＿＿＿＿＿＿＿＿。）

## 3. 閱讀練習 Reading Comprehension

從三個句子中選出一句和原句意思相同的。
（从三个句子中选出一句和原句意思相同的。）
Select one sentence from the given choices that agrees most with the original statement.

__ A. 多數的中國人依然有重男輕女的觀念。
（多数的中国人依然有重男轻女的观念。）

(1) 男女的不同只在身材體重上，一般說來，男人比較重，女人比較輕。
（男女的不同只在身材体重上，一般说来，男人比较重，女人比较轻。）

(2) 在不少人的心目中，生兒子要比生女兒好。
（在不少人的心目中，生儿子要比生女儿好。）

(3) 性別歧視在中國社會已經不是很嚴重的問題了。
（性别歧视在中国社会已经不是很严重的问题了。）

__ B. 有人說：「每個成功的男人背後，總有個女人。」女人可以使男人成功，當然也可以讓自己成功。
（有人说：「每个成功的男人背后，总有个女人。」女人可以使男人成功，当然也可以让自己成 ……）

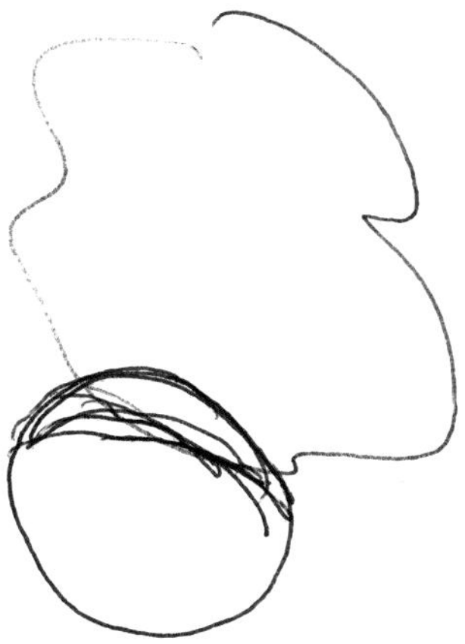

……長短不如在家幫忙丈夫成為一個成功的男人。
……长短不如在家帮忙丈夫成为一个成功的男人。）

……非得背後有個男人不可。
……非得背后有个男人不可。）

……人才有辦法，自己也能有成就。
……人才有办法，自己也能有成就。）

……以前高，比較不那麼受傳統和迷信的影響，盲目地
……前高，比较不那么受传统和迷信的影响，盲目地

……老年人那樣，因為視力不好，看不清楚，只能跟人走。
……年轻人不象老年人那样，因为视力不好，看不清楚，只能跟人走。）

(2) 受的教育越多，對一些傳統的風俗和迷信也就會提出更多的問題。
（受的教育越多，对一些传统的风俗和迷信也就会提出更多的问题。）

(3) 傳統和迷信絕不能影響現代的教育制度。
（传统和迷信绝不能影响现代的教育制度。）

__ D.儘管一般人都認為「婚外情」是一件丟臉的事，現代社會裡還是常發生。
（尽管一般人都认为「婚外情」是一件丢脸的事，现代社会里还是常发生。）

(1) 千萬不要有外遇，不然真是太沒面子了。
（千万不要有外遇，不然真是太没面子了。）

(2) 夫妻婚後的感情不一定就一直不變，有了外遇沒什麼大不了的。
（夫妻婚后的感情不一定就一直不变，有了外遇没什么大不了的。）

(3) 發生「婚外情」是家醜，但是還是常見。
（发生「婚外情」是家丑，但是还是常见。）

__ E. 越來越多的家庭主婦等家中經濟情況好轉，子女長大後，重新走進校園讀書。
（越来越多的家庭主妇等家中经济情况好转，子女长大后，重新走进校园读书。）

(1) 隨著家庭責任的減輕，許多婦女可以重拾書本，再做學生。
（随着家庭责任的减轻，许多妇女可以重拾书本，再做学生。）

(2) 子女的學費越來越貴，家庭主婦當然擔心家中經濟情況。
（子女的学费越来越贵，家庭主妇当然担心家中经济情况。）

(3) 去學校念書的婦女希望能拿個學位，好改善家中的經濟情況。
（去学校念书的妇女希望能拿个学位，好改善家中的经济情况。）

## 4. 漫畫 Cartoons

請標出這兩個漫畫的先後次序，然後依照圖片中所發生的事，寫出故事來。
（请标出这两个漫画的先后次序，然后依照图片中所发生的事，写出故事来。）
Each of the cartoons below consists of four frames, listed in random order. Please number them in their proper order, and then write stories based on each cartoon.

A.

B.

## 5. 問卷調查 Questionnaire

請先在小組中討論下面的問題，決定出答案。然後，老師再統計每組的答案，請各組解釋一下選擇的原因，進行一番討論。

（请先在小组中讨论下面的问题，决定出答案。然后，老师再统计每组的答案，请各组解释一下选择的原因，进行一番讨论。）

The class divides into small groups and decides how to answer the following questionnaire. After the teacher tallies the results, each group discusses their answers with the rest of the class in open discussion.

| | 同意 | 不一定 | 不同意 |
|---|---|---|---|
| a. 女人比男人勇敢<br>（女人比男人勇敢） | ______ | ______ | ______ |
| b. 女人比較喜歡說話<br>（女人比较喜欢说话） | ______ | ______ | ______ |
| c. 女人學外國話學得比較快<br>（女人学外国话学得比较快） | ______ | ______ | ______ |
| d. 女人的分析能力跟男人一樣好<br>（女人的分析能力跟男人一样好） | ______ | ______ | ______ |
| e. 女人喜歡穿漂亮的衣服，<br>因為她們想要吸引男人<br>（女人喜欢穿漂亮的衣服，<br>因为她们想要吸引男人） | ______ | ______ | ______ |
| f. 女人需要男人的保護<br>（女人需要男人的保护） | ______ | ______ | ______ |
| g. 女人應該以先生和孩子為中心<br>（女人应该以先生和孩子为中心） | ______ | ______ | ______ |
| h. 女人和男人的工作能力一樣，<br>所以女人也應該工作<br>（女人和男人的工作能力一样，<br>所以女人也应该工作） | ______ | ______ | ______ |
| i. 女人比較有耐心，所以適合當老師<br>（女人比较有耐心，所以适合当老师） | ______ | ______ | ______ |

## 6. 情況對話 Role Play

兩人一組。請依據下面的情況，任選一個，編演出一段對話。
（两人一组。请依据下面的情况，任选一个，编演出一段对话。）
Choose a partner and present a skit based on one of the following situations:

a. 一個先生告訴他的妻子他有外遇。
（一个先生告诉他的妻子他有外遇。）

b. 一個孩子叫他的父親（或母親）不要離婚。
（一个孩子叫他的父亲（或母亲）不要离婚。）

c. 一個妻子告訴她的先生她已經找到一份工作了，可是她的先生十分反對。
（一个妻子告诉她的先生她已经找到一份工作了，可是她的先生十分反对。）

d. 兩個職業婦女在電話上訴苦，抱怨自己的壓力太大了。
（两个职业妇女在电话上诉苦，抱怨自己的压力太大了。）

e. 兩位已婚男士在酒吧喝酒，抱怨上班的妻子忙著工作，沒時間在一起。
（两位已婚男士在酒吧喝酒，抱怨上班的妻子忙着工作，没时间在一起。）

f. 一對夫婦討論是否要跟男方的父母一起住；先生想這麼做，太太卻不願意。
（一对夫妇讨论是否要跟男方的父母一起住；先生想这么做，太太却不愿意。）

| | | | |
|---|---|---|---|
| 反對 | 反对 | fǎnduì | to disapprove of, to be against |
| 訴苦 | 诉苦 | sùkǔ | to complain about one's grievances |
| 抱怨 | 抱怨 | bàoyuàn | to complain, complaints |
| 是否 | 是否 | shìfǒu | whether or not （= 是不是） |

## 7. 作文 Composition

下面一段是從張系國的「男人的手帕」一書中節錄出來的，請寫出你的讀後感。
（下面一段是从张系国的「男人的手帕」一书中节录出来的，请写出你的读后感。）
The following is taken from Chang Hsi-kuo's book, *Man's Handkerchief.* Read the passage first to see if you agree with the writer, and write your own opinions.

「未來的男人和女人，應該從小培養「自己的家事自己動手」的好習慣。家事的問題解決後，男女之間唯一可能存在的不平等關係，就是性的關係了。但是，有了避孕藥及各種避孕術之後，這種不平等關係也可解除。更重要的是，再過幾十年，我相信男人也可懷孕生產：到那時候，男人和女人就完全平等了...」

「未来的男人和女人，应该从小培养「自己的家事自己动手」的好习惯。家事的问题解决后，男女之间唯一可能存在的不平等关系，就是性的关系了。但是，有了避孕药及各种避孕术之后，这种不平等关系也可解除。更重要的是，再过几十年，我相信男人也可怀孕生产：到那时候，男人和女人就完全平等了...」

| | | | |
|---|---|---|---|
| 培養 | 培养 | péiyǎng | to train, to develop |
| 存在 | 存在 | cúnzài | to exist |
| 避孕 | 避孕 | bìyùn | contraception |
| 解除 | 解除 | jiěchú | to remove, to get rid of |

## 補充資料 Supplementary Materials

### 1. 三八婦女節 Women's Day

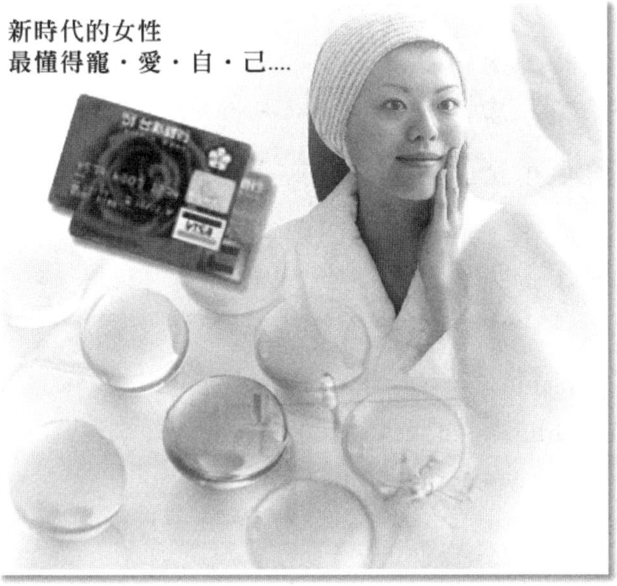

Political Rally on Women's Day

## 2. 婦女關心的問題 Issues That Concern Women

### 父權條款改成公婆條款
### 婦女團體揚言反對到底

【記者陳碧華／台北報導】婦女新知基金會董事長尤美女昨天指出，行政院通過的「民法親屬編」修正案，其中第一千零八十九條只是將「父權條款」改成「公婆條款」，不但不能解決問題，反而增加夫與妻兩個家族之間的糾紛。

行政院將民法第一〇八九條子女監護權「由父行之」，改為「由最近尊親屬議定之，若議定不成才由法院定之」。

尤美女認為這樣的修正不實際。她指出，台灣社會傳統認為「嫁出去的女兒，潑出去的水」，如由最近尊親屬議定，通常會只有公婆出面。萬一夫妻雙方的家庭都出面，也只是徒增兩個家庭的糾紛，不能解決問題。更何況，現在的小家庭很少與尊親屬住在一起，甚至遠隔重洋，要找齊尊親屬一起商議還真不容易，徒然浪費時間。

婦女新知秘書長柏蘭芝也說，對行政院這項修正，婦女團體將反對到底。

Right to Custody

### 女生 准午夜回宿舍
### 校方放寬門禁 十二點才關門

No More Lockouts at 10:30

### 登記婚 儀式婚 立委議論紛紛

【記者梁玉芳／台北報導】民法中有關結婚須有公開儀式及二人以上證人的「儀式婚」規定，婦女團體主張改為「登記婚」，昨天在立法院審查時引起立委辯論，有人主張「登記婚」符合新新人類簡單快速原則，也有人批評「登記婚」將成「騙婚條款」或「通姦脫罪條款」。

也有部分立委贊成兩制並行，如立委謝長廷表示，一般未婚懷孕的小倆口，有時會有不方便公開結婚的苦衷，因此兩種制度應該並存。

立法院司法委員會昨天全天審查民法親屬編修正案，葉菊蘭所提出婦女團體的「新晴版」修正草案中，將九百八十二條結婚的規定改為新人只要有兩位成年證人陪同到戶政機關登記即算成婚，不一定得有儀式昭告天下。

Till Death Do Us Part!

## 3. 台灣的新女性 Noteworthy Women in Taiwan

# 第 十 一 課

# 戴 口 罩 的 騎 士

## 繁体課文 Traditional Text

對許多台灣都市裡上下班以機車為交通工具的騎士而言，戴口罩往往比戴安全帽更重要。在擁擠的馬路上，空氣裡充滿了汽車的廢氣和黑煙，戴上口罩雖然不能完全淨化空氣，但是多少有過濾的作用。骯髒的空氣只是環境污染的一部份；噪音、垃圾和水污染也都是非常嚴重的問題。汽車機車的引擎聲、駕駛們隨手亂按的喇叭聲和商店小販擴音機裡傳出的各種叫賣聲和音樂，使得市區裡沒有一刻安靜的時候。在這麼吵的環境裡，難怪人們容易緊張，脾氣暴躁。即使郊區的環境，也因為工業的廢水和隨地亂倒的垃圾而受到威脅。

過去幾十年台灣強調經濟的發展，卻忽略了環境的保護。這是為進步而付出的代價。但是生活水準提高以後，大家都希望能有一個美好整潔的居住環境。於是近年來人們的環保意識逐漸提高了；遊行、抗議的活動不時出現，給政府帶來很大的壓力。淨化環境不只是政府的事，更需要每個人的配合。大家都應該有公德心，不要『自掃門前雪』。幾個淨化環境成功的例子，給關心環保的人帶來極大的信心。現在趕快開始行動，以免再遲就來不及了！

## 简体课文 Simplified Text

对许多台湾都市里上下班以机车为交通工具的骑士而言，戴口罩往往比戴安全帽更重要。在拥挤的马路上，空气里充满了汽车的废气和黑烟，戴上口罩虽然不能完全净化空气，但是多少有过滤的作用。肮脏的空气只是环境污染的一部份；噪音、垃圾和水污染也都是非常严重的问题。汽车机车的引擎声、驾驶员随手乱按的喇叭声和商店小贩扩音机里传出的各种叫卖声和音乐，使得市区里没有一刻安静的时候。在这么吵的环境里，难怪人们容易紧张，脾气暴躁。即使郊区的环境，也因为工业的废水和随地乱倒的垃圾而受到威胁。

过去几十年台湾强调经济的发展，却忽略了环境的保护。这是为进步而付出的代价。但是生活水平提高以后，大家都希望能有一个美好整洁的居住环境。于是近年来人们的环保意识逐渐提高了；游行、抗议的活动不时出现，给政府带来很大的压力。净化环境不只是政府的事，更需要每个人的配合。大家都应该有公德心，不要「自扫门前雪」。几个净化环境成功的例子，给关心环保的人带来极大的信心。现在赶快开始行动，以免再迟就来不及了！

# 生詞 Vocabulary

| | | | | | |
|---|---|---|---|---|---|
| 1. | 口罩 | 口罩 | kǒuzhào | *N.* | gauze mask (worn over nose and mouth) |
| 2. | 騎士 | 骑士 | qíshì | *N.* | (motorcycle, horse) rider |
| 3. | 工具 | 工具 | gōngjù | *N.* | means, tool, instrument |
| 4. | 擁擠 | 拥挤 | yōngjǐ | *Vs.* | crowded |
| 5. | 充滿 | 充满 | chōngmǎn | *Vpt.* | full of, permeated with |
| 6. | 廢氣 | 废气 | fèiqì | *N.* | exhaust fume |
| 7. | 煙 | 烟 | yān | *N.* | smog; smoke; cigarette |
| 8. | 淨化 | 净化 | jìnghuà | *V.* | to purify |
| 9. | 過濾 | 过滤 | guòlǜ | *V.* | to filter |
| 10. | 作用 | 作用 | zuòyòng | *N.* | function |
| 11. | 骯髒 | 肮脏 | āngzāng | *Vs.* | dirty |
| 12. | 環境 | 环境 | huánjìng | *N.* | environment; *Vs.* environmental |
| 13. | 污染 | 污染 | wūrǎn | *N.* | pollution; *V.* to pollute, to contaminate |
| 14. | 噪音 | 噪音 | zàoyīn | *N.* | noise |
| 15. | 垃圾 | 垃圾 | lèsè, lājī | *N.* | garbage |
| 16. | 嚴重 | 严重 | yánzhòng | *Vs.* | serious, critical |
| 17. | 引擎 | 引擎 | yǐnqíng | *N.* | engine |
| 18. | 隨手 | 随手 | suíshǒu | *Adv.* | unintentionally, conveniently |
| 19. | 喇叭 | 喇叭 | lǎbā | *N.* | motor-horn; brass-wind instruments in general; loudspeaker |
| 20. | 擴音機 | 扩音机 | kuòyīnjī | *N.* | megaphone, audio amplifier |
| 21. | 使得 | 使得 | shǐdé | *V.* | to make, to cause |
| 22. | 一刻 | 一刻 | yíkè | *N.* | a moment of |
| 22. | 脾氣 | 脾气 | píqì | *N.* | temperament, disposition |
| 23. | 暴躁 | 暴躁 | bàozào | *Vs.* | irritable, fretful |
| 24. | 即使 | 即使 | jíshǐ | *Conj.* | even if, even though |
| 25. | 郊區 | 郊区 | jiāoqū | *N.* | suburban districts, suburbs |
| 26. | 廢水<br>污水 | 废水 | fèishuǐ<br>wūshuǐ | *N.*<br>*N.* | (industrial) waste water<br>(domestic) sewage, polluted water |
| 27. | 威脅 | 威胁 | wēixié | *V.* | to threaten; *N.* threat |

| | | | | | |
|---|---|---|---|---|---|
| 28. | 強調 | 强调 | qiángdiào | *V.* | to stress, to emphasize |
| 29. | 發展 | 发展 | fāzhǎn | *N.* | development; *V.* to develop |
| 30. | 忽略 | 忽略 | hūlüè | *V.* | to neglect, to ignore |
| 31. | 保護 | 保护 | bǎohù | *N.* | protection; *V.* to protect |
| 32. | 付出 | 付出 | fùchū | *V.* | to pay |
| 33. | 代價 | 代价 | dàijià | *N.* | price |
| 34. | 水準<br>水平 | 水准<br>水平 | shuǐzhǔn<br>shuǐpíng | *N.*<br>*N.* | standard, level (Taiwan usage)<br>standard, level (Mainland China usage) |
| 35. | 整潔 | 整洁 | zhěngjié | *Vs.* | clean and tidy |
| 36. | 居住 | 居住 | jūzhù | *Vi.* | residential; to live, to reside |
| 37. | 意識 | 意识 | yìshì | *N.* | consciousness; to awake to, to realize |
| 38. | 逐漸 | 逐渐 | zhújiàn | *Adv.* | gradually, by degrees |
| 39. | 抗議 | 抗议 | kàngyì | *N.* | protest; *V.* to protest |
| 40. | 公德心 | 公德心 | gōngdéxīn | *N.* | concern for public good, regard for public welfare |
| 41. | 掃 | 扫 | sǎo | *V.* | to sweep |
| 42. | 趕快 | 赶快 | gǎnkuài | *Adv.* | quickly, at once |
| 43. | 以免 | 以免 | yǐmiǎn | *Conj.* | in order to avoid, lest |
| 44. | 來不及 | 来不及 | láibùjí | *Vs.* | there is not enough time (to do something), it is too late (to do something) |

# 文法 Grammar

Each pattern below is illustrated by sample sentences. When blanks are provided, complete the sentences. When English sentences are provided, give Chinese counterparts.

## 1. 對...而言 duì ... éryán: (Prep.) in so far as ... is concerned

a. 對初學外國語言的學生而言，教科書的選擇是非常重要的。
（对初学外国语言的学生而言，教科书的选择是非常重要的。）
To students who are beginning the study of a foreign language, selecting good textbooks is very important.

b. 對這個農村的居民而言，去廟裡求神絕不是迷信。
（对这个农村的居民而言，去庙里求神决不是迷信。）
To these villagers, going to temples to supplicate gods is not superstitious.

c. 對現代化大都市的居民而言，如何解決環境污染和交通擁擠問題都是他們所關心的。
（对现代化大都市的居民而言，如何解决环境污染和交通拥挤问题都是他们所关心的。）
In so far as residents of large modern cities are concerned, how to clean up environmental pollution and reduce traffic congestion are two of the key issues affecting them.

d. 對路上行人而言，________________ 嚴重地影響到他們的健康。
（对路上行人而言，________________ 严重地影响到他们的健康。）

e. 對某些汽車製造廠而言，________________________________。
（对某些汽车制造厂而言，________________________________。）

f. As far as most college students are concerned, campus dormitories are not very desirable places to live.

g. To most village farmers, visiting large cities is just too expensive.

## 2. 以 . . . 為 . . . yǐ ... wéi ...: (Prep. Phrase) it is ..., that is ..., treating ... as ...

a. 我們班上以他的現代漢語程度為最高。
（我们班上以他的现代汉语程度为最高。）
His proficiency in modern Chinese is regarded as the highest in our class.

b. 中國北方以麵食為主，而南方以米飯為主。
（中国北方以面食为主，而南方以米饭为主。）
Wheat is the main staple in northern China, while rice is the main staple in southern China.

c. 本市以住在市場旁邊的居民受到髒亂的威脅最重。
（本市以住在市场旁边的居民受到脏乱的威胁最重。）
It's the residents in the proximity of the markets who are most seriously affected by the garbage.

d. 由於水的缺乏許多人不得不以________________為______________。
（由于水的缺乏许多人不得不以________________为______________。）

e. 十多年來，因為身體的關係，她都以醫院為________________。
（十多年来，因为身体的关系，她都以医院为________________。）

f. 西洋樂器中，以____________________最為__________________。
（西洋乐器中，以____________________最为__________________。）

g. Our store deals primarily in jade antiques.

h. All banks in Taiwan take the Japanese Yen as the norm.

## 3. 隨 suí + Noun: (Adv. Phrase) taking along, whilst ..., might as well.

*(The nouns usually refer to body parts, indicating a casual relationship between two events.)*

a. 出去的時候，請你隨手把門關上。
（出去的时候，请你随手把门关上。）
Please close the door behind you as you leave!

b. 每位旅客可以隨身帶幾件行李上飛機？
（每位旅客可以随身带几件行李上飞机？）
How many pieces of carry-on luggage is each passenger allowed?

c. 他不過隨口說了幾句，請你別放在心上。
（他不过随口说了几句，请你别放在心上。）
He was just speaking impulsively. Please do not take it to heart!

d. 到外國去旅行千萬別忘了隨身________________________。
（到外国去旅行千万别忘了随身________________________。）

e. 隨地丟東西、倒垃圾會____________________________。
（随地丢东西、倒垃圾会____________________________。）

f. 有問題請隨時__________________________________。
（有问题请随时__________________________________。）

## 4. 使得 shǐdé: (Causative Verb) to cause, such that

a. 他的教學法使得學生對這門課的興趣提高了許多。
（他的教学法使得学生对这门课的兴趣提高了许多。）
His teaching method raised his students' interest in this course.

b. 經濟的快速發展使得人民的生活水準大大地提高了。
（经济的快速发展使得人民的生活水准大大地提高了。）
Rapid economic development greatly elevated the standard of living.

c. 緊張的工作和吵鬧的居住環境使得他脾氣更暴躁了。
（紧张的工作和吵闹的居住环境使得他脾气更暴躁了。）
Tense working conditions and noisy living surroundings worsened his bad temper.

d. 天氣的變化使得________________________________。
（天气的变化使得________________________________。）

e. 市民不斷地抗議使得______________________________。
（市民不断地抗议使得______________________________。）

f. Wastewater from factories has made the Yellow River heavily polluted.

g. New parks and trees have made our city a much more pleasant place to live.

## 5. 即使 jíshǐ: (Conj.) even if

*(This usually pairs with 也 or 還)*

a. 即使你真的做错事了，也不會有人看不起你的。
（即使你真的做错事了，也不会有人看不起你的。）
Even if you did do something wrong, nobody will despise you for it.

b. 即使居住環境再怎麼不理想，大家也要回到原來生長的地方。
（即使居住环境再怎么不理想，大家也要回到原来生长的地方。）
Even if the living conditions are undesirable, everyone still returns to the place they originally came from.

c. 人民如果不能配合政府，即使有再好的政策也沒有用。
（人民如果不能配合政府，即使有再好的政策也没有用。）
If people do not comply with government policies, those policies, no matter how good they may be, are useless.

d. 缺乏信心的人即使有__________________也不__________________。
（缺乏信心的人即使有__________________也不__________________。）

e. 即使生活水準提高了，__________________________________。
（即使生活水准提高了，__________________________________。）

f. Even if it rains tomorrow, it will not help with the drought in the south.

g. Even if it should take me one month to finish *The Dream of the Red Chamber*（紅樓夢）, I would not regret it a bit.

## 6. 卻 què: (Adv.) however, yet (indicating something unexpected or out of the ordinary)

a. 你看這天氣多奇怪，東邊下雨，西邊卻又出太陽了。
（你看这天气多奇怪，东边下雨，西边却又出太阳了。）
See how strange the weather is; it's raining in the east yet sunny in the west.

b. 他心裡有許多話要說，一時卻又什麼也表達不出來。
（他心里有许多话要说，一时却又什么也表达不出来。）
He had many things on his mind that he wanted to express, but for a moment was unable to utter a word.

c. 騎士明明知道戴安全帽的重要，卻從來不肯聽從。
（骑士明明知道戴安全帽的重要，却从来不肯听从。）
Motorcyclists are clearly aware of the importance of wearing safety helmets, yet they refuse to comply with the regulations.

d. 大家都知道污染的嚴重性卻______________________________。
（大家都知道污染的严重性却______________________________。）

e. 上班時間統一會造成交通擁擠，政府卻____________________ 。
（上班时间统一会造成交通拥挤，政府却____________________ 。）

f. The school is aware of the dirty tap water, but they are not willing to supply filtered water.

g. On holidays, garbage piles up in the streets, but nothing is being done about it.

## 7. 給...帶來... gěi ... dàilái: (Prep. Phrase) to bring about

a. 孩子的成功給父母帶來很大的安慰。
（孩子的成功给父母带来很大的安慰。）
Children's success brings much comfort and joy to parents.

b. 不時出現的遊行和抗議的活動給政府帶來很多壓力。
（不时出现的遊行和抗议的活动给政府带来很多压力。）
Constant rallies and demonstrations put great pressure on the government.

c. 《綠色和平》的成功給____________________帶來__________________ 。
（《绿色和平》的成功给____________________带来__________________ 。）

d. 高堆如山的垃圾給____________________帶來__________________ 。
（高堆如山的垃圾给____________________带来__________________ 。）

e. The discovery of crude oil （石油） brought much wealth to this small country.

f. The economic success in this region brought confidence to everyone in the nation.

## 8. 不只...更... bùzhǐ ... gèng ...: (Adv.) not only ... but furthermore ...

a. 我不只同意你的看法，更願意支持你們的活動。
（我不只同意你的看法，更愿意支持你们的活动。）
Not only do I agree with your views, I am also willing to support your actions.

b. 她不只會書面翻譯，更會即時口譯。
（她不只会书面翻译，更会即时口译。）
Not only does she translate, she can even do simultaneous interpreting.

c. 新的規則不只不准小販在馬路上擺攤子，更不准任何人在路上叫賣報紙。
（新的规则不只不准小贩在马路上摆摊子，更不准任何人在路上叫卖报纸。）
The new rulings not only do not permit roadside stands, and even peddling newspapers in the street is outlawed.

d. 湖水受污染後，不只不適合人喝，更威脅了湖中魚蝦的生命。
（湖水受污染后，不只不适合人喝，更威胁了湖中鱼虾的生命。）
Not only is polluted lake water unfit for human consumption, it even threatens the lives of what's living in the lake.

e. 第三世界的人民不只需要__________________，更__________________。
（第三世界的人民不只需要__________________，更__________________。）

f. 骯髒的空氣不只______________________，更____________________。
（肮脏的空气不只______________________，更____________________。）

g. He is not only conversant in European languages, he can even speak three African dialects.

h. Tourism not only brings wealth, it also promotes international understanding.

## 練習 Exercises

### I. 找出原因 Find the Cause

Match the effects below with the situations that caused them.

| | | | |
|---|---|---|---|
| 1. 廢氣 | 废气 | 6. 廢水 | 废水 |
| 2. 黑煙 | 黑烟 | 7. 垃圾 | 垃圾 |
| 3. 喇叭聲 | 喇叭声 | 8. 酸雨 | 酸雨 |
| 4. 引擎聲 | 引擎声 | 9. 污水 | 污水 |
| 5. 二手菸 | 二手烟 | | |

_____ a. 擠滿了汽車、機車的街道上。
（挤满了汽车、机车的街道上。）

_____ b. 在一節窗戶關緊了開著冷氣的火車中抽煙。
（在一节窗户关紧了开着冷气的火车中抽烟。）

_____ c. 小吃店和餐廳為了衛生，全部使用免洗餐具，吃完了就丟掉。
（小吃店和餐厅为了卫生，全部使用免洗餐具，吃完了就丢掉。）

_____ d. 因為方便，把不要的東西都丟到河裡，讓河水沖走。
（因为方便，把不要的东西都丢到河里，让河水冲走。）

_____ e. 在海邊建核能發電廠。
（在海边建核能发电厂。）

_____ f. 商店和超市都使用塑膠購物袋。
（商店和超市都使用塑胶购物袋。）

## 2. 填充 Fill in the blanks with the given words.

| | | | |
|---|---|---|---|
| 整潔 | 整洁 | 抗議 | 抗议 |
| 郊區 | 郊区 | 威脅 | 威胁 |
| 結果 | 结果 | 公德心 | 公德心 |
| 環境 | 环境 | 強調 | 强调 |
| 忽略 | 忽略 | | |

近年來許多城市都因為垃圾問題而頭大。就拿北市來說吧！市政府一直______美化市容的工作，花了大筆錢來種植樹木，卻______了環境保護的工作。______市區雖然有了綠葉和鳥語，可是路邊垃圾到處可見，很不______。經過一些環保人士的______，缺乏______的市民逐漸減少；市政府也增加經費，加派清潔工人。然而，隨著而來的問題就是垃圾過多，不知該如何處理。每天一車車的垃圾運往______的垃圾場，嚴重地______到附近居民的住家______。

（近年来许多城市都因为垃圾问题而头大。就拿北市来说吧！市政府一直______美化市容的工作，花了大笔钱来种植树木，却______了环境保护的工作。______市区虽然有了绿叶和鸟语，可是路边垃圾到处可见，很不______。经过一些环保人士的______，缺乏______的市民逐渐减少；市政府也增加经费，加派清洁工人。然而，随着而来的问题就是垃圾过多，不知该如何处理。每天一车车的垃圾运往______的垃圾场，严重地______到附近居民的住家______。）

## 3. 討論 Discussion

就下面的情況和四個解決辦法進行討論。老師可先帶學生讀過，並在黑板上統計出學生的選擇後，再請學生說出他們選擇的原因。
（就下面的情况和四个解决办法进行讨论。老师可先带学生读过，并在黑板上统计出学生的选择后，再请学生说出他们选择的原因。）
Read the following paragraph and discuss the given four possible solutions in class. Select one according to your preference and justify your choice.

某小鎮開了一家新的化學工廠。隨著這家工廠的開張，鎮民的工作機會增加了，他們的生活也逐漸好起來了。這個小鎮旁邊有條小河，是鎮民最主要的水源。一天，一個住在鎮上也在工廠上班的工人在河邊釣魚時卻發現成群的死魚。為了找到魚的死因，這個人順著河水往上走，居然發現這家化學工廠的排水管就在水邊，而且管中排出有惡臭的廢水。這個工人馬上去找他的老板，也就是工廠的負責人，要求他解決這個問題。廢水處理設備非常貴，工廠老板不願意花這個錢，老板甚至威脅這個工人說如果再給他找麻煩，就把工人開除。

（某小镇开了一家新的化学工厂。随着这家工厂的开张，镇民的工作机会增加了，他们的生活也逐渐好起来了。这个小镇旁边有条小河，是镇民最主要的水源。一天，一个住在镇上也在工厂上班的工人在河边钓鱼时却发现成群的死鱼。为了找到鱼的死因，这个人顺着河水往上走，居然发现这家化学工厂的排水管就在水边，而且管中排出有恶臭的废水。这个工人马上去找他的老板，也就是工厂的负责人，要求他解决这个问题。废水处理设备非常贵，工厂老板不愿意花这个钱，老板甚至威胁这个工人说如果再给他找麻烦，就把工人开除。）

| | | | |
|---|---|---|---|
| 水源 | 水源 | shuǐyuán | headwaters |
| 釣魚 | 钓鱼 | diàoyú | fishing |
| 排水管 | 排水管 | páishuǐguǎn | drain pipe |
| 惡臭 | 恶臭 | èchòu | foul smell, stench |
| 開除 | 开除 | kāichú | to fire (an employee) |
| 擔心 | 担心 | dānxīn | to worry about |
| 偷偷 | 偷偷 | tōutōu | secretly |
| 報導 | 报导 | bàodǎo | to report; news report |

Your Decision: 如果你是這個工人，你會怎麼辦？
（如果你是这个工人，你会怎么办？）

a. 算了，為了幾條死魚而丟了工作，不值得。而且魚會死，人不一定會死，根本不要擔心。
（算了，为了几条死鱼而丢了工作，不值得。而且鱼会死，人不一定会死，根本不要担心。）

b. 偷偷寫封信給當地的新聞記者，要他們來報導這件事。
（偷偷写封信给当地的新闻记者，要他们来报导这件事。）

c. 告知鎮民及工廠的工人，到工廠前面遊行、抗議，要求馬上解決這個問題。
（告知镇民及工厂的工人，到工厂前面游行、抗议，要求马上解决这个问题。）

d. 這樣的環境不能再住下去了，還是搬家，找個可以釣魚的地方和新工作。
（这样的环境不能再住下去了，还是搬家，找个可以钓鱼的地方和新工作。）

## 4. 情況對話 Role Play

三到五人一組，一人扮演小學老師，在地球日那天和一群二年級的學生討論環保問題。

（三到五人一组，一人扮演小学老师，在地球日那天和一群二年级的学生讨论环保问题。）

The class divides into groups of three to five students, one playing the role of teacher, the others, second-grade students. It is Earth Day, and the teacher is discussing important environmental issues with students in class.

| | | | |
|---|---|---|---|
| 浪費 | 浪费 | làngfèi | to waste |
| 回收（垃圾） | 回收（垃圾） | huíshōu | to recycle |
| 罐頭 | 罐头 | guàntóu | (tin) can |
| 鋁罐 | 铝罐 | lǚguàn | aluminum can |
| 塑膠 | 塑胶 | sùjiāo | plastic |
| 玻璃瓶 | 玻璃瓶 | bōlípíng | glass bottle |
| 廢紙 | 废纸 | fèizhǐ | waste paper |
| 再生紙 | 再生纸 | zàishēng zhǐ | recycled paper |

## 5. 漫畫 Cartoon

根據下面漫畫回答問題：

（根据下面漫画回答问题）

Answer the following questions based on the cartoon.

a. 你看得懂這個漫畫嗎？
（你看得懂这个漫画吗？）

b. 這個漫畫指出現代社會的什麼問題？
（这个漫画指出现代社会的什么问题？）

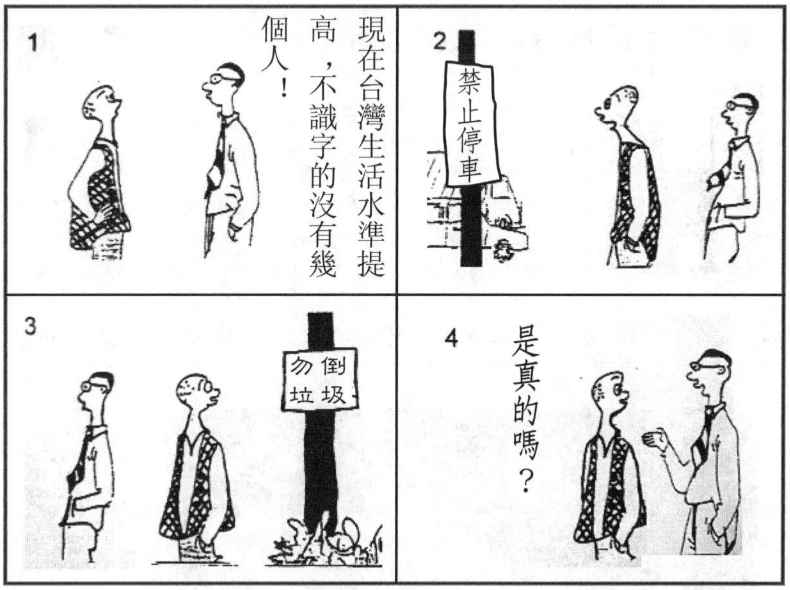

## 6. 作文 Composition

用第一人稱寫一篇地球的獨白，並請把下列生詞放入文章中。
（用第一人称写一篇地球的独白，并请把下列生词放入文章中。）

Write a monologue for the planet Earth, using first-person point of view. Be sure to use all the vocabulary given below in your composition.

| | |
|---|---|
| 威脅 | 威胁 |
| 亂+V | 乱+V |
| 代價 | 代价 |
| 使得 | 使得 |
| 忽略 | 忽略 |
| 消失 | 消失 |
| 嚴重 | 严重 |
| 即使 | 即使 |

堆積如山的垃圾
Garbage Heaps Everywhere

# 補充資料 Supplementary Materials

## 1. 減少污染 Reduce Pollution

| 減少污染 jiǎnshǎo wūrǎn Reduce Pollution | | |
|---|---|---|
| 垃圾分類 | 可燃、不可燃 | classification of garbage (combustible and non-combustible) |
| 垃圾回收 | 紙、鋁罐、玻璃 | Recycling (paper, aluminum, glass) |
| 減少製造垃圾 | 塑膠袋、免洗碗 | produce less garbage |

Conspicuous Consumption!

## 2. 回收 Recycling

紙類回收
Recycling Paper

Flammables and
Non-Flammables

Separating Throw-Aways

## 第 十 二 課

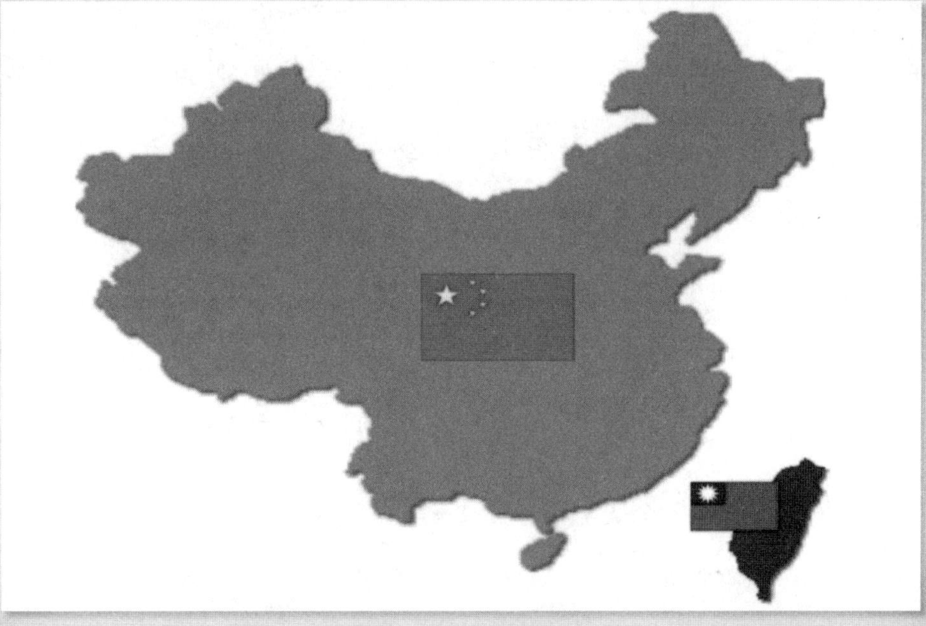

# 海 峽 兩 岸

## 繁体課文 Traditional Text

海峽兩岸於民國七十六年解除戒嚴令，並開放民眾赴大陸探親後，打破對立了將近四十年的僵局，展開了新頁。由於探親人數逐年增加，民間接觸漸多，因此民國八十年台北設立了「海基會」、北京設立了「海協會」，次年制定了兩岸關係條例。到此，台灣和大陸在政策事務之上，建立起相應且具有法制基礎的交流體系。

這二十年來，兩岸促進了不少民間交流。中華民國政府放寬了赴大陸來台探親的限制，同時也積極鼓勵兩岸在文化、學術、藝術、科技等多方面的交流，開放台灣大陸學者互訪。在「三通」問題（通商、通郵、通航）之上，通航部分雖然有定點定時的限制，但從赴大陸投資的台商人數及郵電往來的數量來看，反映了兩岸經貿關係日益密切。

民間交流已有相當大的成效，然而台海彼此之間的政治分歧尚未解決，大陸對台灣試射飛彈，台灣提出一邊一國，令兩岸陷入緊張的情況。台海關係的發展是長時間的問題，不是單方可決定控制的；若要全面長治久安，政治和解是最重要的一步。面對全球日益激烈的競爭，兩岸「經濟合則兩利」「政治和則雙贏」，因此雙方應以溝通、合作的方式創造兩利雙贏的局面。

## 简体课文 Simplified Text

海峡两岸于民国七十六年解除戒严令，并开放民众赴大陆探亲后，打破对立了将近四十年的僵局，展开了新页。由于探亲人数逐年增加，民间接触渐多，因此民国八十年台北设立了「海基会」、北京设立了「海协会」，次年制定了两岸关系条例。到此，台湾和大陆在政策事务之上，建立起相应且具有法制基础的交流体系。

这二十年来，两岸促进了不少民间交流。中华民国政府放宽了赴大陆来台探亲的限制，同时也积极鼓励两岸在文化、学术、艺术、科技等多方面的交流，开放台湾大陆学者互访。在「三通」问题（通商、通邮、通航）之上，通航部分虽然有定点定时的限制，但从赴大陆投资的台商人数及邮电往来的数量来看，反映了两岸经贸关系日益密切。

民间交流已有相当大的成效，然而台海彼此之间的政治分歧尚未解决，大陆对台湾试射飞弹，台湾提出一边一国，令两岸陷入紧张的情况。台海关系的发展是长时间的问题，不是单方可决定控制的；若要全面长治久安，政治和解是最重要的一步。面对全球日益激烈的竞争，两岸「经济合则两利」「政治和则双赢」，因此双方应以沟通、合作的方式创造两利双赢的局面。

## 生詞 Vocabulary

| | | | | | |
|---|---|---|---|---|---|
| 1. | 海峽 | 海峡 | hǎixiá | *N.* | strait (here referring to the Taiwan Strait located between Taiwan island and Mainland China) |
| 2. | 岸<br>東岸 | 岸 | àn<br>dōng'àn | *B.*<br>*N.* | coast<br>east coast |
| 3. | 於 | 于 | yú | *Prep.* | in |
| 4. | 民國 | 民国 | mínguó | *N.* | the Republic of China, founded in 1912. 民國三十八年 = 西元1949年 |
| 5. | 解除 | 解除 | jiěchú | *V.* | to terminate, to alleviate |
| 6. | 戒嚴法 | 戒严法 | jièyánfǎ | *N.* | martial law |
| 7. | 赴 | 赴 | fù | *V.* | to go to, to attend |
| 8. | 大陸 | 大陆 | dàlù | *N.* | Mainland China; mainland, continent |
| 9. | 探親 | 探亲 | tànqīn | *V-sep.* | to visit one's family or relatives |
| 10. | 打破 | 打破 | dǎpò | *V.* | to break, to put an end to |
| 11. | 對立 | 对立 | duìlì | *Vs-pred.* | antagonistic, hostile |
| 12. | 僵局 | 僵局 | jiāngjú | *N.* | a deadlock, an impasse, a stalemate |
| 13. | 展開 | 展开 | zhǎnkāi | *V.* | to initiate, to implement |
| 14. | 接觸 | 接触 | jiēchù | *V.* | to contact; *N.* contact |
| 15. | 設立 | 设立 | shèlì | *V.* | to establish, to set up |
| 16. | 海基會 | 海基会 | Hǎijīhuì | *N.* | Foundation for Exchanges across straits (海峽交流基金會Hǎixiá Jiāoliú Jījīnhuì ) |
| 17. | 海協會 | 海协会 | Hǎixiéhuì | *N.* | Association for Exchanges Across the Taiwan Straits （海峽兩岸關係協會 Hǎixiá Liǎng'àn Guānxī Xiéhuì ） |
| 18. | 制定 | 制定 | zhìdìng | *V.* | to draw up, to formulate |
| 19. | 政策 | 政策 | zhèngcè | *N.* | policy |
| 20. | 條例 | 条例 | tiáolì | *N.* | regulations and rules |
| 21. | 法制 | 法制 | fǎzhì | *N.* | legal system |
| 22. | 基礎 | 基础 | jīchǔ | *N.* | foundation |
| 23. | 體系 | 体系 | tǐxì | *N.* | system |
| 24. | 促進 | 促进 | cùjìn | *V.* | to promote, to advance |

| | | | | | |
|---|---|---|---|---|---|
| 25. | 中華民國<br><br>中華人民<br>共和國 | 中华民国 | Zhōnghuá<br>Mínguó<br>Zhōnghuá<br>Rénmín<br>Gònghéguó | *N.*<br><br>*N.* | the Republic of China<br><br>the People's Republic of China |
| 26. | 放寬 | 放宽 | fàngkuān | *V.* | to relax restrictions |
| 27. | 鼓勵 | 鼓励 | gǔlì | *V.* | to urge, to encourage |
| 28. | 學術 | 学术 | xuéshù | *N.* | academic |
| 29. | 科技 | 科技 | kējì | *N.* | science and technology |
| 30. | 三通<br><br>通郵<br>通航<br>通商 | 三通 | sāntōng<br><br>tōng yóu<br>tōng hang<br>tōng shāng | *N.*<br><br>*N.*<br>*N.*<br>*N.* | "Three Linkages" or "Three Links," which are:<br>to open up postal services<br>to open up transportation services<br>to open up trade |
| 31. | 投資 | 投资 | tóuzī | *V.* | to invest; *N.* investment |
| 32. | 郵電 | 邮电 | yóudiàn | *N.* | post and telecommunications |
| 33. | 往來 | 往来 | wǎnglái | *N.* | dealings, contact |
| 34. | 反映 | 反映 | fǎnyìng | *V.* | to reflect |
| 35. | 經貿<br>經濟<br>貿易 | 经贸 | jīng mào<br>jīngjì<br>màoyì | *N.*<br>*N.*<br>*N.* | economy and trade （經濟＋貿易）<br>economy<br>trade |
| 36. | 日益密切 | 日益密切 | rìyìmìqiè | *Id.* | to increase in strides |
| 37. | 成效 | 成效 | chéngxiào | *N.* | effects, results, outcomes |
| 38. | 政治 | 政治 | zhèngzhì | *N.* | politics, political affairs |
| 39. | 分歧 | 分歧 | fēnqí | *N.* | differences, discrepancy |
| 40. | 試射 | 试射 | shìshè | *N.* | test-fire |
| 41. | 飛彈 | 飞弹 | fēidàn | *N.* | missile |
| 42. | 令 | 令 | lìng | *V.* | to make, to cause |
| 43. | 陷入 | 陷入 | xiànrù | *Vi.* | to sink into, to fall into |
| 44. | 控制 | 控制 | kòngzhì | *V.* | to control |
| 45. | 長治久安 | 长治久安 | chángzhì jiǔ'ān | *Id.* | long period of political stability, the long term peace and stability |
| 46. | 和解 | 和解 | héjiě | *Vi.* | to reconcile |
| 47. | 面對 | 面对 | miànduì | *V.* | to confront |
| 48. | 激烈 | 激烈 | jīliè | *Vs.* | intense |
| 49. | 利 | 利 | lì | *B.* | advantage, benefit |

| | | | | | |
|---|---|---|---|---|---|
| 50. | 贏 | 赢 | yíng | *V.* | to win |
| 51. | 溝通 | 沟通 | gōutōng | *Vi.* | to communicate with; *N.* communication |
| 52. | 合作 | 合作 | hézuò | *N.* | cooperation |
| 53. | 創造 | 创造 | chuàngzào | *V.* | to create |
| 54. | 局面 | 局面 | júmiàn | *N.* | situation, status quo |

# 文法 Grammar

Each pattern below is illustrated by sample sentences. When blanks are provided, complete the sentences. When English sentences are provided, give Chinese counterparts.

## 1. 於 yú: (Prep.)

(*A classical element still used in literary materials, occurring either before or after verb phrases, corresponding to modern* 在)

a. 熊貓產於中國西南山區。
(熊猫产于中国西南山区。)
Pandas are found in the southwest mountainous regions of China.

b. 他一九八七年畢業於北京大學。
(他一九八七年毕业于北京大学。)
He graduated from Beijing University in 1987.

c. 他生於一八一八年，死於一九〇〇年，一生都為教育而努力。
(他生于一八一八年，死于一九〇〇年，一生都为教育而努力。)
He was born in 1818, died in 1900, and devoted all his life to education.

d. 他最近一直忙於準備第一次國際貿易大會。
(他最近一直忙于准备第一次国际贸易大会。)
Lately he's been rather preoccupied with the preparation of the First International Trade Congress.

e. 限制大陸商品進口台灣的法律已於一九八五年解除了。
(限制大陆商品进口台湾的法律已于一九八五年解除了。)
The law prohibiting the importation of Chinese mainland goods into Taiwan was revoked in 1985.

f. 從台灣直接打到中國的電話已於一九九〇年正式接通了。
（从台湾直接打到中国的电话已于一九九〇年正式接通了。）
Direct phone calls to the mainland from Taiwan were officially established in 1990.

g. 美國於一七七六年________________________________。
（美国于一七七六年________________________________。）

h. 陳教授每天生活於 ______________________________。
（陈教授每天生活于 ______________________________。）

i. The People's Republic of China was established in 1949.

j. The U.S. transcontinental railway was completed in 1889.

## 2. 之 zhī + Noun:

(*Nouns that enter into this literary pattern are called localizers and include* 內、外、中、上、下、前、後、*but not* 裡)

a. 每位旅客的行李嚴格限制在二十公斤之內。
（每位旅客的行李严格限制在二十公斤之内。）
Each passenger's luggage is strictly limited to twenty kilograms.

b. 除了電氣品之外，其他禮品都沒有特別的進口限制。
（除了电气品之外，其他礼品都没有特别的进口限制。）
Outside of home appliances, there are no special restrictions on the kind of gifts one can import.

c. 戒嚴法解除之後，兩國敵對的態度也隨著減輕了不少。
（戒严法解除之后，两国敌对的态度也随着减轻了不少。）
Ever since the removal of the martial law, tension between the two countries has lessened somewhat accordingly.

d. 回到家鄉之前，他完全沒想到會再一次見到年老的父親。
（回到家乡之前，他完全没想到会再一次见到年老的父亲。）
Before he reached his home town, he never expected to see his elderly father again.

e. 天生聰明之外，還得 ____________________________。
（天生聪明之外，还得____________________________。）

f. 在中國古代社會，皇帝之上________________________。
（在中国古代社会，皇帝之上________________________。）

g. Two out of every three people in China speak Mandarin as their native dialect.

h. Under the Chinese president, there are five Yuanzhang （院長） in charge of different areas of the government.

## 3. 令 lìng: (Causative Verb) to cause, to make

*(Generally occurs only with adjectives)*

a. 接到女朋友的來信令他大為不高興。
（接到女朋友的来信令他大为不高兴。）
The letter from his girlfriend displeased him greatly.

b. 他那對任何事都不關心的態度令父母非常擔心。
（他那对任何事都不关心的态度令父母非常担心。）
His indifferent attitude made his parents very worried.

c. 擁擠的馬路、吵鬧的環境、等等都是令現代化大都市的居 民頭痛的問題。
（拥挤的马路、吵闹的环境、等等都是令现代化大都市的居民头痛的问题。）
Crowded streets and noisy neighborhoods are some of the problems that give urban residents headaches.

d. 他的演唱會令所有的年輕學生為他瘋狂。
（他的演唱会令所有的年轻学生为他疯狂。）
His recital made all the young students ecstatic.

e. 亞洲四小龍在經濟上的發展令______________________________。
（亚洲四小龙在经济上的发展令______________________________。）

f. 那位律師在談判時的表現令人______________________________。
（那位律师在谈判时的表现令人______________________________。）

g. His job performance disappointed those who trained him.

h. What some tourists from Taiwan did on the mainland offended the local authorities.

## 4. 從…來看 cóng...láikàn: viewed from, based on, judging from

a. 從國家安全的角度來看，台、美、中、日四國之間有許多利益及衝突點。
（从国家安全的角度来看，台、美、中、日四国之间有许多利益及冲突点。）
Viewed from a national security perspective, there exist many beneficial points as well as conflicts in the relations among China, Taiwan, Japan, and the United States.

b. 從官方公布的消息來看,新任總統並未談到兩國之間的軍事關係。
（从官方公布的消息来看,新任总统并未谈到两国之间的军事关系。）
Judging from official news releases, the new president has not touched on any military relations between the two countries.

c. 從兩岸關係的歷史和現實來看,只有兩岸關係良性互動才能確保台海安全。
（从两岸关系的历史和现实来看,只有两岸关系良性互动才能确保台海安全。）
Based on the history and the status quo of the cross-strait relations, national security on both sides can only be ascertained by increased non-hostile interactions.

d. 從____________________________來看，現今的職場上，仍存在著男女同工不同酬的現象。
（从____________________________来看，现今的职场上，仍存在着男女同工不同酬的现象。）

e. 從____________________________來看，大多數受訪者的意見都希望通訊器材能縮小體積不要佔空間。
（从____________________________来看，大多数受访者的意见都希望通讯器材能缩小体积不要占空间。）

f. 中國人喜歡福氣，其實這是一個很健康的態度，就是凡事都從____________________________。
（中国人喜欢福气，其实这是一个很健康的态度，就是凡事都从____________________________。）

## 5. 因此 yīncǐ: (Conj.) therefore, because of it

a. （由於） 缺少工作的經驗，因此剛從大學畢業的學生找工作比較困難。
（（由于） 缺少工作的经验，因此刚从大学毕业的学生找工作比较困难。）
Those graduating seniors who lack work experience will have a difficult time finding jobs.

b. 我們在一起工作多年了，因此我們很了解他的脾氣。
（我们在一起工作多年了，因此我们很了解他的脾气。）
Because we've all been colleagues for years, we know his temperament well.

c. 小高雖然沒考上大學，但是他沒因此失去信心。
（小高虽然没考上大学，但是他没因此失去信心。）
Xiao Gao didn't get into a college, but he didn't lose confidence as a result.

d. 他的同學們都考上了有名的學校，____________________________。
（他的同学们都考上了有名的学校，____________________________。）

e. 王家今年有兩個孩子參加聯考，____________________________。
（王家今年有两个孩子参加联考，____________________________。）

f. She was travelling abroad and thus unable to attend her roommate's wedding.

g. John Jiang was not feeling well on the day of the exam and therefore did poorly.

# 練習 Exercises

## 1. 請用中文解釋或說明下面的詞彙。
Define the following words in Chinese:

| | | | |
|---|---|---|---|
| a. 對立的局面 | 对立的局面 | e. 探親 | 探亲 |
| b. 學術交流 | 学术交流 | f. 日益密切 | 日益密切 |
| c. 台商 | 台商 | g. 貿易往來 | 贸易往来 |
| d. 和解 | 和解 | h. 積極的接觸 | 积极的接触 |

## 2. 填充 **Fill in the blanks with the given words.**

| | | | | |
|---|---|---|---|---|
| a. 接觸<br>接触 | b. 赴<br>赴 | c. 記者<br>记者 | d. 解除<br>解除 | e. 海峽兩岸<br>海峡两岸 |
| f. 終於<br>终于 | g. 態度<br>态度 | h. 任何<br>任何 | i. 積極<br>积极 | |

（新華社北京6月23日電）中華全國新聞工作者協會負責人今天接受 ________ 訪問時表示，________ 新聞界的雙向交流是協會全體會員一向的主張，台灣 ________ 戒嚴法後，________ 打開了兩岸記者交流的大門。負責人說，這樣直接的________，可增加兩岸人民彼此的了解。協會對來訪的台灣記者，表示極為歡迎的________，並且 ________ 地幫助安排各種採訪工作，不會有 ________歧視或限制。對大陸 ________ 台採訪的記者，協會負責人則希望台灣當局能儘快簡化申請的手續及辦理的過程。

（（新华社北京6月23日电）中华全国新闻工作者协会负责人今天接受 ________ 访问时表示，________ 新闻界的双向交流是协会全体会员一向的主张，台湾 ________ 戒严法后，________ 打开了两岸记者交流的大门。负责人说，这样直接的________，可增加两岸人民彼此的了解。协会对来访的台湾记者，表示极为欢迎的________，并且 ________ 地帮助安排各种采访工作，不会有 ________歧视或限制。对大陆 ________ 台采访的记者，协会负责人则希望台湾当局能儘快简化申请的手续及办理的过程。）

| | | | |
|---|---|---|---|
| 新華社 | 新华社 | xīnhuáshè | New China News Agency |
| 協會 | 协会 | xiéhuì | association, society |
| 採訪 | 采访 | cǎifǎng | gather material |
| 當局 | 当局 | dāngjú | the authorities |
| 手續 | 手续 | shǒuxù | procedures, formalities |
| 過程 | 过程 | guòchéng | process, course |

## 3. 閱讀練習 Reading Comprehension

下面是一封從大陸寄到台灣的家信，請先讀一遍，再討論問題。
（下面是一封从大陆寄到台湾的家信，请先读一遍，再讨论问题。）
The following is a letter sent from Mainland China to Taiwan. Read the letter first, and then discuss the given questions in class:

其威：

相別多年，忽接二哥轉來你的信，知道你近況，又喜又悲。當年才二十多歲，轉眼已經過花甲，這一年，我們這兒有許多台胞回來探親。對台灣的生活情況知道一些，也聽說不少人再婚。你不必覺得心不安。四十年時間不算短，誰想得到居然還有再見面的一天！

我在中學任教35年，現在退休和立兒、媳婦陳芳、孫女阿紅同住。立生於你離家的那年冬天，算算比你女兒明惠大了20歲。你有一子一女可說是萬事足了。立高中畢業后即在中國旅行社工作，陳芳也在同一單位，紅紅上初中，生活不錯，家中三間半屋，彩電冰箱都有，挺舒適的。

你回來千萬不要大包小包地帶，在國內旅行并不方便。決定好日期後，國內車票可交由立代辦，他人熟地熟，買票絕對沒有問題。千言萬語等見面再談吧！帶明惠和她媽一塊兒來！

祝
安康快樂

雨香
2002.08.05

a. 信中提到許多人名：其威、立、陳芳、紅、明惠和雨香。他們大概是什麼年紀？是什麼關係？
（信中提到许多人名：其威、立、陈芳、红、明惠和雨香。他们大概是什么年纪？是什么关系？）

b. 這封信是誰寫給誰的？他們大概有多少年沒見了？請說說他們各人的近況？
（这封信是谁写给谁的？他们大概有多少年没见了？请说说他们各人的近况？）

c. 信中有一句「又喜又悲」，想想看應該是什麼事令寫信的人高興？什麼事困擾著他，讓他悲傷？
（信中有一句「又喜又悲」，想想看应该是什么事令写信的人高兴？什么事困扰着他，让他悲伤？）

d. 你覺得他們應該見面嗎？能不能想像出他們見面的情形？
（你觉得他们应该见面吗？能不能想像出他们见面的情形？）

e. 如果你是其威，你會不會回老家？如果你是雨香，你會不會寫出一封這樣的信？如果你是明惠的媽，你對這個情況又會怎麼辦？
（如果你是其威，你会不会回老家？如果你是雨香，你会不会写出一封这样的信？如果你是明惠的妈，你对这个情况又会怎么办？）

## 4. 情況對話 Role Play

就上面第三大題信中所提到的情況，任選兩個人，編演一段對話。
（就上面第三大题信中所提到的情况，任选两个人，编演一段对话。）
Find a partner and choose any two of the seven people mentioned in the above letter as basis for the role play. Present a dialogue between these two people in class.

## 5. 作文 Composition

從下面任選一個歷史事件，到圖書館找資料，寫一篇報告，說明發生的時間、地點、原因及影響或重要性。
（从下面任选一个历史事件，到图书馆找资料，写一篇报告，说明发生的时间、地点、原因及影响或重要性。）
Write a short paper on one of the following historical incidents. Be sure to include in your paper the time, place, cause, significance, and consequence of this particular incident.

| | | | |
|---|---|---|---|
| 鴉片戰爭 | 鸦片战争 | Yāpiàn Zhànzhēng | the Opium War |
| 五四運動 | 五四运动 | Wǔsì Yùndòng | the May Fourth Movement |
| 文化大革命 | 文化大革命 | Wénhuà Dàgémìng | the Cultural Revolution |
| 法國大革命 | 法国大革命 | Fàguó Dàgémìng | the French Revolution |
| 南北戰爭 | 南北战争 | Nánběi Zhànzhēng | the American Civil War |
| 東西德統一 | 东西德统一 | Dōngxīdé Tǒngyī | the Reunion of East and West Germany |

## 6. 報紙標題閱讀 Reading Headlines

請從下面報紙標題中選出和本課主題『海峽兩岸的交流』有關的新聞。並說明一下新聞中可能談到的內容。如有生詞，請查字典。

（请从下面报纸标题中选出和本课主题『海峡两岸的交流』有关的新闻。并说明一下新闻中可能谈到的内容。如有生词，请查字典。）

Identify which of the following headlines are connected with the main topic of this lesson – "Communications across the Taiwan Strait"– and explain what the article may be about. Use dictionaries if necessary.

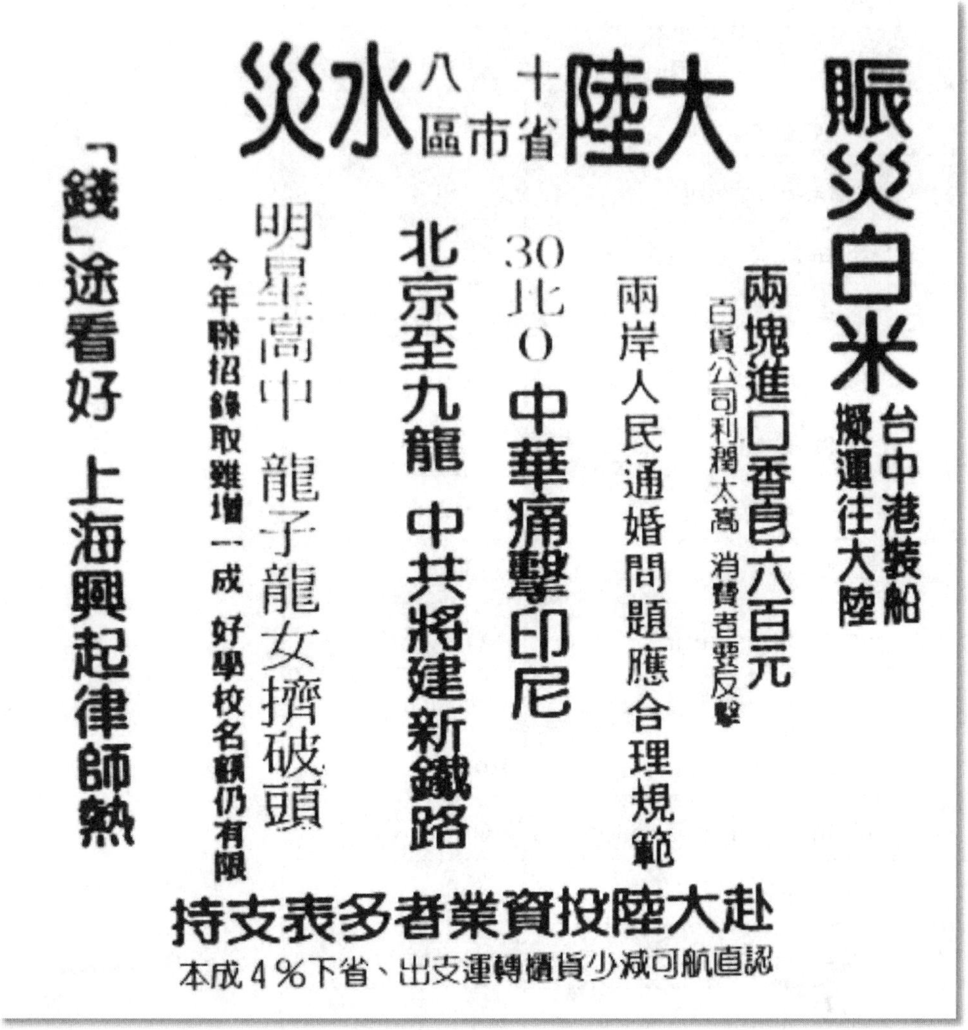
大陸十省八區市水災

賑災白米 台中港裝船 擬運往大陸

兩塊進口香皂六百元 百貨公司利潤太高 消費者要反擊

兩岸人民通婚問題應合理規範

30比0 中華痛擊印尼

北京至九龍 中共將建新鐵路

明星高中 龍子龍女擠破頭 今年聯招錄取雖增一成 好學校名額仍有限

「錢」途看好 上海興起律師熱

赴大陸投資業者多表支持 認直航可減少貨櫃轉運支出、省下4%成本

# 補充資料 Supplementary Materials

## I. 兩岸用語 Contrastive Vocabulary

| 兩岸用語 Contrastive Vocabulary | | |
|---|---|---|
| 台灣 | 大陸 | 英語 |
| 國語 guóyǔ | 普通話 pǔtōnghuà | Mandarin |
| 警察 jǐngchá | 公安 gōng'ān | police |
| 冰棒 bīngbàng | 冰棍 bīnggùn | popsicle |
| 計程車 jìchéngchē | 出租汽車 chūzū qìchē | taxi |
| 聯考 liánkǎo | 高考 gāokǎo | college exam |
| 小販 xiǎofàn | 個體戶 gètǐhù | private business |
| 錄影機 lùyǐngjī | 錄像機 lùxiàngjī | VCR |
| 水準 shuǐzhǔn | 水平 shuǐpíng | standard, level |
| 工作 gōngzuò | 幹活 gànhuó | work |
| 電腦 diànnǎo | 計算機 jìsuànjī | computer |
| 餐廳 cāntīng | 飯店 fàndiàn | restaurant |
| 韓國 Hánguó | 朝鮮 Cháoxiǎn | Korea |
| 速食麵 sùshímiàn | 方便麵 fāngbiànmiàn | instant noodles |
| 生字 shēngzì | 詞匯 cíhuì | vocabulary |
| 錄音帶 lùyīndài | 磁帶 cídài | cassette tapes |
| 聯絡 liánluò | 聯系 liánxì | get in touch |
| 二樓 èrlóu | 二層 èrcéng | 2nd floor |
| 墮胎 duòtāi | 人流 rénliú | abortion |
| 雷射 léishè | 激光 jīguāng | laser |

## 中共：台灣可參加北京婦女大會

【特派記者賴錦宏／北京二十三日電】中共全國婦聯國際部官員今天表示，台灣婦女團體應可參加九月在北京召開的聯合國婦女大會，由於報名日期尚未截止，還不能確定有那些台灣婦女團體能參加；所有參加會議的團體名稱將在五月初公布。

中共全國婦聯國際部馬姓官員指出，作為中國的一部分，台灣當然應有婦女團體參加九月聯合世界婦女大會。近幾年兩岸婦女團體交流發展得很快，中共全國婦聯高層領導人多次在會見台灣婦女界代表時，口頭邀請台灣婦女界率團參加九月的北京婦女大會。

On Entering Taiwan

「大陸地區人民進入台灣地區許可辦法」將在近日內公布實施，該辦法還有如下重點：

- 大陸人民來台，年逾七十、患重病，需人隨行照顧，基於人道，降為六十歲，並放寬其配偶或子女一人同行。
- 基於人道放寬申請探病條件，「七十歲」降為「六十歲」，並放寬原規定「配偶」同行，改為「配偶或子女一人」同行。

大陸地區人民在台灣地區申請延期照料的年齡由七十歲降為六十歲。

## 拿中共護照 怎說？

**陸委會官員：「雙重身分」問題更嚴重**

【記者何明國/台北報導】

如國人持有「中華人民共和國」護照，算不算雙重國籍？陸委會發言人高孔廉一時答不上來，僅表示「這不是一個簡單的答案」。

另據陸委會官員表示，兩岸關係既不是國際關係，也不是國內關係，而是特殊關係，在國際法上，國人持有中共護照應稱不上雙重國籍問題，倒不如稱之為「雙重身分」。

陸委會表示，國人持有中共護照，而中共對我仍有敵意，這已嚴重涉及忠貞問題，比「雙重國籍」還嚴重。

Dual Citizenship

Tug of War, or Ping Pong?

# 第 十 三 課

# 台 灣 的 族 群 與 語 言

## 繁体課文 Traditional Text

你曾經搭過台北的捷運嗎？每次下車前，車上總會播放一段包括四種語言的廣播，提醒乘客下一站的站名。這時你一定會好奇，為什麼除了國語和英語之外還有兩種陌生的語言？其實，這樣的設計和台灣多族群的社會環境有關。

台灣和瑞士一樣，是一個多族群的國家，大致上可分為台灣原住民以及漢民族。原住民是最早定居在台灣的居民，共有十族。其中的平埔族，因為與漢人通婚，漢化較深所以幾乎已經全部消失。高山族則有卑南、雅美、賽夏、泰雅、布農等九族，他們多半居住在山地，較少與漢人接觸，因此能夠保有自己的語言和文化。

至於後來移居到台灣的漢人，又可分為三支：一是明朝末年從福建移民而來的福佬人，二是清朝乾隆時移居到台灣的客家人，最後則是在1949年從大陸撤退到台灣的外省人。

原本這三大族群各有屬於自己的語言，福佬人說的是閩南話、客家人說的是客家話，而外省人說的則是自己家鄉的方言或是帶有濃厚鄉音的國語，也有人說比較標準的國語。當時政府把北京官話當作標準語，大力推行國語政策，因此閩南話、客家話等方言並不受到重視，但是近年來本土意識抬頭，強調族群融合，於是母語教育開始受到重視，愈來愈多的人以說自己的語言為榮，這是台灣很特殊的現象。

## 简体课文 Simplified Text

你曾经搭过台北的捷运吗？每次下车前，车上总会播放一段包括四种语言的广播，提醒乘客下一站的站名。这时你一定会好奇，为什么除了国语和英语之外还有两种陌生的语言？其实，这样的设计和台湾多族群的社会环境有关。

台湾和瑞士一样，是一个多族群的国家，大致上可分为台湾原住民以及汉民族。原住民是最早定居在台湾的居民，共有十族。其中的平埔族，因为与汉人通婚，汉化较深所以几乎已经全部消失。高山族则有卑南、雅美、赛夏、泰雅、布农等九族，他们多半居住在山地，较少与汉人接触，因此能够保有自己的语言和文化。

至于后来移居到台湾的汉人，又可分为三支：一是明朝末年从福建移民而来的福佬人，二是清朝乾隆时移居到台湾的客家人，最后则是在1949年从大陆撤退到台湾的外省人。

原本这三大族群各有属于自己的语言，福佬人说的是闽南话、客家人说的是客家话，而外省人说的则是自己家乡的方言或是带有浓厚乡音的国语，也有人说比较标准的国语。当时政府把北京官话当作标准语，大力推行国语政策，因此闽南话、客家话等方言并不受到重视，但是近年来本土意识抬头，强调族群融合，于是母语教育开始受到重视，愈来愈多的人以说自己的语言为荣，这是台湾很特殊的现象。

# 生詞 Vocabulary

| | | | | | |
|---|---|---|---|---|---|
| 1 | 捷運 | 捷运 | jiéyùn | *N.* | mass rapid transport, underground train |
| 2. | 播放 | 播放 | bòfàng | *V.* | to broadcast, to play (video or audio) (more formal than 放) |
| 3. | 廣播<br>廣播電台 | 广播 | guǎngbò<br>guǎngbòdiàntái | *V.*<br>*N.* | to broadcast (as of radio); *N.* broadcast<br>radio station |
| 4. | 提醒 | 提醒 | tíxǐng | *V.* | to remind |
| 5. | 乘客 | 乘客 | chéngkè | *N.* | passengers |
| 6. | 設計<br>服裝設計 | 设计 | shèjì<br>fúzhuāngshèjì | *V.*<br>*N.* | to design; *N.* a design<br>fashion design |
| 7. | 族群 | 族群 | zúqún | *N.* | community, people of common traits, ethnic groups |
| 8. | 瑞士 | 瑞士 | Ruìshì | *N.* | Switzerland |
| 9. | 大致上 | 大致上 | dàzhìshàng | *Adv.* | on the whole, roughly speaking |
| 10. | 原住民 | 原住民 | yuánzhùmín | *N.* | aborigines, tribal/minority people |
| 11. | 漢<br>漢朝<br>漢字 | 汉 | hàn<br>Hàncháo<br>Hànzì | *N.*<br>*N.*<br>*N.* | the Han (ethnic majority in China)<br>Han Dynasty<br>Chinese characters |
| 12. | 民族<br>少數民族 | 民族 | mínzú<br>shǎoshùmínzú | *N.*<br>*N.* | race, people, of the people<br>minority people |
| 13. | 定居 | 定居 | dìngjū | *Vi.* | to settle down and take residence |
| 14. | 族<br><br>上班族<br>紅唇族 | 族 | zú<br><br>shàngbānzú<br>hóngchúnzú | *B.*<br><br>*N.*<br>*N.* | tribes, groups, communities of common traits<br>those who work in the office from 9-5<br>those who chew betel nuts |
| 15. | 平埔族 | 平埔族 | Píngpǔzú | *N.* | the Pingpu tribe (hill people in Taiwan who settled down on the plains, and mixed with Han and Hakka people) |
| 16. | 通婚 | 通婚 | tōnghūn | *V-sep.* | to marry across ethnic lines, to inter-marry (X與Y通婚) |
| 17. | 漢化 | 汉化 | Hànhuà | *Vp.* | to Sinicize, to be assimilated into the Han culture |
| 18. | 卑南 | 卑南 | Bēinán | *N.* | the Puyuma tribe |
| 19. | 雅美 | 雅美 | Yǎměi | *N.* | the Yami tribe |
| 20. | 賽夏 | 赛夏 | Sàixià | *N.* | the Saisiyat tribe |

| | | | | | |
|---|---|---|---|---|---|
| 21. | 泰雅 | 泰雅 | Tàiyǎ | *N.* | the Atayal tribe |
| 22. | 布農 | 布农 | Bùnóng | *N.* | the Bunun tribe |
| 23. | 移居 | 移居 | yíjū | *V.* | to emigrate, to relocate (one's household) |
| 24. | 明朝 | 明朝 | míngcháo | *N.* | Ming Dynasty (1368-1644) |
| 25. | 末年 | 末年 | mònián | *N.* | the last few years of |
| 26. | 福建 | 福建 | Fújiàn | *N.* | the Fujian Province in southeast China |
| 27. | 移民<br>移民熱潮 | 移民 | yímín<br>yímínrècháo | *Vi.*<br>*N.* | to emigrate/immigrate; *N.* emigrants/immigrants<br>high activity of emigration/immigration |
| 28. | 福佬人 | 福佬人 | Fúlǎo rén | *N.* | people from southern Fukien/Hokkien province, often written also as 河洛人 |
| 29. | 乾隆 | 乾隆 | Qiánlóng | *N.* | Emperor Qianlong (1736-1795) |
| 30. | 客家人 | 客家人 | Kèjiā rén | *N.* | the Hakka people |
| 31. | 撤退 | 撤退 | chètuì | *Vi.* | to retreat, withdraw |
| 32. | 屬於 | 属于 | shǔyú | *V.* | to belong to |
| 33. | 閩南話 | 闽南话 | Mǐnnán huà | *N.* | southern Fujian dialect, widely spoken in Taiwan |
| 34. | 濃厚<br>濃厚的興趣 | 浓厚 | nónghòu<br>nónghòu de xìngqù | *Vs.* | heavy, strong (accent, emotion, interest, etc.)<br>keen interest |
| 35. | 鄉音 | 乡音 | xiāngyīn | *N.* | regional accent |
| 36. | 大力<br>大力支持 | 大力 | dàlì<br>dàlìzhīchí | *Adv.* | with all efforts, to do the best one can<br>to strongly support |
| 37. | 推行 | 推行 | tuīxíng | *V.* | to promote, implement |
| 38. | 方言 | 方言 | fāngyán | *N.* | regional dialects |
| 39. | 本土<br>本土文化<br>本土語言 | 本土 | běntǔ<br>běntǔwénhuà<br>běntǔyǔyán | *Vs-attr.*<br>*N.*<br>*N.* | local<br>local culture<br>local language/dialect |
| 40. | 抬頭 | 抬头 | táitóu | *Vi.* | to gain strength, rise in status |
| 41. | 母語<br>母語教育 | 母语 | mǔyǔ<br>mǔyǔjiàoyù | *N.*<br>*N.* | mother tongue<br>education in one's mother tongue |
| 42. | 以…為榮 | 以…为荣 | yǐ...wéiróng | *Id.* | proud of …, to take pride in … |
| 43. | 現象<br>普遍現象 | 现象 | xiànxiàng<br>pǔbiànxiànxiàng | *N.*<br>*N.* | phenomenon<br>commonplace |

## 文法 Grammar

Each pattern below is illustrated by sample sentences. When blanks are provided, complete the sentences. When English sentences are provided, give Chinese counterparts.

### 1. A和B有關 A hé B yǒuguān: (Prep. Phrase) is related to, has to do with (colloquial counterpart: A跟B有（直接）關係)

a 他心情不好和考試成績有關。
（他心情不好和考试成绩有关。）
His bad mood has to do with his test grades.

b. 這件事和政府官員收取賄賂有關。
（这件事和政府官员收取贿赂有关。）
This matter is related to the issue of government officials taking bribes.

c. 健康和營養及運動有關。
（健康和营养及运动有关。）
Good health is related to nutrition and exercise.

d. 台北夏天的氣候非常潮濕，和__________________________有關。
（台北夏天的气候非常潮湿，和__________________________有关。）

e. His success has nothing to do with his family background.（無關）

f. It's possible that this crime is related to politics.

### 2. 大致上 dàzhìshàng: (Adv.) on the whole, roughly speaking, in rough terms, basically

a. 地下鐵的工程大致上全部完工了，明年就可以通車。
（地下铁的工程大致上全部完工了，明年就可以通车。）
The construction of the underground train system is, on the whole, complete. It will be operational next year.

b. 我可以把事情的經過大致上告訴你。
（我可以把事情的经过大致上告诉你。）
I can tell you basically what happened.

c. 這一套書大致上我都讀過了。
（这一套书大致上我都读过了。）
I have looked through this whole set of books.

d. I agree with your point of view on the whole.

e. All romanization systems are basically the same.

f. 大致上________________________________，所以六月我就可以出國了。
（大致上________________________________，所以六月我就可以出国了。）

## 3. –化 –huà: (Suffix) to -ize, to make it ...

a. 政府最近正在推動城市綠化美化運動。
（政府最近正在推动城市绿化美化运动。）
Recently the government has been promoting its campaign to beautify and "greenify" the city.

b. 因為都市化的結果，人們生活的空間愈來愈狹小。
（因为都市化的结果，人们生活的空间愈来愈狭小。）
As a result of urbanization, people's living spaces are getting tighter and tighter.

c. 這不過是件小事，你可別把問題複雜化了。
（这不过是件小事，你可别把问题复杂化了。）
This is not a serious problem. Don't make it more complicated.

d. 他雖然是個男人，個性卻非常女性化。
（他虽然是个男人，个性却非常女性化。）
Although he is a man, his personality is rather effeminate.

e. Shanghai is a highly modernized city.

f. Westernization movements are losing ground these days.

## 4. 至於、對於、關於 zhìyú, duìyú, guānyú: (Prep.) As to, to, about, concerning, etc.

*(至於 switches to a new topic; 對於 introduces a noun to which an emotion or opinion is expressed; 關於 brings in a noun about which a statement is expressed or an action is [to be] taken.)*

a. 至於那件事情，我看下次再說吧！
（至于那件事情，我看下次再说吧！）
We'll talk about that next time, OK?

b. 對你的要求，我會再考慮看看。
（对你的要求，我会再考虑看看。）
I'll think about what you requested.

c. 我想多了解關於二次大戰的歷史。
（我想多了解关于二次大战的历史。）
I would like to learn more about the history of World War II.

d. 對於這次意外，______________________________________________。
（对于这次意外，______________________________________________。）

e. 至於__________________________________________，我想就算了吧！
（至于__________________________________________，我想就算了吧！）

f. 我計劃出版一本關於__________________________________________。
（我计划出版一本关于__________________________________________。）

g. I am not interested in commenting on this political scandal.

h. I'll study Southern Min first, but I also have to think about Hakka.

i. Your Majesty, what would you like us to do with your personal property?

## 5. A 把B當作C A bǎ B dāngzuò C: (Prep. Phrase) B is mistaken as/treated like C by A

a. 我不小心把鹽當作糖，所以果汁的味道有一點奇怪。
（我不小心把盐当作糖，所以果汁的味道有一点奇怪。）
I mistook salt for sugar, so the juice tastes a bit funny.

b. 中國人把龍鳳當作吉祥的象徵。
（中国人把龙凤当作吉祥的象征。）
Chinese people regard dragons and phoenixes as auspicious symbols.

c. 因為她無法生育，所以把小狗當作小孩子一樣疼愛。
（因为她无法生育，所以把小狗当作小孩子一样疼爱。）
She is infertile, and therefore she treats her pet dog like her own child.

d. 糟糕！我把資料當作廢紙丟掉了。
（糟糕！我把资料当作废纸丢掉了。）
Oh dear! I threw away the documents because I thought they were just scrap paper.

e. I really don't understand why he regards me as an opponent.

f. Imported beer is so cheap nowadays that he drinks it like water.

## 6. 受到…（X的）重視/輕視/影響/鼓勵 shòudào... (X de) zhòngshì/qīngshì/yǐngxiǎng/gǔlì: (Verb Phrase) to be thought highly of, taken seriously / looked down upon / influenced / encouraged (by X)

a. 最近這幾年，環保愈來愈受到重視。
（最近这几年，环保愈来愈受到重视。）
Environmental issues have received greater attention over the last few years.

b. 他因為功課不好而受到同學的輕視。
（他因为功课不好而受到同学的轻视。）
His classmates look down on him because of his grades.

c. 李大年能有今天的成就是受到他父親的影響。
（李大年能有今天的成就是受到他父亲的影响。）
Li Danian owes his achievements today to his father's influence.

d. 受到朋友的鼓勵，陳先生決定報考研究所。
（受到朋友的鼓励，陈先生决定报考研究所。）
Spurred by his friends' encouragement, Mr. Chen decided to apply to a masters' degree program.

e. 受到電視的影響，______________________________。
（受到电视的影响，______________________________。）

f. ______________________________受到老師的重視。
（______________________________受到老师的重视。）

## 7. 愈A愈B yù A yù B: (Prep. Phrase) the more A, the more B

*(colloquial=越A越B)*

a. 在台灣，近視的人愈來愈多。
（在台湾，近视的人愈来愈多。）
More and more people in Taiwan are suffering from near-sightedness.

b. 他想到幾天前被騙的事，愈想愈氣，真想報警。
（他想到几天前被骗的事，愈想愈气，真想报警。）
The more he thinks about how he got cheated the other day, the angrier he gets. He would really like to report it to the police.

c. 最近老王愈睡愈晚，不知道是在忙什麼。
（最近老王愈睡愈晚，不知道是在忙什么。）
Recently Lao Wang has been staying up later and later. I wonder what is keeping him so busy.

## 8. 以A為B yǐ A wéi B: (Prep. Phrase) take/with/regard A as B

a. 東方人以米飯為主食，西方人則以麵包為主食。
（东方人以米饭为主食，西方人则以面包为主食。）
Rice is the main staple in the East, whereas bread is the staple in the West.

b. 這家公司只以學歷為錄用的標準。
（这家公司只以学历为录用的标准。）
This company regards having a diploma as the sole requirement.

c. 今年的慶祝活動以全國中學生為主。
（今年的庆祝活动以全国中学生为主。）
High school students are the focus of this year's celebration activities.

d. 我們都應該以王冕的好學為榜樣。
（我们都应该以王冕的好学为榜样。）
We all regard Wang Mian's industriousness as exemplary.

## 練習 Exercises

### I. 填空 Fill in the blanks with the words below.

強調　移民　消失　重視　推行　屬於　包括　提醒　鄉音　播放
强调　移民　消失　重视　推行　属于　包括　提醒　乡音　播放

a. 老虎＿＿＿＿＿＿食肉性的動物。
（老虎＿＿＿＿＿＿食肉性的动物。）

b. 最近台灣興起一股＿＿＿＿＿＿熱潮，愈來愈多人想住在國外。
（最近台湾兴起一股＿＿＿＿＿＿热潮，愈来愈多人想住在国外。）

c. 新政上任之後，＿＿＿＿＿＿了許多新政策。
（新政上任之后，＿＿＿＿＿＿了许多新政策。）

d. 環境保護問題受到了各界人士的＿＿＿＿＿＿。
（环境保护问题受到了各界人士的＿＿＿＿＿＿。）

e. 老師再三＿＿＿＿＿＿，努力練習是學好語言的唯一方法。
（老师再三＿＿＿＿＿＿，努力练习是学好语言的唯一方法。）

f. 他是山東人，說起普通話帶有濃厚的＿＿＿＿＿＿。
（他是山东人，说起普通话带有浓厚的＿＿＿＿＿＿。）

g. 吃飯的時候，爸爸喜歡＿＿＿＿＿＿一些輕鬆的音樂。
（吃饭的时候，爸爸喜欢＿＿＿＿＿＿一些轻松的音乐。）

h. 由於原住民沒有文字，所以他們的文化正逐漸＿＿＿＿＿＿中。
（由于原住民没有文字，所以他们的文化正逐渐＿＿＿＿＿＿中。）

i 別忘了＿＿＿＿＿＿我收聽明天早上的廣播節目。
（别忘了＿＿＿＿＿＿我收听明天早上的广播节目。）

j. 這本書的內容非常豐富，＿＿＿＿＿＿歷史、地理、自然科學等方面。
（这本书的内容非常丰富，＿＿＿＿＿＿历史、地理、自然科学等方面。）

## 2. 閱讀練習 Read the passage below and then do the exercises accordingly.

### 蘭嶼過台灣

在台灣東南方的西太平洋上，距台東九十一公里有個綠色小島，人們叫它蘭嶼。

島上的雅美族人，世代靠捕魚、種芋頭維生，家家自給自足，大人生活中沒有所謂「賺錢」，蘭嶼的孩子更有令人羨慕的快樂童年。

但是近年來，這樣的日子已一去不復返。自從開放觀光後，民國六十年有小飛機飛往蘭嶼，民國七十一年蘭嶼開始供電。隨著交通便利，一批批「文明世界」的觀光客來了又去，帶走了珍貴的羅漢松、珠光鳳蝶，留下了文明世界的商業氣息：旅舍、別館、餐廳、藝品店紛紛在蘭嶼出現，雅美人逐漸不能滿足只有芋頭、飛魚的生活，他們開始想嚐嚐從台灣進口的蛋糕、米飯，也希望有電視看、有電扇吹。尤其是青少年，對台灣更是向往。

無奈的是，蘭嶼只有四所小學、一所國中，除了捕魚、種芋頭沒有其它的工作機會，因此在孩子們國中畢業後，無論升學或就業，去台灣是唯一的一條路。

但是，台灣真的是蘭嶼人的天堂嗎？許多雅美人到了台灣工作求學之後，才赫然發現，事實並不如想像中的美好，儘管政府對於原住民子弟提供了優厚的教育補助，龐大的升學壓力，仍然使人吃不消。由於知識水準不高，只能做較低層的工作，不但辛苦薪資也不多，而且還可能受本地人的欺騙。

種種的挫折與不適應，有人夢醒、有人心灰意冷。物質生活改變了蘭嶼的社會結構、人際關係及價值觀，愈來愈多的年輕人漸漸不會說母語、不了解有關雅美的傳說和禁忌、不穿傳統服飾……，他們已經不像傳統雅美人，可是另一方面，他們又無法完全融入漢文化社會，進退兩難成了「邊緣人」。

類似的情形不斷地在各個原住民部落中發生，或許有一天，這些美麗珍貴的文化都將消失，成為永遠的傳說。

（改寫自張瓊方〈蘭嶼過台灣〉光華雜誌，80年7月）

### 兰屿过台湾

在台湾东南方的西太平洋上，距台东九十一公里有个绿色小岛，人们叫它兰屿。

岛上的雅美族人，世代靠捕鱼、种芋头维生，家家自给自足，大人生活中没有所谓「赚钱」，兰屿的孩子更有令人羡慕的快乐童年。

但是近年来，这样的日子已一去不复返。自从开放观光后，民国六十年有小飞机飞往兰屿，民国七十一年兰屿开始供电。随着交通便利，一批批「文明世界」的观光客来了又去，带走了珍贵的罗汉松、珠光凤蝶，留下了文明世界的商业气息：旅舍、别馆、餐厅、艺品店纷纷在兰屿出现，雅美人逐渐不能满足只有芋头、飞鱼的生活，他们开始想嚐嚐从台湾进口的蛋糕、米饭，也希望有电视看、有电扇吹。尤其是青少年，对台湾更是向往。

无奈的是，兰屿只有四所小学、一所国中，除了捕鱼、种芋头没有其它的工作机会，因此在孩子们国中毕业后，无论升学或就业，去台湾是唯一的一条路。

但是，台湾真的是兰屿人的天堂吗？许多雅美人到了台湾工作求学之后，才赫然发现，事实并不如想像中的美好，儘管政府对於原住民子弟提供了优厚的教育补助，庞大的升学压力，仍然使人吃不消。由於知识水准不高，只能做较低层的工作，不但辛苦薪资也不多，而且还可能受本地人的欺骗。

种种的挫折与不适应，有人梦醒、有人心灰意冷。物质生活改变了兰屿的社会结构、人际关係及价值观，愈来愈多的年轻人渐渐不会说母语、不了解有关雅美的传说和禁忌、不穿传统服饰......，他们已经不像传统雅美人，可是另一方面，他们又无法完全融入汉文化社会，进退两难成了「边缘人」。

类似的情形不断地在各个原住民部落中发生，或许有一天，这些美丽珍贵的文化都将消失，成为永远的传说。

（改写自张琼方〈兰屿过台湾〉光华杂誌，80年7月）

(1) 判斷正誤 **True or False**

Based on the passage, mark the statements T for true, or F for false.

1. _____ 雅美族人很能融入台灣的生活，不再想念故鄉蘭嶼。
（雅美族人很能融入台湾的生活，不再想念故乡兰屿。）

2. _____ 以前在蘭嶼人的心中，並沒有「賺錢」的觀念。
（以前在兰屿人的心中，并没有「赚钱」的观念。）

3. _____ 政府提供了許多補助，使得雅美人完全沒有就學問題。
（政府提供了许多补助，使得雅美人完全没有就学问题。）

4. _____ 許多年輕人受到電視的影響而不再接受傳統文化。
（许多年轻人受到电视的影响而不再接受传统文化。）

5. _____ 如果有關單位再不設法解決原住民的問題，有一天原住民文化可能會消失。
（如果有关单位再不设法解决原住民的问题，有一天原住民文化可能会消失。）

(2) 討論 **Discussion**

Answer these questions based on your reading of the passage as well as your own experiences.

1. 在過去，雅美族人如何生存？
（在过去，雅美族人如何生存？）

2. 現在他們的問題在哪裡？
（现在他们的问题在哪里？）

3. 你認為現代文明和傳統文化何者比較重要？為什麼？
（你认为现代文明和传统文化何者比较重要？为什么？）

4. 如果你是一個雅美族人，面對文章中提到的情形，你會怎麼做？
（如果你是一个雅美族人，面对文章中提到的情形，你会怎么做？）

## 3. 情況對話 Role Play

**Role A** （飾演兒子）
你有一個交往多年的女友，跟你是不同族群；因為你的父母常常告訴你，除非是同族群的女孩，否則其他的女孩子他們都不接受，所以你一直不敢告訴父母女朋友的事，最近你打算向女朋友求婚，所以你得告訴父母並說服他們答應婚事。

（你有一个交往多年的女友，跟你是不同族群；因为你的父母常常告诉你，除非是同族群的女孩，否则其它的女孩子他们都不接受，所以你一直不敢告诉父母女朋友的事，最近你打算向女朋友求婚，所以你得告诉父母并说服他们答应婚事。）

A son. You have a girlfriend who you have dated for many years and who is of a different ethnicity. Because your parents often tell you they would only accept a girlfriend of the same ethnicity, you have never dared to tell your parents about your partner. You just decided to propose to your girlfriend, so you need to tell your parents about her and also persuade them to accept the marriage.

**Role B** （飾演父親）
你擔心兒子娶一個不同族群的女孩子，可能因為語言與文化的差異給家裡帶來麻煩，所以反對兒子跟不同族群的女孩交往。

（你担心儿子娶一个不同族群的女孩子，可能因为语言与文化的差异给家里带来麻烦，所以反对儿子跟不同族群的女孩交往。）

A father. You are worried that, if your son marries a girl of a different race, the language and cultural differences would cause discord within the family. You forbid your son from associating with the girl.

## 4. 討論專區 From a Different Perspective

Based on the questions below, discuss race-related issues in your own country.

(1) 如果貴國也有不同的種族，請談一談這些族群間有沒有什麼問題?你們的政府的種族政策是什麼?
（如果贵国也有不同的种族，请谈一谈这些族群间有没有什么问题?你们的政府的种族政策是什么?）

(2) 請同學回家後找一篇文章，有關貴國少數民族或原住民的問題，閱讀後與同學分享。
（请同学回家后找一篇文章，有关贵国少数民族或原住民的问题，阅读后与同学分享。）

## 5. 分析漫畫 Studying a Cartoon

After analyzing the cartoon, answer the questions below.

a. 圖中的媽媽，從圖(1)到圖(3)，有什麼變化? 為什麼?
（图中的妈妈，从图(1)到图(3)，有什么变化? 为什么?）

b. 請談一談在你的文化中有哪些語言禁忌、或有意思的語言現象?
（请谈一谈在你的文化中有哪些语言禁忌、或有意思的语言现象?）

c. 你曾經因為不知道其他種族文化的語言禁忌，而鬧出笑話嗎?請談一談你的經驗。
（你曾经因为不知道其它种族文化的语言禁忌，而闹出笑话吗?请谈一谈你的经验。）

# 補充資料 Supplementary Materials

## 1. 原住民各族問候語原住民各族問候語 Greetings by Various Tribes

| 族別 | 你好! | 謝謝! |
|---|---|---|
| 卑南族 Puyuma | ais ba riu ria | a ais to（日語） |
| 阿美族 Amis | ga ai ho | a rai |
| 賽夏族 Saisiyat | su wu ais u hai | ar mar lo |
| 泰雅族 Atayal | lau ka a su | mah ais u ba lai |
| 布農族 Bunun | masialkasu | mih misang |
| 雅美族 Yami | ko kai | ai yoi |
| 排灣族 Paiwan | nasa run wa sun | masaro |
| 魯凱族 Rukai | mua dinadina aiso | maura nuna |
| 鄒族 Tsou | miko wumonoon | a vu vu hu |
| 邵族 Thao | iu hu makeidan | iaka lin kin |

## 2. 台灣各族群介紹台灣各族群介紹 Ethnic Groups in Taiwan

1. 本省台灣人：明朝末年從大陸沿海各省移民而來的福建人，來台灣已有300多年的歷史，是台灣最大的族群。
（本省台湾人：明朝末年从大陆沿海各省移民而来的福建人，来台湾已有300多年的历史，是台湾最大的族群。）

2. 客家人：原居大陸中原地區，因逃避戰亂，於清朝乾隆時移居到台灣，多居住在新竹、桃園、屏東、高雄等地，一般來說客家族群有著極大的向心力。
（客家人：原居大陆中原地区，因逃避战乱，于清朝乾隆时移居到台湾，多居住在新竹、桃园、屏东、高雄等地，一般来说客家族群有着极大的向心力。）

3. 外省人：指1949年以後隨國民政府撤退到台灣的人，成員包括大陸各個省份，次於客家人，是台灣地區第三大族群。
（外省人：指1949年以后随国民政府撤退到台湾的人，成员包括大陆各个省份，次于客家人，是台湾地区第三大族群。）

4. 阿美族：分佈在台灣東部，是台灣原住民中人口最多的一族，母系社會為其特色，愛好歌舞，目前流行的山地歌謠，多半是阿美族人的創作。
（阿美族：分布在台湾东部，是台湾原住民中人口最多的一族，母系社会为其特色，爱好歌舞，目前流行的山地歌谣，多半是阿美族人的创作。）

5. 泰雅族：分佈在台灣北部中英山脈的兩側，以及花蓮、宜蘭等山區，人口約六萬餘人，以狩獵採集為生。
（泰雅族：分布在台湾北部中英山脉的两侧，以及花莲、宜兰等山区，人口约六万余人，以狩猎采集为生。）

6. 賽夏族：分佈在苗栗和新竹縣境內，人口約三千，生性愛好和平。
（赛夏族：分布在苗栗和新竹县境内，人口约三千，生性爱好和平。）

7. 布農族：散居在南投、花蓮、台東、高雄等縣境內，布農族喜歡居住在深山中，為父系社會。
（布农族：散居在南投、花莲、台东、高雄等县境内，布农族喜欢居住在深山中，为父系社会。）

8. 曹族：又稱鄒族，分佈在嘉義、南投縣境內，人口約五千左右，和布農族一樣為父系社會。
（曹族：又称邹族，分布在嘉义、南投县境内，人口约五千左右，和布农族一样为父系社会。）

9. 雅美族：大多集中住在蘭嶼島上，人口約兩千人，是台灣原住民中最原始的一支，以捕魚為生，男性多穿丁字帶，漁舟下水禮是每年的大事。
（雅美族：大多集中住在兰屿岛上，人口约两千人，是台湾原住民中最原始的一支，以捕鱼为生，男性多穿丁字带，渔舟下水礼是每年的大事。）

10. 卑南族：分布在台東縣，人口約六千，為母系社會，男女婚嫁是由男方嫁到女方家。以農耕為生，是所有高山原住民漢化最深的民族。
（卑南族：分布在台东县，人口约六千，为母系社会，男女婚嫁是由男方嫁到女方家。以农耕为生，是所有高山原住民汉化最深的民族。）

11. 排灣族：散居於高雄、屏東等山區，人口約五萬多。排灣族是一個有階級觀念的社會，分貴族和平民。崇拜百步蛇，木雕藝術最為出色。
（排湾族：散居于高雄、屏东等山区，人口约五万多。排湾族是一个有阶级观念的社会，分贵族和平民。崇拜百步蛇，木雕艺术最为出色。）

12. 魯凱族：由於和排灣族住的很近，所以受排灣族的影響很大，也是一個有階級觀念的社會。人口數約為六千。
（鲁凯族：由于和排湾族住的很近，所以受排湾族的影响很大，也是一个有阶级观念的社会。人口数约为六千。）

## 3. Locations of Minority Tribes in Taiwan

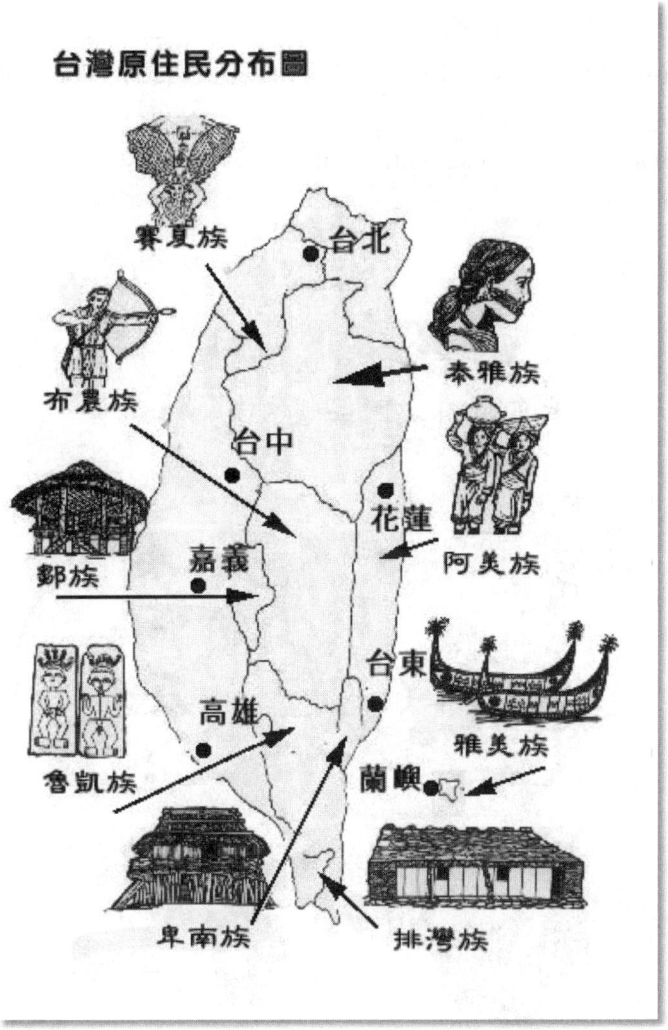


## 4. 什麼是台灣國語？What is Taiwanese Mandarin?

A. 台灣國語語音特徵 Phonetic Features

- No retroflexives: [zh, ch, sh, r] pronounced as [z, c, s, zz]
  池＝詞；使＝死
- Final [-n] pronounced as [-ng]: 很 [heng], 嫩 [neng]
- Some pronounce [f] as [h]: 飛＝灰；發＝花
- Some add final [u]: 吃＝粗；次＝醋
- Some pronounce [r] as [l]: 熱＝樂；肉＝漏
- No neutral tone: 關係 [guānxì]，精神 [jīngshén]，東西 [dōngxī]

B. 台灣國語詞彙特徵 Vocabulary Features

- No suffix [-r]: 電影（兒），信封（兒），蓋（兒）
- Extra suffix [zi]: 蝦子，鴨子，靴子
- Suffix [zi] instead of [er]: 繩兒→繩子，桌兒→桌子
- Also see Supplementary Materials, Lesson 12 of this volume for a list of Contrastive Vocabulary.

C. 台灣國語語法特徵 Grammatical Features of Taiwanese Mandarin

a. 有 as an auxiliary verb

•我有碰到你的学生喔。
（我有碰到你的学生喔。）
•我們現在在週年慶，您消費1000元以上我們就有送贈品喔。
（我们现在在周年庆，您消费1000元以上我们就有送赠品喔。）
•網路現在有正常了嗎？
（网络现在有正常了吗？）
•研究生宿舍有在回收電池嗎?
（研究生宿舍有在回收电池吗?）
•今天真是有夠倒楣。
（今天真是有够倒霉。）

台灣國語「有」
（台湾国语「有」）

b. 説 as a complementizer

•我發現說用了電蚊香可是蚊子還是不會死。
（我发现说用了电蚊香可是蚊子还是不会死。）
•說麻州今天早上有地震喔？
（说麻州今天早上有地震喔？）
•在美國唸大學說一年要一百萬台幣啦。
（在美国念大学说一年要一百万台币啦。）
•當我看到這報導，真是嚇了一跳說。
（当我看到这报导，真是吓了一跳说。）
•小妍在加班，好可憐說。
（小妍在加班，好可怜说。）

c. 給 as a special preposition

•你要不要給我載？
（你要不要给我载？）
•最近身體有點虛，我要吃點好料來給他補一下。
（最近身体有点虚，我要吃点好料来给他补一下。）
•老師，他給我打！

（老师，他给我打！）
• 時間給他過得好快！
（时间给他过得好快！）
• 我有給他講我們搬家了。
（我有给他讲我们搬家了。）
• 這幾天常熬夜，所以經過Starbucks都會順路給他買上一杯去上課。
（这几天常熬夜，所以经过Starbucks都会顺路给他买上一杯去上课。）

d. 在 as a special progressive marker
• 你怎麼不吃蝦子呢？這份定食就是蝦子在貴。
（你怎么不吃虾子呢？这份定食就是虾子在贵。）
• 趕快來看，趕快來買，這邊的東西都是五十塊一百塊在賣的喔！
（赶快来看，赶快来买，这边的东西都是五十块一百块在卖的喔！）
• 我們的孩子是婆婆在帶，房租是我先生在付。
（我们的孩子是婆婆在带，房租是我先生在付。）
• 個人偏愛第二集，最常在聽的也是這張。
（个人偏爱第二集，最常在听的也是这张。）
• 這些仿冒的錶在鑑定的時候有困難在。
（这些仿冒的表在鉴定的时候有困难在。）

e. 用 as an auxiliary verb
• 如果你去退貨，許多售貨小姐會勸你用換的。
（如果你去退货，许多售货小姐会劝你用换的。）
• 那種蛋糕很好吃，每次端出來以後大家就用搶的。
（那种蛋糕很好吃，每次端出来以后大家就用抢的。）
• 考數學不能用背的。
（考数学不能用背的。）
• 不是每個研究生都能住宿舍，要用抽籤的。
（不是每个研究生都能住宿舍，要用抽签的。）
• 年輕的時候比較衝，什麼事都用吵架的。
（年轻的时候比较冲，什么事都用吵架的。）

"太神奇！簡訊用說的"
（"太神奇！简讯用说的"）

f. 會 as a special modal verb

- A：謝謝！ B：不會。
  (A：谢谢！ B：不会。)
- 這個牛肉乾不會辣，你放心啦！
  （这个牛肉干不会辣，你放心啦！）
- 這個褲子的長度我覺得還好，不會長啊。
  （这个裤子的长度我觉得还好，不会长啊。）
- 現在超級市場的橘子會不會甜哪？
  （现在超级市场的橘子会不会甜哪？）
- A：這題難不難？B：不會難啊，書上找一找就有了。
  （A：这题难不难？B：不会难啊，书上找一找就有了。）

g. 不行 as a modal verb

- A: 數學作業寫完你就可以輕鬆一點啦！B: 不行輕鬆，還有國語要寫。
  （A: 数学作业写完你就可以轻松一点啦！B: 不行轻松，还有国语要写。）
- 那台電腦現在不行用，有人在燒光碟。
  （那台计算机现在不行用，有人在烧光盘。）
- 好吧，這一段如果不行播，我們會剪掉。
  （好吧，这一段如果不行播，我们会剪掉。）
- 他說他今天重感冒，不行來錄音。
  （他说他今天重感冒，不行来录音。）
- 為什麼研究生宿舍的跑步機我們不行用？
  （为什么研究生宿舍的跑步机我们不行用？）

h. 不錯 as an auxiliary verb

- 聽說他們的東西還不錯喝啦，可是有點貴。
  （听说他们的东西还不错喝啦，可是有点贵。）
- 他們的便當還不錯吃的樣子。
  （他们的便当还不错吃的样子。）
- 今天去看了宮崎駿的新作「神隱少女」，挺不錯看的喔！
  （今天去看了宫崎骏的新作「神隐少女」，挺不错看的喔！）
- Laufma的背包，還不錯背，老闆說背包的襯墊可以透氣。
  （Laufma的背包，还不错背，老板说背包的衬垫可以透气。）
- 我覺得中華電信真的在日本不錯用耶。
  （我觉得中华电信真的在日本不错用耶。）

i. V看看 as a verb reduplication form

- 車站附近新開一家拉堤咖啡館，拿了它們發的特價傳單去喝看看。
  （车站附近新开一家拉堤咖啡馆，拿了它们发的特价传单去喝看看。）
- 你彈看看這台鋼琴的聲音怎麼樣。
  （你弹看看这台钢琴的声音怎么样。）

• 喜歡可以試穿看看喔！
（喜欢可以试穿看看喔！）
• 這倒是不錯的idea，可以注意看看有沒有這樣的設計公司或者廣告公司。
（这倒是不错的idea，可以注意看看有没有这样的设计公司或者广告公司。）
• 真希望所有美國人都來學中文看看，就知道我們學英文的痛苦。
（真希望所有美国人都来学中文看看，就知道我们学英文的痛苦。）

j. 來去 as a double auxiliary verb
• 希望大家不要泛政治化，用意識型態的想法來去看民進黨。
（希望大家不要泛政治化，用意识型态的想法来去看民进党。）
• 查了一下潮汐表，發現下午2:35有個大退潮。嗯！想想來去海邊看看書好了。
（查了一下潮汐表，发现下午2:35有个大退潮。嗯！想想来去海边看看书好了。）
• 另有20餘座博物館推出特惠參觀辦法，歡迎大家告訴大家，一起來去博物館。
（另有20余座博物馆推出特惠参观办法，欢迎大家告诉大家，一起来去博物馆。）
• 十二點半了，來去吃飯嘍！
（十二点半了，来去吃饭喽！）
• 班上有人要一起來去吃咖啡或喝越南河粉的嗎？
（班上有人要一起来去吃咖啡或喝越南河粉的吗？）

# 第 十 四 課

# 台 灣 的 經 濟

## 繁体課文 Traditional Text

站在台灣許多大城市的高樓大廈、車水馬龍之中，讓人很難想像，才不過五十幾年前，許多地方還是一片人煙稀少的稻田和平房。自從第二次世界大戰後，台灣脫離日本的殖民統治，經過政府及人民的推動和努力，終於創造了今天安定富裕的局面，這一切都有賴於普及的國民教育、勤勞而節儉的人民、和正確的發展政策。台灣因為天然資源有限，而且人口密度高，無法自給自足，於是對外貿易便成為創造台灣經濟奇蹟的最大功臣。

隨著經濟的高速成長，台灣人民的生活品質也不斷的提高，電視、電話、私家汽車及家用電腦均十分普遍，每年出國旅遊人次，更佔總人口的百分之二十六以上；儘管經過九〇年代後期的東亞金融風暴，造成房地產和股市的不景氣，但台灣經濟所受到的不利影響仍較為輕微。

在脫離貧窮、締造奇蹟之後，台灣的未來，仍有許多問題急需解決：包括長期忽視的環保問題、天然資源的破壞、海峽兩岸的情勢，以及社會中部分人的「暴發户心態」、年輕一代的享樂主義，和工作倫理的喪失等等。這些都須要靠大家運用智慧和毅力，共同面對，讓台灣能夠儘快在世界上站穩腳步，擁有更寬廣的國際視野。

## 简体课文 Simplified Text

站在台湾许多大城市的高楼大厦、车水马龙之中，让人很难想象，才不过五十几年前，许多地方还是一片人烟稀少的稻田和平房。自从第二次世界大战后，台湾脱离日本的殖民统治，经过政府及人民的推动和努力，终于创造了今天安定富裕的局面，这一切都有赖于普及的国民教育、勤劳而节俭的人民、和正确的发展政策。台湾因为天然资源有限，而且人口密度高，无法自给自足，于是对外贸易便成为创造台湾经济奇迹的最大功臣。

随着经济的高速成长，台湾人民的生活品质也不断的提高，电视、电话、私家汽车及家用计算机均十分普遍，每年出国旅游人次，更占总人口的百分之二十六以上；尽管经过九〇年代后期的东亚金融风暴，造成房地产和股市的不景气，但台湾经济所受到的不利影响仍较为轻微。

在脱离贫穷、缔造奇迹之后，台湾的未来，仍有许多问题急需解决：包括长期忽视的环保问题、天然资源的破坏、海峡两岸的情势，以及社会中部分人的「暴发户心态」、年轻一代的享乐主义，和工作伦理的丧失等等。这些都须要靠大家运用智慧和毅力，共同面对，让台湾能够尽快在世界上站稳脚步，拥有更宽广的国际视野。

## 生詞 Vocabulary

| | | | | | |
|---|---|---|---|---|---|
| 1. | 車水馬龍 | 车水马龙 | chēshuǐ mǎlóng | *Id.* | bustling with heavy traffic |
| 2. | 想像<br>想像力<br>想像中 | 想象 | xiǎngxiàng<br>xiǎngxiànglì<br>xiǎngxiàng zhōng | *V.*<br>*N.* | to imagine<br>imagination<br>as imagined, as expected |
| 3. | 人煙稀少 | 人烟稀少 | rényān xīshǎo | *Id.* | sparsely populated |
| 4. | 稻田 | 稻田 | dàotián | *N.* | rice paddies |
| 5. | 平房 | 平房 | píngfáng | *N.* | standard, low-profile houses, bungalows |
| 6. | 世界大戰 | 世界大战 | shìjiè dàzhàn | *N.* | World War (prefixed by 第一次, etc.) |
| 7. | 脫離 | 脱离 | tuōlí | *V.* | to be freed from |
| 8. | 殖民<br>殖民地<br>殖民政策 | 殖民 | zhímín<br>zhímíndì<br>zhímín zhèngcè | *N.*<br>*N.*<br>*N.* | colonization<br>a colony<br>colonial policy |
| 9. | 統治 | 统治 | tǒngzhì | *V.* | to govern (as in political authority) |
| 10. | 經過 | 经过 | jīngguò | *V.* | to experience, to pass by |
| 11. | 政府<br>聯邦政府<br>中央政府 | 政府 | zhèngfǔ<br>liánbāngzhèngfǔ<br>zhōngyāngzhèngfǔ | *N.*<br>*N.*<br>*N.* | government<br>the federal government<br>the central government |
| 12. | 推動 | 推动 | tuīdòng | *V.* | to promote, to push ahead |
| 13. | 創造 | 创造 | chuàngzào | *V.* | to create, to implement |
| 14. | 安定 | 安定 | āndìng | *Vs.* | peaceful, turmoil-free |
| 15. | 局面<br>安定局面<br>動盪局面 | 局面 | júmiàn<br>āndìngjúmiàn<br>dòngdàngjúmiàn | *N.*<br>*N.*<br>*N.* | situation, status quo<br>in a stable state<br>in turmoil |
| 16. | 有賴於 | 有赖于 | yǒulàiyú | *Prep.* | due to, owing to |
| 17. | 普及 | 普及 | pǔjí | *Vs.* | widespread, universal |
| 18. | 勤勞 | 勤劳 | qínláo | *Vs.* | diligent, industrious |
| 19. | 節儉 | 节俭 | jiéjiǎn | *Vs.* | frugal, thrifty |
| 20. | 天然資源 | 天然资源 | tiānrán zīyuán | *N.* | natural resources |
| 21. | 有限<br>有限公司 | 有限 | yǒuxiàn<br>yǒuxiàn gōngsī | *Vs.*<br>*N.* | limited<br>Co., Ltd. |
| 22. | 密度 | 密度 | mìdù | *N.* | density |

| | | | | | |
|---|---|---|---|---|---|
| 23. | 無法 | 无法 | wúfǎ | *Adv.* | not to be in a position to, unable to |
| 24. | 自給自足 | 自给自足 | zìjǐ zìzú | *Id.* | to be self-reliant |
| 25. | 奇蹟 | 奇迹 | qíjī | *N.* | miracle |
| 26. | 功臣 | 功臣 | gōngchén | *N.* | most important factor (lit. a court official of important achievements) |
| 27. | 高速<br>高速公路<br>高速鐵路 | 高速 | gāosù<br>gāosùgōnglù<br>gāosùtiělù | *Vs-attr.*<br>*N.*<br>*N.* | high speed<br>autobahn, freeway<br>bullet train (system) |
| 28. | 成長<br>負面成長 | 成长 | chéngzhǎng<br>fùmiàn chéngzhǎng | *N.*<br>*N.* | growth; *V.* to grow<br>negative growth |
| 29. | 不斷 | 不断 | búduàn | *Adv.* | continually, incessantly |
| 30. | 私家<br>私家偵探 | 私家 | sījiā<br>sījiā zhēntàn | *Vs-attr.*<br>*N.* | private<br>private detective |
| 31. | 均 | 均 | jūn | *Adv.* | (literary) equivalent to 都, all |
| 32. | 十分 | 十分 | shífēn | *Adv.* | extremely (literary) |
| 33. | 人次 | 人次 | réncì | *N.* | head count |
| 34. | 後期 | 后期 | hòuqí | *N.* | the latter phase (of an event/period) |
| 35. | 金融風暴 | 金融风暴 | jīnróng fēngbào | *N.* | financial crisis (lit. storm) |
| 36. | 房地產 | 房地产 | fángdìchǎn | *N.* | real estate, realty |
| 37. | 股市 | 股市 | gǔshì | *N.* | stock market |
| 38. | 不景氣<br>經濟不景氣<br>景氣不看好 | 不景气 | bù jǐngqì<br>jīngjì bú jǐngqì<br>jǐngqì bú kànhǎo | *Vs.* | in a financial crunch, business slow-down (usu. negative)<br>economic downturn<br>prospects not promising |
| 39. | 較為 | 较为 | jiàowéi | *Adv.* | (to be) relatively… |
| 40. | 輕微 | 轻微 | qīngwéi | *Vs.* | mild, slight |
| 41. | 貧窮 | 贫穷 | pínqióng | *Vs.* | poor, impoverished, poverty-stricken |
| 42. | 締造 | 缔造 | dìzào | *V.* | to create, to make, to materialize |
| 43. | 未來 | 未来 | wèilái | *N.* | future; in the future |
| 44. | 長期<br>長期臥床 | 长期 | chángqí<br>chángqí wòchuáng | *N.* | long-term<br>to be bedridden |
| 45. | 忽視 | 忽视 | hūshì | *V.* | to neglect |
| 46. | 環保 | 环保 | huánbǎo | *N.* | environmental protection |
| 47. | 破壞 | 破坏 | pòhuài | *V.* | to violate, to abuse, to destroy |

| | | | | | |
|---|---|---|---|---|---|
| 48. | 情勢 | 情势 | qíngshì | *N.* | situation, condition |
| 49. | 部分 | 部分 | bùfèn | *N.* | a small minority of; a section, a part |
| 50. | 暴發戶 | 暴发户 | bàofāhù | *N.* | overnight millionaire (lit. sudden-explosion-in-wealth family) |
| 51. | 心態 | 心态 | xīntài | *N.* | mental state, state of mind |
| 52. | 享樂 | 享乐 | xiǎnglè | *Vi.* | to indulge in pleasure |
| 53. | 主義<br>帝國主義<br>社會主義<br>軍國主義 | 主义 | zhǔyì<br>dìguó zhǔyì<br>shèhuì zhǔyì<br>jūnguó zhǔyì | *N.*<br>*N.*<br>*N.*<br>*N.* | -ism, ideology<br>imperialism<br>socialism<br>militarism |
| 54. | 倫理 | 伦理 | lúnlǐ | *N.* | ethics |
| 55. | 喪失 | 丧失 | sàngshī | *V.* | to lose (sight of) |
| 56. | 運用 | 运用 | yùnyòng | *V.* | to exercise, to employ |
| 57. | 智慧<br>智慧財產 | 智慧 | zhìhuì<br>zhìhuìcáichǎn | *N.*<br>*N.* | wisdom, sound judgment<br>intellectual property |
| 58. | 毅力 | 毅力 | yìlì | *N.* | resolution |
| 59. | 面對 | 面对 | miànduì | *V.* | to confront, to face squarely |
| 60. | 儘快 | 尽快 | jìnkuài | *Adv.* | as soon as possible |
| 61. | 穩 | 稳 | wěn | *Vs-pred.* | -fast, firmly |
| 62. | 腳步 | 脚步 | jiǎobù | *N.* | pace, stride, foothold |
| 63. | 擁有 | 拥有 | yǒngyǒu | *V.* | to possess |
| 64. | 寬廣 | 宽广 | kuānguǎng | *Vs.* | panoramic, wide and deep |
| 65. | 視野 | 视野 | shìyě | *N.* | viewpoint, perspective, vision |

# 文法 Grammar

Each pattern below is illustrated by sample sentences. When blanks are provided, complete the sentences.

## 1. 才不過 cái búguò: (Adv.+ Verb) merely, a mere...

*(Literally, 才 means "only" and 不過 means "no more than." The colloquial counterpart is 只不過.)*

a. 台灣經歷才不過數十年的努力，經濟起飛的成果值得世界刮目相看。
（台湾经历才不过数十年的努力，经济起飞的成果值得世界刮目相看。）
Taiwan's economic success, having taken only a few decades to achieve, has drawn envious international attention.

b. 才不過幾年，台灣的景氣竟然衰退得這麼厲害。
（才不过几年，台湾的景气竟然衰退得这么厉害。）
In just a few years, Taiwan's economy suffered a serious downturn.

c. 由於近幾年的經濟不景氣，這家企業才不過一年的時間已經裁員了三次。
（由于近几年的经济不景气，这家企业才不过一年的时间已经裁员了三次。）
Due to the recent economic downturn, this company had three job cuts within merely one year.

d. 才不過短短的一個星期，我們的經改政策出現了大轉彎。
（才不过短短的一个星期，我们的经改政策出现了大转弯。）
Our economic reform program produced major changes in merely one short week.

e. 現在大陸一年已經有三百萬台PC市場，台灣才不過一百萬台。
（现在大陆一年已经有三百万台PC市场，台湾才不过一百万台。）
Today, China has a ____________________________, and Taiwan a mere ________________.

f. 生產汽車的廠家據說有十幾家，但規模達到十萬輛的才不過三家。
（生产汽车的厂家据说有十几家，但规模达到十万辆的才不过三家。）
Though they say there are more than ten car manufacturers, ________________.

## 2. 終於 zhōngyú: (Adv.) finally, eventually

a. 台灣歷經近12年的努力，終於獲准加入WTO世界貿易組織。
（台湾历经近12年的努力，终于获准加入WTO世界贸易组织。）
Taiwan's application to join the WTO was finally approved after nearly 12 years of hard effort.

b. 因為政府的資金介入，這陣子的股市表現終於由黑轉紅。
（因为政府的资金介入，这阵子的股市表现终于由黑转红。）
Because of the government's investment in the stock market, it finally began to show signs of an upturn.

c. 農業經濟改革政策終於拍版定案。
（农业经济改革政策终于拍版定案。）
The program to upgrade agricultural economy has finally been fully established.

d. 新政府振興經濟方案，終於在朝野的期待下出爐。
（新政府振兴经济方案，终于在朝野的期待下出炉。）
The new government's plans to revitalize the economy have finally taken center stage after much anticipation from both the administration and people at large.

e. 房地產低迷的情況終於在年底有了起色。
（房地产低迷的情况终于在年底有了起色。）
The slow real estate industry has ______________________________.

f. 經濟成長終於在2002年第1季止跌回升，呈現正向成長。
（经济成长终于在2002年第1季止跌回升，呈现正向成长。）
The economy finally ______________________________ and indicated positive trends.

### 3. 一切 yíqiè: (Pron.) all, every, everything, any(thing)

*(The difference between* 一切 *and* 所有 *is that* 一切 *can be used alone, but* 所有 *must be followed by a noun. For example,* 你是我的一切 *is correct, but not* 你是我的所有*.)*

a. 目前失業率居高不下，許多人將一切責任歸咎於政府的無能。
（目前失业率居高不下，许多人将一切责任归咎于政府的无能。）
Many people blame the government's incompetence for today's increasingly high unemployment rates.

b. 恐怖事件的一切都讓投資人人心惶惶，保持觀望的態度。
（恐怖事件的一切都让投资人人心惶惶，保持观望的态度。）
Everything related to terrorist attacks makes investors anxious and more cautious.

c. 政府所做的一切努力都是為了人民的生計。
（政府所做的一切努力都是为了人民的生计。）
Every government measure is taken with the people's livelihood in mind.

d. 經濟部長願意擔下一切經改方向錯誤的責任。
（经济部长愿意担下一切经改方向错误的责任。）
The economics minister accepted all responsibility for the misdirection of the economic reform program.

e. 健全產業經濟發展是一切改革的基礎。
（健全产业经济发展是一切改革的基础。）
Healthy growth in the manufacturing sector is ______________________________.

f. 對台灣來說，沒有經濟就沒有一切；只有經濟發展台灣才有前途。
（对台湾来说，没有经济就没有一切；只有经济发展台湾才有前途。）
______________________________; Taiwan's future depends on _________________________.

## 4. 受到…的影響 shòudào...de yǐngxiǎng: (Prep. Phrase.)affected by, due to (the fact that)

a. 台灣的農業受到WTO的影響，讓農民難以生存。
（台湾的农业受到WTO的影响，让农民难以生存。）
WTO's effect on Taiwanese agriculture has made it hard for Taiwan's farmers to survive.

b. 受到波斯灣情勢日趨緊張的影響，石油價格也蠢蠢欲動。
（受到波斯湾情势日趋紧张的影响，石油价格也蠢蠢欲动。）
As the tension in the Persian Gulf region increases, the price of petroleum threatens to rise.

c. 受到失業率居高不下的影響，經濟復甦效果仍然有限。
（受到失业率居高不下的影响，经济复苏效果仍然有限。）
High unemployment rates reduce the chances for economic recovery.

d. 亞洲國家經濟受到出口激增的影響，2002年經濟成長大幅上揚。
（亚洲国家经济受到出口激增的影响，2002年经济成长大幅上扬。）
Helped by an increase in exports, Asian countries showed significant economic growth in 2002.

e. 由於受到新台幣大幅波動及工資上漲的影響，台商大量赴海外投資。
（由于受到新台币大幅波动及工资上涨的影响，台商大量赴海外投资。）
Due to fluctuating Taiwanese currency and wage increases, a large number of ___________________ in Taiwan _______________________________________________.

f. 受到消費需求不足的影響，台灣經濟出現了五十年來第一次負增長。
（受到消费需求不足的影响，台湾经济出现了五十年来第一次负增长。）
______________________________________________, Taiwanese economy showed its first negative growth in 50 years.

## 5. 儘快 jǐnkuài: (Adv.) as quickly/soon as possible

a. 在一片經濟不景氣聲中，老百姓無不希望台灣的經濟儘快復甦。
（在一片经济不景气声中，老百姓无不希望台湾的经济尽快复苏。）
Amidst various signs of a shrinking economy, everyone in Taiwan is hoping for a fast recovery.

b. 政府必須儘快修法通過,勞工權益才得以受到重視。
（政府必须尽快修法通过,劳工权益才得以受到重视。）
The government must soon amend relevant laws so that the rights of the blue-collar workers can be addressed.

c. 為了振興經濟，國家經濟改革的大方向應儘快決定。
（为了振兴经济，国家经济改革的大方向应尽快决定。）
To stimulate the economy, the major direction of economic reforms must be decided upon as soon as possible.

d. 專家呼籲各級政府應當儘快改善消費供給，營造良好消費和投資環境。
（专家呼吁各级政府应当尽快改善消费供给，营造良好消费和投资环境。）
Experts call for the improvement of consumer supplies at various levels of administration in order to create a better environment for consumption and investment.

e. 銀行界對匯率問題也有兩派主張，一種是儘快調整，一種是緩慢調整。
（银行界对汇率问题也有两派主张，一种是尽快调整，一种是缓慢调整 。）
Bankers approach the issue of foreign exchange rates differently; some ______________________________ and others ________________________________.

f. 假如不能儘快改善國內的環境、提昇國際競爭力，將會在現實的國際競爭環境中逐漸喪失舞台。
（假如不能尽快改善国内的环境、提升国际竞争力，将会在现实的国际竞争环境中逐漸丧失舞台。）
If we cannot ____________________________________________, we shall lose our competitive edge in ____________________________________________.

# 練習 Exercises

## 1. 填充 Fill in the blanks with the given words.

台灣的污濁水流與經濟奇蹟同受國際社會注意

| | | | |
|---|---|---|---|
| 美麗之島 | 美丽之岛 | 經濟奇蹟 | 经济奇迹 |
| 環境污染 | 环境污染 | 指標意義 | 指标意义 |
| 環保問題 | 环保问题 | 象徵 | 象征 |
| 代價 | 代价 | | |

（中央社舊金山五日專電）台灣的____________舉世皆知，但伴隨高度經濟發展而來的____________也引起國際社會的注意。舊金山灣區發行量最大的舊金山紀事報今天就以「台灣的污濁水流」為題，報導了台灣的嚴重____________。

紀事報說，台灣過去二十年建立了亞洲最富庶的經濟，但現在卻要為她的快速發展付出____________；過去被稱為____________的台灣，今天卻為她污染的河川而飽受折磨。

紀事報表示，核四廠興建與否將對台灣環保具有____________，如陳水扁總統決定停止計畫，將____________了台灣過去強調經濟發展重於一切的政策，有了一百八十度的轉變。

（（中央社旧金山五日专电）台湾的____________举世皆知，但伴随高度经济发展而来的____________也引起国际社会的注意。旧金山湾区发行量最大的旧金山纪事报今天就以「台湾的污浊水流」为题，报导了台湾的严重____________。

纪事报说，台湾过去二十年建立了亚洲最富庶的经济，但现在却要为她的快速发展付出____________；过去被称为____________的台湾，今天却为她污染的河川而饱受折磨。

纪事报表示，核四厂兴建与否将对台湾环保具有____________，如陈水扁总统决定停止计划，将____________了台湾过去强调经济发展重于一切的政策，有了一百八十度的转变。）

## 2. 新聞標題 Headline News in Taiwan

Indicate what each headline is about.

a. 搖頭丸(Ecstasy)—毒品新貴和PUB次文化相互依存
（摇头丸(Ecstasy)—毒品新贵和PUB次文化相互依存）

________________________________________________.

b. 抹去輕狂烙印　　少年法庭百人除紋
（抹去轻狂烙印　　少年法庭百人除纹）

______________________________________________.

c. 台北國際電信展　　超炫登場
（台北国际电信展　　超炫登场）

______________________________________________.

d. 颱風影響　　進出口貿易降低
（台风影响　　进出口贸易降低　）

______________________________________________.

e. 看好我半導體業發展　　法商來台探路
（看好我半导体业发展　　法商来台探路）

______________________________________________.

f. 曾文溪水源區強制離牧　　逾200養豬場將被拆
（曾文溪水源区强制离牧　　逾200养猪场将被拆）

______________________________________________.

g. 台電濫墾建電塔　　人心惶惶
（台电滥垦建电塔　　人心惶惶）

______________________________________________.

h. 地震頻仍　　高雄房市又倍感銷售壓力
（地震频仍　　高雄房市又倍感销售压力）

______________________________________________.

## 3. 情況對話 Role Play

兩位同學一組，依照以下情境設計一段對話。
（兩位同学一组，依照以下情境设计一段对话。）
Form teams of two and compose dialogues based on the following situations.

（情境一）

一位曾經在八十年代留學台灣的外國學生現在在美國一家公司任職，今年一月到台北參加某產品展示會。出了桃園中正國際機場，搭上計程車到台北市，一路上和司機談台灣近年來的轉變和他印象中的台灣。

（一位曾经在八十年代留学台湾的外国学生现在在美国一家公司任职，今年一月到台北参加某产品展示会。出了桃园中正国际机场，搭上出租车到台北市，一路上和司机谈台湾近年来的转变和他印象中的台湾。）

（情境二）

紐約時報駐亞洲特派記者在台灣一漁港採訪當地的海豚野放活動。這是亞洲第一隻擱淺獲救並經復原後成功野放的海豚。記者訪問當地市長談論台灣在動物保育方面工作的成績。

（纽约时报驻亚洲特派记者在台湾一渔港采访当地的海豚野放活动。这是亚洲第一只搁浅获救并经复原后成功野放的海豚。记者访问当地市长谈论台湾在动物保育方面工作的成绩。）

## 4. 討論『經濟發展與環境保護』Join a Debate

將學生分成A、B、C三組，針對「經濟發展與環境保護」議題進行討論；討論方式（如果班上人數六人以上），老師事先準備三種卡片，有企業家、環保人士及政府官員，讓學生隨機抽取，拿到代表企業家的卡片，該名學生就扮演企業家，依此類推，最後把學生分成三組，分別是兩位企業家、兩位環保人士、及政府官員兩位，針對上述的議題進行辯論。

（將学生分成A、B、C三组，针对「经济发展与环境保护」议题进行讨论；讨论方式（如果班上人数六人以上），老师事先准备三种卡片，有企业家、环保人士及政府官员，让学生随机抽取，拿到代表企业家的卡片，该名学生就扮演企业家，依此类推，最后把学生分成三组，分别是两位企业家、两位环保人士、及政府官员两位，针对上述的议题进行辩论。）

Have students form three groups to discuss the conflict between economic development and protecting the environment. If the class contains at least six students, the teacher should prepare three types of cards that represent business people, environmentalists, and government officials respectively. In class, each student picks a random card and takes the role indicated by the card. Once roles are assigned, the teacher separates the students into groups ( businesspeople, environmentalists, and government officials) that will debate the topic.

## 5. 看資料討論 Analyze the Graphic

以下是台灣與大陸近十幾年來，在經濟成長方面的比較，請同學看完圖後回答問題。（資料來源：中華民國政府主計處）

（以下是台湾与大陆近十几年来，在经济成长方面的比较，请同学看完图后回答问题。（资料来源：中华民国政府主计处））

The chart below compares economic growth rates for Taiwan and mainland China in the last few decades. Analyze the chart to answer the questions that follow.

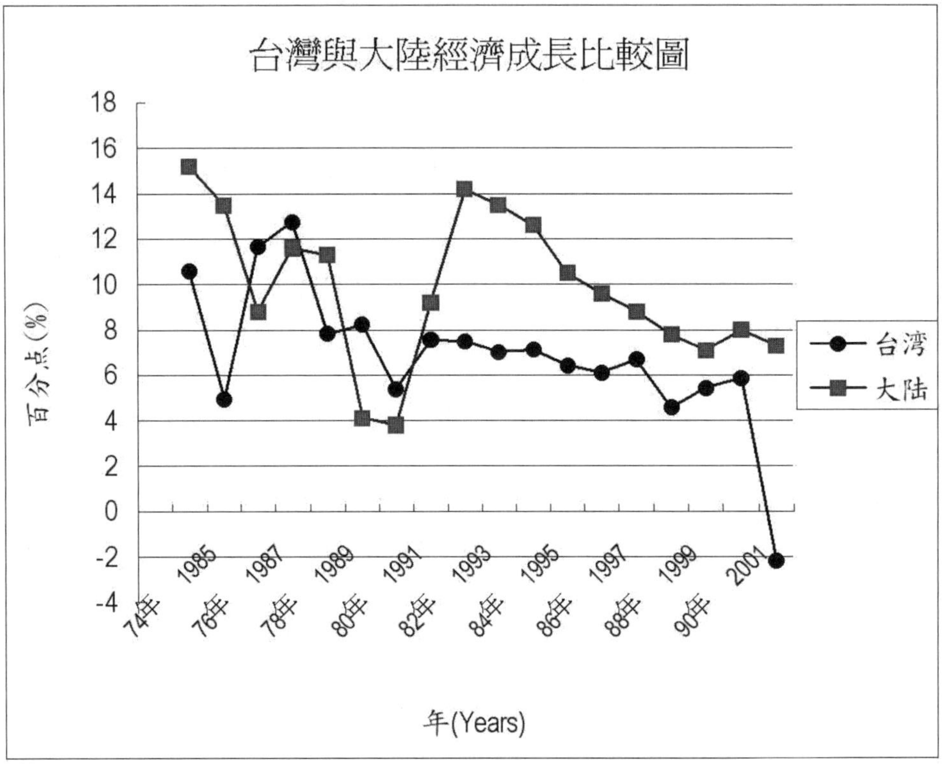


(1) 請問「台灣」與「大陸」這幾十年來，各自在「經濟成長」方面的表現如何?
（请问「台湾」与「大陆」这几十年来，各自在「经济成长」方面的表现如何?）

(2) （續上題）你覺得可能是哪些因素造成彼此不同的表現?
（（续上题）你觉得可能是哪些因素造成彼此不同的表现?）

(3) 面对台湾的经济情况，如果你是台湾的政府官员，你有什麼因应对策?
（面對台灣的經濟情況，如果你是台灣的政府官員，你有什么因應對策?）

(4) 請簡單說明你們國家的經濟發展情況?
（请简单说明你们国家的经济发展情况?）

## 6. 閱讀以下短文後，進行討論 A Mild Protest

Read the letter below, then answer the questions that follow.

台胞給台灣政府的一封

親愛的台灣政府，

你們在立法院討論著「台灣到底開不開放三通」時，我們這群台胞早已往來於兩岸間無數次，為自己的生活及未來努力；過多的工作時數、陌生且競爭的環境，都打不垮我們，更何況是小小的「三通」問題。

很多台灣人都以為大陸還是以前那個人煙稀少、需要大家幫助的貧窮國家，其實不然，現在的大陸，不但到處可見高樓大廈，人民的生活品質也不斷地提高；只要來過大陸的人，一定會被眼前的現代化景象嚇一大跳。不少台胞來大陸奮鬥，一待就是好幾年，但不要以為在這裡賺錢容易，其實這裡競爭的壓力絕不低於台灣，甚至比台灣還激烈，一不小心，就可能從商界消失。

台胞的辛苦應該受到肯定而不是歧視，應該受到政府的幫助而不是威脅，政府應該放棄多年的政治意識形態，幫助台灣人找到生意的第二春。否則當國際企業家大量進入大陸找尋商機時，台灣這群缺乏資金又受到很多限制的中小企業家註定要退出大陸這個大商圈。

亲爱的台湾政府，

你们在立法院讨论着「台湾到底开不开放三通」时，我们这群台胞早已往来于两岸间无数次，为自己的生活及未来努力；过多的工作时数、陌生且竞争的环境，都打不垮我们，更何况是小小的「三通」问题。

很多台湾人都以为大陆还是以前那个人烟稀少、需要大家帮助的贫穷国家，其实不然，现在的大陆，不但到处可见高楼大厦，人民的生活品质也不断地提高；只要来过大陆的人，一定会被眼前的现代化景象吓一大跳。不少台胞来大陆奋斗，一待就是好几年，但不要以为在这里赚钱容易，其实这里竞争的压力绝不低于台湾，甚至比台湾还激烈，一不小心，就可能从商界消失。

台胞的辛苦应该受到肯定而不是歧视，应该受到政府的帮助而不是威胁，政府应该放弃多年的政治意识形态，帮助台湾人找到生意的第二春。否则当国际企业家大量进入大陆找寻商机时，台湾这群缺乏资金又受到很多限制的中小企业家注定要退出大陆这个大商圈。

| | | | |
|---|---|---|---|
| 打不垮 | 打不垮 | dǎbùkuǎ | irrepressible |
| 景象 | 景象 | jǐngxiàng | scene; sight; picture |
| 奮鬥 | 奋斗 | fèndòu | fight to achieve a goal; struggle; strive |
| 肯定 | 肯定 | kěndìng | affirm; approve |
| 政治意識形態 | 政治意识形态 | zhèngzhì yìshì xíngtài | political ideology |
| 第二春 | 第二春 | dì'èrchūn | second attempt |
| 商機 | 商机 | shāngjī | business opportunity |
| 註定 | 注定 | zhùdìng | be destined; be doomed |

(1) 你去過大陸嗎?請你談一談你所看到的大陸?
如果你沒去過，也請談一談你印象中（知道）的大陸?
（你去过大陆吗?请你谈一谈你所看到的大陆?
如果你没去过，也请谈一谈你印象中（知道）的大陆?）

(2) 如果你是台灣的政府官員，面對台胞這樣的情形，你會怎麼辦?
（如果你是台湾的政府官员，面对台胞这样的情形，你会怎么办?）

(3) 如果你是個企業家，面對家庭與工作之間，該如何選擇?
（如果你是个企业家，面对家庭与工作之间，该如何选择?）

(4) 如果你是中小企業家，面對這樣的競爭環境，你會如何處理?
（如果你是中小企业家，面对这样的竞争环境，你会如何处理?）

(5) 你認為台灣的經濟奇蹟經驗可以為大陸的經濟改革帶來什麼啟示?
（你认为台湾的经济奇迹经验可以为大陆的经济改革带来什么启示?）

## 7. 請閱讀以下短文，並討論問題 Read and Discuss

Read the short passages below and discuss the questions that follow.

(A)

民國七十六年（西元1987年）是台灣政局變化非常重要的一年，該年取消戒嚴，並有各種社會運動，如勞工運動、環保抗爭、消費者運動、農民運動，時斷時續，同時政治抗爭更是常見。這些運動與抗爭造成投資環境的惡化，成為部分企業出走海外的一個原因。

（民国七十六年（公元1987年）是台湾政局变化非常重要的一年，该年取消戒严，并有各种社会运动，如劳工运动、环保抗争、消费者运动、农民运动，时断时续，同时政治抗争更是常见。这些运动与抗争造成投资环境的恶化，成为部分企业出走海外的一个原因。）

(1) 台灣的經濟快速發展，也造成了哪些問題？
（台湾的经济快速发展，也造成了哪些问题？）

(2) 為什麼有些企業會選擇改向海外投資呢？
（为什么有些企业会选择改向海外投资呢？）

(3) 如果你是一位大企業負責人，你會選擇在台灣投資嗎？
（如果你是一位大企业负责人，你会选择在台湾投资吗？）

(B)

民國七十六年（西元1987年）也是台灣與大陸兩岸人民開始來往的一年。政府於這一年宣布台灣同胞可到大陸探親，於是兩岸民間交往便熱絡起來。到八十五年為止，台商到大陸投資的金額，據台灣官方登記，為六十億美元；若據中共官方統計，則逾二百億美元。

（民国七十六年（公元1987年）也是台湾与大陆两岸人民开始来往的一年。政府于这一年宣布台湾同胞可到大陆探亲，于是两岸民间交往便热络起来。到八十五年为止，台商到大陆投资的金额，据台湾官方登记，为六十亿美元；若据中共官方统计，则逾二百亿美元。）

(1) 為什麼會有許多台灣企業到大陸投資呢？
（为什么会有许多台湾企业到大陆投资呢？）

(2) 台灣企業到大陸投資的金額數目，在台灣和在大陸的估計，為什麼會有這麼大的差別呢？
（台湾企业到大陆投资的金额数目，在台湾和在大陆的估计，为什么会有这么大的差别呢？）

(3) 兩岸除了有經濟上的交流以外，還有什麼樣的交流？
（两岸除了有经济上的交流以外，还有什么样的交流？）

# 補充資料 Supplementary Materials

## 1. 台灣重要統計數據一覽表：人口概況

| 類別 | 種類 | 單位 | 資料 | 資料涵蓋時間 |
|---|---|---|---|---|
| 人口概況 | 戶籍登記人口數 | 人 | 22,173,000 | 截至民國八十九年六月 |
| -- | 出生率 | 千分比 | 12.59 | 截至民國八十九年六月 |
| -- | 死亡率 | 千分比 | 5.51 | 截至民國八十九年六月 |

## 2. 台灣重要統計數據一覽表：經濟建設

| 類別 | 單位 | 資料 | 資料涵蓋時間 |
|---|---|---|---|
| 平均每人國民生產毛額(P) | 新臺幣元 | 427,330 | 民國八十八年 |
| -- | 美元 | 13,248 | 民國八十八年 |
| 平均每人國民所得(P) | 新臺幣元 | 392,342 | 民國八十八年 |
| -- | 美元 | 12,163 | 民國八十八年 |
| 經濟成長率(P) | 百分比 | 5.43 | 民國八十九年六月 |
| 國民儲蓄率(P) | 百分比 | 27.84 | 民國八十九年六月 |
| 出口 | 新臺幣百萬元 | 3,917,445 | 民國八十八年 |
| -- | 百萬美元 | 121,591 | 民國八十八年 |
| 進口 | 新臺幣百萬元 | 3,576,416 | 民國八十八年 |
| -- | 百萬美元 | 110,690 | 民國八十八年 |
| 外匯存底(P) | 億美元 | 1,138.3 | 截至民國八十九年六月 |
| 國人出國人數 | 千人次 | 6,559 | 民國八十八年 |
| 來台旅客數 | 千人次 | 2,411 | 民國八十八年 |

## 3. 台灣重要統計數據一覽表：政治及外交

| 種類 | 單位 | 資料 | 資料涵蓋時間 |
|---|---|---|---|
| 政黨數 | 個 | 91 | 截至民國八十九年五月 |
| 人民團體數 | 個 | 3,435 | 截至民國八十九年四月 |
| 邦交國數 | 個 | 29 | 截至民國八十九年九月 |
| 參與非政府間國組織數 | 個 | 970 | 截至民國八十九年六月 |
| 參與政府間國際組織數 | 個 | 16 | 截至民國八十九年六月 |

## 4. 台灣重要指標：國際舞台

| | 全球地位 |
|---|---|
| 國家競爭力 | 24 |
| 國內經濟 | 40 |
| 對外投資 | 21 |
| 生活品質 | 33 |
| 環保 | 39 |
| 全球化 | 34 |
| | 亞洲地位 |
| 經濟自由 | 3 |
| 經濟成長 | 5 |
| 失業率 | 3（高） |

# Vocabulary Index

| A | | | Lesson |
|---|---|---|---|
| āndìng | 安定 | 安定 | 14 |
| āndìngjúmiàn | 安定局面 | 安定局面 | 14 |
| ānjìng | 安靜 | 安静 | 1 |
| ānwèi | 安慰 | 安慰 | 8 |
| àn | 岸 | 岸 | 12 |
| ànshí | 按時 | 按时 | 8 |
| āngzāng | 骯髒 | 肮脏 | 11 |
| **B** | | | |
| bāshì | 巴士 | 巴士 | 6 |
| bāzì | 八字 | 八字 | 8 |
| bǎi | 擺 | 摆 | 2 |
| bǎinián hǎohé | 百年好合 | 百年好合 | 5 |
| bàibài | 拜拜 | 拜拜 | 8 |
| bān | 班 | 班 | 6 |
| bànyǎn | 扮演 | 扮演 | 9 |
| bāoluó wànxiàng | 包羅萬象 | 包罗万象 | 8 |
| bāozi | 包子 | 包子 | 3 |
| bǎohù | 保護 | 保护 | 11 |
| bǎoshǒu | 保守 | 保守 | 5 |
| bàofāhù | 暴發戶 | 暴发户 | 14 |
| bàozào | 暴躁 | 暴躁 | 11 |
| bàozhāng | 報章 | 报章 | 10 |
| bēijù | 悲劇 | 悲剧 | 5 |
| Bēinán | 卑南 | 卑南 | 13 |
| běntǔ | 本土 | 本土 | 13 |
| běntǔwénhuà | 本土文化 | 本土文化 | 13 |
| běntǔyǔyán | 本土語言 | 本土语言 | 13 |
| bǐcǐ | 彼此 | 彼此 | 5 |
| bǐrú | 比如 | 比如 | 3 |
| bǐsài | 比賽 | 比赛 | 7 |
| bìbèi | 必備 | 必备 | 4 |
| bìxū | 必須 | 必须 | 4 |
| biānpào | 鞭炮 | 鞭炮 | 9 |
| biāozhǔn | 標準 | 标准 | 7 |
| biǎomiàn | 表面 | 表面 | 10 |
| biǎomiàn shàng | 表面上 | 表面上 | 10 |
| biǎoyǎn | 表演 | 表演 | 2 |
| bówùguǎn | 博物館 | 博物馆 | 6 |
| bówùyuàn | 博物院 | 博物院 | 6 |
| bòfàng | 播放 | 播放 | 13 |
| búduàn | 不斷 | 不断 | 14 |
| bújiàndé | 不見得 | 不见得 | 6 |
| bújìn xiāngtóng | 不盡相同 | 不尽相同 | 7 |
| búlì | 不利 | 不利 | 10 |
| búlùn | 不論 | 不论 | 5 |
| bùfèn | 部分 | 部分 | 14 |
| bù jǐngqì | 不景氣 | 不景气 | 14 |
| bùjiǔde jiānglái | 不久的將來 | 不久的将来 | 6 |
| Bùnóng | 布農 | 布农 | 13 |
| bùrú | 不如 | 不如 | 10 |

| C | | | |
|---|---|---|---|
| cǎiyòng | 採用 | 采用 | 7 |
| cān | 餐 | 餐 | 3 |
| cāntīng | 餐廳 | 餐厅 | 3 |
| cānyǐndiàn | 餐飲店 | 餐饮店 | 3 |
| chádài | 茶袋 | 茶袋 | 4 |
| cháyè | 茶葉 | 茶叶 | 4 |
| cháyì guǎn | 茶藝館 | 茶艺馆 | 4 |
| chánglóng | 長龍 | 长龙 | 6 |
| chángqí | 長期 | 长期 | 14 |
| chángqí wòchuáng | 長期臥床 | 长期卧床 | 14 |
| chángzhì jiǔ'ān | 長治久安 | 长治久安 | 12 |
| cháo | 巢 | 巢 | 9 |
| cháo | 潮 | 潮 | 6 |
| chǎo mǐfěn | 炒米粉 | 炒米粉 | 3 |
| chēhuò | 車禍 | 车祸 | 6 |
| chēshuǐ mǎlóng | 車水馬龍 | 车水马龙 | 14 |
| chètuì | 撤退 | 撤退 | 13 |
| chéngdù | 程度 | 程度 | 6 |
| chéngjì | 成績 | 成绩 | 7 |
| chéngjiù | 成就 | 成就 | 10 |
| chéngkè | 乘客 | 乘客 | 13 |
| chéngwéi | 成為 | 成为 | 3 |
| chéngxiào | 成效 | 成效 | 12 |
| chéngzhǎng | 成長 | 成长 | 14 |
| chōngmǎn | 充滿 | 充满 | 11 |
| chōngtiān | 沖天 | 冲天 | 9 |
| chòu | 臭 | 臭 | 3 |
| chūfādiǎn | 出發點 | 出发点 | 7 |
| chūxiàn | 出現 | 出现 | 10 |
| chūzū (qì)chē | 出租(汽)車 | 出租(汽)车 | 6 |

| | | | |
|---|---|---|---|
| chuánqí | 傳奇 | 传奇 | 9 |
| chuánshuō | 傳說 | 传说 | 9 |
| chuántǒng | 傳統 | 传统 | 3 |
| chuàngzào | 創造 | 创造 | 12, 14 |
| chūnjié | 春節 | 春节 | 9 |
| cìshù | 次數 | 次数 | 4 |
| chūnjuǎn | 春捲 | 春卷 | 3 |
| cóngcǐ | 從此 | 从此 | 9 |
| cùjìn | 促進 | 促进 | 12 |
| **D** | | | |
| dǎpò | 打破 | 打破 | 12 |
| dàlì | 大力 | 大力 | 13 |
| dàlìzhīchí | 大力支持 | 大力支持 | 13 |
| dàlù | 大陸 | 大陆 | 12 |
| dàqīngzǎo | 大清早 | 大清早 | 1 |
| dàzhìshàng | 大致上 | 大致上 | 13 |
| dàibiǎo | 代表 | 代表 | 10 |
| dàijià | 代價 | 代价 | 11 |
| dàilái | 帶來 | 带来 | 7 |
| dānrèn | 擔任 | 担任 | 10 |
| dānshēn | 單身 | 单身 | 5 |
| dāngdì | 當地 | 当地 | 8 |
| dàochù kějiàn | 到處可見 | 到处可见 | 3 |
| dàodǐ | 到底 | 到底 | 5 |
| dàojiào | 道教 | 道教 | 8 |
| dàolù | 道路 | 道路 | 6 |
| dàotián | 稻田 | 稻田 | 14 |
| děng | 等 | 等 | 3 |
| dèngzi | 凳子 | 凳子 | 3 |
| dī | 低 | 低 | 2 |
| díquè | 的確 | 的确 | 8 |
| díshì | 的士 | 的士 | 6 |

| | | | |
|---|---|---|---|
| dìfāngxìng | 地方性 | 地方性 | 8 |
| dìguó zhǔyì | 帝國主義 | 帝国主义 | 14 |
| dìqū | 地區 | 地区 | 3 |
| dìxiàtiě | 地下鐵 | 地下铁 | 6 |
| dìzào | 締造 | 缔造 | 14 |
| diǎn | 點 | 点 | 9 |
| diǎnrán | 點燃 | 点燃 | 9 |
| diànmiàn | 店面 | 店面 | 3 |
| dìnghūn | 訂婚 | 订婚 | 5 |
| dìngjū | 定居 | 定居 | 13 |
| dōng'àn | 東岸 | 东岸 | 12 |
| dūshì | 都市 | 都市 | 6 |
| dúlì | 獨立 | 独立 | 10 |
| dòngdàng-júmiàn | 動盪局面 | 动盪局面荡 | 14 |
| duānwǔ | 端午 | 端午 | 9 |
| duàn | 段 | 段 | 10 |
| duì | 對 | 对 | 5 |
| duìlì | 對立 | 对立 | 12 |
| duìxiàng | 對象 | 对象 | 5 |
| duōbàn | 多半 | 多半 | 1 |
| duōyuán rùxué | 多元入學 | 多元入学 | 7 |
| **E** | | | |
| èguǐ | 惡鬼 | 恶鬼 | 9 |
| ěrsāi | 耳塞 | 耳塞 | 9 |
| **F** | | | |
| fājué | 發掘 | 发掘 | 7 |
| fāshēng | 發生 | 发生 | 6 |
| fāzhǎn | 發展 | 发展 | 11 |
| fǎzhì | 法制 | 法制 | 12 |
| fǎnér | 反而 | 反而 | 7 |
| fǎnyìng | 反映 | 反映 | 12 |
| fāngshì | 方式 | 方式 | 3 |
| fāngyán | 方言 | 方言 | 13 |
| fángdìchǎn | 房地產 | 房地产 | 14 |
| fǎngmàopǐn | 仿冒品 | 仿冒品 | 2 |
| fàngkuān | 放寬 | 放宽 | 12 |
| fēidàn | 飛彈 | 飞弹 | 12 |
| fēifǎ | 非法 | 非法 | 12 |
| fēiguānfāng | 非官方 | 非官方 | 12 |
| fèichú | 廢除 | 废除 | 7 |
| fèiqì | 廢氣 | 废气 | 11 |
| fèishuǐ | 廢水 | 废水 | 11 |
| fēnqí | 分歧 | 分歧 | 12 |
| fēng | 蜂 | 蜂 | 9 |
| fēnghuà qū | 風化區 | 风化区 | 8 |
| fēngkuáng | 瘋狂 | 疯狂 | 9 |
| fēngpào | 蜂炮 | 蜂炮 | 8 |
| fēngshuǐ | 風水 | 风水 | 8 |
| fēngsú | 風俗 | 风俗 | 9 |
| féng | 逢 | 逢 | 9 |
| fó | 佛 | 佛 | 8 |
| fójiào | 佛教 | 佛教 | 8 |
| fǒuzé | 否則 | 否则 | 9 |
| fú | 福 | 福 | 12 |
| Fújiàn | 福建 | 福建 | 13 |
| Fúlǎo rén | 福佬人 | 福佬人 | 13 |
| fúzhuāngshèjì | 服裝設計 | 服装设计 | 13 |
| fùmiàn chéngzhǎng | 負面成長 | 负面成长 | 14 |
| fù | 赴 | 赴 | 12 |
| fùchū | 付出 | 付出 | 11 |
| fùnǚ | 婦女 | 妇女 | 1 |
| fùyù | 富裕 | 富裕 | 12 |

| G | | | |
|---|---|---|---|
| gǎi | 改 | 改 | 6 |
| gǎibiàn | 改變 | 改变 | 7 |
| gǎishàn | 改善 | 改善 | 6 |
| gǎnkuài | 趕快 | 赶快 | 11 |
| gǎnzǒu | 趕走 | 赶走 | 9 |
| gāocháo | 高潮 | 高潮 | 8 |
| gāosù | 高速 | 高速 | 14 |
| gāosùgōnglù | 高速公路 | 高速公路 | 14 |
| gāosùtiělù | 高速鐵路 | 高速铁路 | 14 |
| gèháng gèyè | 各行各業 | 各行各业 | 10 |
| gèshì gèyàng | 各式各樣 | 各式各样 | 4 |
| gèzhǒng | 各種 | 各种 | 2 |
| gēnběn | 根本 | 根本 | 6 |
| gōngchén | 功臣 | 功臣 | 14 |
| gōngchéngshī | 工程師 | 工程师 | 10 |
| gōngdéxīn | 公德心 | 公德心 | 11 |
| gōngfū | 功夫 | 功夫 | 1 |
| gōngjù | 工具 | 工具 | 11 |
| gōngpíng | 公平 | 公平 | 7 |
| gōngyìng | 供應 | 供应 | 3 |
| gōutōng | 溝通 | 沟通 | 12 |
| gūjì | 估計 | 估计 | 8 |
| gǔlì | 鼓勵 | 鼓励 | 12 |
| gǔsè gǔxiāng | 古色古香 | 古色古香 | 4 |
| gǔshì | 股市 | 股市 | 14 |
| gùgōng bówùguàn | 故宮博物院 | 故宫博物院 | 6 |
| gùkè | 顧客 | 顾客 | 2 |
| guānguāng | 觀光 | 观光 | 6 |
| guānguāngkè | 觀光客 | 观光客 | 6 |
| guānniàn | 觀念 | 观念 | 5 |
| guānxīn | 關心 | 关心 | 6 |
| guānyuán | 官員 | 官员 | 10 |
| guǎndào | 管道 | 管道 | 5 |
| guǎngbò | 廣播 | 广播 | 13 |
| guǎngbō-diàntái | 廣播電台 | 广播电台 | 13 |
| guǎngdà | 廣大 | 广大 | 8 |
| guàng | 逛 | 逛 | 2 |
| guàngjiē | 逛街 | 逛街 | 2 |
| guīzé | 規則 | 规则 | 6 |
| guǐ | 鬼 | 鬼 | 9 |
| guō | 鍋 | 锅 | 7 |
| guójì | 國際 | 国际 | 6 |
| guólì | 國立 | 国立 | 7 |
| guǒ | 裹 | 裹 | 10 |
| guòfèn | 過分 | 过分 | 6 |
| guòlǜ | 過濾 | 过滤 | 11 |

| H | | | |
|---|---|---|---|
| Hǎijīhuì | 海基會 | 海基会 | 12 |
| hǎixiá | 海峽 | 海峡 | 12 |
| Hǎixiéhuì | 海協會 | 海协会 | 12 |
| hàn | 漢 | 汉 | 13 |
| hànbǎo | 漢堡 | 汉堡 | 3 |
| Hàncháo | 漢朝 | 汉朝 | 13 |
| Hànhuà | 漢化 | 汉化 | 13 |
| Hànzì | 漢字 | 汉字 | 13 |
| hángyè | 行業 | 行业 | 10 |
| hé bāzì | 合八字 | 合八字 | 8 |
| héjiě | 和解 | 和解 | 12 |
| héshì | 合適 | 合适 | 2 |
| hézuò | 合作 | 合作 | 12 |
| hóngbāo | 紅包 | 红包 | 5 |

| | | | |
|---|---|---|---|
| hóngchúnzú | 紅唇族 | 红唇族 | 13 |
| hóngniáng | 紅娘 | 红娘 | 5 |
| hòuqí | 後期 | 后期 | 14 |
| hūlüè | 忽略 | 忽略 | 11 |
| hūshì | 忽視 | 忽视 | 14 |
| hūxī | 呼吸 | 呼吸 | 1 |
| hú | 壺 | 壶 | 4 |
| huācǎo | 花草 | 花草 | 2 |
| huādēng | 花燈 | 花灯 | 9 |
| huánbǎo | 環保 | 环保 | 14 |
| huánjìng | 環境 | 环境 | 11 |
| hūnlǐ | 婚禮 | 婚礼 | 5 |
| hūnyīn | 婚姻 | 婚姻 | 5 |
| huò | 禍 | 祸 | 12 |
| **J** | | | |
| jīchē | 機車 | 机车 | 6 |
| jīchǔ | 基礎 | 基础 | 12 |
| jīdū | 基督 | 基督 | 8 |
| jīdūjiào | 基督教 | 基督教 | 8 |
| jīhū | 幾乎 | 几乎 | 4 |
| jījí | 積極 | 积极 | 5 |
| jīliè | 激烈 | 激烈 | 12 |
| jíróng kāfēi | 即溶咖啡 | 速溶咖啡 | 4 |
| jíshǐ | 即使 | 即使 | 11 |
| jíwéi | 極為 | 极为 | 8 |
| jǐ | 擠 | 挤 | 2 |
| jìbài | 祭拜 | 祭拜 | 8 |
| jìchéngchē | 計程車 | 出租车 | 6 |
| jìzhě | 記者 | 记者 | 10 |
| jiāshì | 家事 | 家事 | 10 |
| jiātíng | 家庭 | 家庭 | 4 |
| jiāzhǎng | 家長 | 家长 | 7 |
| jià | 嫁 | 嫁 | 5 |

| | | | |
|---|---|---|---|
| jiàshǐ | 駕駛 | 驾驶 | 6 |
| jiàzhí | 價值 | 价值 | 4 |
| jiǎnqīng | 減輕 | 减轻 | 7 |
| jiǎnshǎo | 減少 | 减少 | 6 |
| jiànjiàn | 漸漸 | 渐渐 | 8 |
| jiànlì | 建立 | 建立 | 6 |
| jiànkāng | 健康 | 健康 | 1 |
| jiànměicāo | 健美操 | 健美操 | 1 |
| jiāngjú | 僵局 | 僵局 | 12 |
| jiānglái | 將來 | 将来 | 6 |
| jiǎngjià | 講價 | 讲价 | 2 |
| jiǎngjiù | 講究 | 讲究 | 4 |
| jiāoliú | 交流 | 交流 | 8 |
| jiāoqū | 郊區 | 郊区 | 11 |
| jiāowǎng | 交往 | 交往 | 5 |
| jiāoyǒu | 交友 | 交友 | 5 |
| jiǎobù | 腳步 | 脚步 | 14 |
| jiǎoluò | 角落 | 角落 | 8 |
| jiǎosè, juésè | 角色 | 角色 | 9 |
| jiàohuì | 教會 | 教会 | 8 |
| jiàotáng | 教堂 | 教堂 | 5 |
| jiàowéi | 較為 | 较为 | 14 |
| jiàoyù gǎigé | 教育改革 | 教育改革 | 7 |
| jiēchù | 接觸 | 接触 | 12 |
| jiēshòu | 接受 | 接受 | 5 |
| jiētóu | 街頭 | 街头 | 4 |
| jiéguǒ | 結果 | 结果 | 7 |
| jiéjiǎn | 節儉 | 节俭 | 14 |
| jiéqìng | 節慶 | 节庆 | 9 |
| jiérì | 節日 | 节日 | 9 |
| jiéyùn | 捷運 | 捷运 | 13 |
| jiěchú | 解除 | 解除 | 12 |
| jiějué | 解決 | 解决 | 6 |

| | | | |
|---|---|---|---|
| jiěkě | 解渴 | 解渴 | 4 |
| jièyánfǎ | 戒嚴法 | 戒严法 | 12 |
| jīnróng fēngbào | 金融風暴 | 金融风暴 | 14 |
| jǐnguǎn | 儘管 | 尽管 | 10 |
| jìnbù | 進步 | 进步 | 10 |
| jìnkuài | 儘快 | 尽快 | 14 |
| jìnxíng | 進行 | 进行 | 7 |
| jīngjì | 經濟 | 经济 | 3, 12 |
| jīngjì bú jǐngqì | 經濟不景氣 | 经济不景气 | 14 |
| jīng mào | 經貿 | 经贸 | 12 |
| jīngrén | 驚人 | 惊人 | 9 |
| jīngshén | 精神 | 精神 | 8 |
| jīngguò | 經過 | 经过 | 14 |
| jìnghuà | 淨化 | 净化 | 11 |
| jǐngqì bú kànhǎo | 景氣不看好 | 景气不看好 | 14 |
| jìngzhēng | 競爭 | 竞争 | 7 |
| jiùshì | 舊式 | 旧式 | 5 |
| jūmín | 居民 | 居民 | 8 |
| jūzhù | 居住 | 居住 | 11 |
| júmiàn | 局面 | 局面 | 12, 14 |
| jǔxíng | 舉行 | 举行 | 5, 7 |
| jù | 具 | 具 | 9 |
| juébù | 絕不 | 绝不 | 4 |
| juédìng | 決定 | 决定 | 5 |
| juéduì | 絕對 | 绝对 | 4 |
| jūnguó zhǔyì | 軍國主義 | 军国主义 | 14 |
| jūn | 均 | 均 | 14 |

| K | | | |
|---|---|---|---|
| kāizhāng | 開張 | 开张 | 3 |
| kàngyì | 抗議 | 抗议 | 11 |
| kào | 靠 | 靠 | 10 |
| kē | 棵 | 棵 | 1 |
| kējì | 科技 | 科技 | 12 |
| kēxì | 科系 | 科系 | 7 |
| Kèjiā rén | 客家人 | 客家人 | 13 |
| kèmǎn | 客滿 | 客满 | 6 |
| kōngqì | 空氣 | 空气 | 1 |
| kòngzhì | 控制 | 控制 | 12 |
| kǒuhào | 口號 | 口号 | 5 |
| kǒuwèi | 口味 | 口味 | 3 |
| kǒuzhào | 口罩 | 口罩 | 11 |
| kuàicān | 快餐 | 快餐 | 3 |
| kuānguǎng | 寬廣 | 宽广 | 14 |
| kùnnán | 困難 | 困难 | 8 |
| kuòyīnjī | 擴音機 | 扩音机 | 11 |

| L | | | |
|---|---|---|---|
| lǎbā | 喇叭 | 喇叭 | 11 |
| láibùjí | 來不及 | 来不及 | 11 |
| lánqiú | 籃球 | 篮球 | 1 |
| lǎobǎn | 老板 | 老板 | 2 |
| lǎogōng | 老公 | 老公 | 5 |
| lǎopó | 老婆 | 老婆 | 5 |
| lǎoshào | 老少 | 老少 | 1 |
| lèsè, lājī | 垃圾 | 垃圾 | 11 |
| lèqù | 樂趣 | 乐趣 | 2 |
| lèisì | 類似 | 类似 | 9 |
| líhūn | 離婚 | 离婚 | 5 |
| lì | 利 | 利 | 12 |
| lìzi | 例子 | 例子 | 10 |

| Q | | | |
|---|---|---|---|
| qíjī | 奇蹟 | 奇迹 | 14 |
| qílóu | 騎樓 | 骑楼 | 6 |
| qíshí | 其實 | 其实 | 3 |
| qíshì | 歧視 | 歧视 | 10 |
| qíshì | 騎士 | 骑士 | 11 |
| qízhōng | 其中 | 其中 | 1 |
| qìyèjiā | 企業家 | 企业家 | 10 |
| qiānwàn | 千萬 | 千万 | 9 |
| Qiánlóng | 乾隆 | 干隆 | 13 |
| qiáng | 強 | 强 | 10 |
| qiángdiào | 強調 | 强调 | 11 |
| qīnqi | 親戚 | 亲戚 | 5 |
| qínláo | 勤勞 | 勤劳 | 14 |
| qīngchá | 清茶 | 清茶 | 4 |
| qīngcháo | 清朝 | 清朝 | 9 |
| qīngmíng | 清明 | 清明 | 9 |
| qīngwéi | 輕微 | 轻微 | 14 |
| qíngkuàng | 情況 | 情况 | 6 |
| qíngshì | 情勢 | 情势 | 14 |
| qìngzhù | 慶祝 | 庆祝 | 9 |
| qiúchǎng | 球場 | 球场 | 1 |
| qiúhūn | 求婚 | 求婚 | 5 |
| qǔ | 娶 | 娶 | 5 |
| qǔdài | 取代 | 取代 | 7 |
| qǔdé | 取得 | 取得 | 7 |
| quēfá | 缺乏 | 缺乏 | 7 |
| quēshǎo | 缺少 | 缺少 | 5 |
| qún | 群 | 群 | 1 |

| R | | | |
|---|---|---|---|
| rán'ér | 然而 | 然而 | 4 |
| réncháo | 人潮 | 人潮 | 6 |
| réncì | 人次 | 人次 | 14 |
| rényān xīshǎo | 人煙 稀少 | 人烟 稀少 | 14 |
| réngrán | 仍然 | 仍然 | 9 |
| rìyìmìqiè | 日益 密切 | 日益 密切 | 12 |
| rìyòngpǐn | 日用品 | 日用品 | 2 |
| rónghé | 融合 | 融合 | 8 |
| rú | 如 | 如 | 6 |
| rúhé | 如何 | 如何 | 6 |
| rújiā | 儒家 | 儒家 | 8 |
| rù | 入 | 入 | 4 |
| rùxué kǎoshì | 入學 考試 | 入学 考试 | 7 |
| Ruìshì | 瑞士 | 瑞士 | 13 |

| S | | | |
|---|---|---|---|
| sāichē | 塞車 | 塞车 | 6 |
| Sàixià | 賽夏 | 赛夏 | 13 |
| sāntōng | 三通 | 三通 | 12 |
| sànbù | 散步 | 散步 | 1 |
| sàngshī | 喪失 | 丧失 | 14 |
| sǎo | 掃 | 扫 | 11 |
| shāngpǐn | 商品 | 商品 | 2 |
| shàng... | 上 | 上 | 8 |
| shàngbǎiwàn | 上百萬 | 上百万 | 8 |
| shàngbānzú | 上班族 | 上班族 | 10 |
| shàngxiàbān | 上下班 | 上下班 | 6 |
| shāoxiāng | 燒香 | 烧香 | 8 |
| shǎoshù-mínzú | 少數 民族 | 少数 民族 | 13 |
| shàonián | 少年 | 少年 | 1 |
| shé | 蛇 | 蛇 | 6 |
| shéxíng | 蛇行 | 蛇行 | 6 |
| shèchū | 射出 | 射出 | 9 |
| shèhuì | 社會 | 社会 | 4 |

| | | | |
|---|---|---|---|
| shèhuì zhǔyì | 社會主義 | 社会主义 | 14 |
| shèjì | 設計 | 设计 | 13 |
| shèlì | 設立 | 设立 | 12 |
| shēnqǐng | 申請 | 申请 | 7 |
| shēnyè | 深夜 | 深夜 | 3 |
| shén | 神 | 神 | 8 |
| shénwèi | 神位 | 神位 | 8 |
| shènzhì | 甚至 | 甚至 | 6 |
| shēngchǎn | 生產 | 生产 | 10 |
| shēngxué zhǔyì | 升學主義 | 升学主义 | 7 |
| shēngyīn | 聲音 | 声音 | 1 |
| shībài | 失敗 | 失败 | 7 |
| shídài | 時代 | 时代 | 5 |
| shífēn | 十分 | 十分 | 14 |
| shíwù | 食物 | 食物 | 3 |
| shíyòng | 實用 | 实用 | 4 |
| shǐdé | 使得 | 使得 | 11 |
| shìchǎng | 市場 | 市场 | 2 |
| shìhé | 適合 | 适合 | 4 |
| shìjiè dàzhàn | 世界大戰 | 世界大战 | 14 |
| shìjièxìng | 世界性 | 世界性 | 8 |
| shìshè | 試射 | 试射 | 12 |
| shìyě | 視野 | 视野 | 14 |
| shóuxí, shúxí | 熟悉 | 熟悉 | 3 |
| shǒuxiān | 首先 | 首先 | 4 |
| shòu huānyíng | 受歡迎 | 受欢迎 | 3 |
| shūjí | 書籍 | 书籍 | 2 |
| shǔyú | 屬於 | 属于 | 13 |
| shù | 樹 | 树 | 1 |
| shùliàng | 數量 | 数量 | 9 |
| shuāngfāng | 雙方 | 双方 | 5 |

| | | | |
|---|---|---|---|
| shuǐpíng | 水平 | 水平 | 11 |
| shuǐzhǔn | 水準 | 水准 | 11 |
| shùnzhe | 順著 | 顺着 | 1 |
| sījī | 司機 | 司机 | 6 |
| sījiā | 私家 | 私家 | 14 |
| sījiā zhēntàn | 私家偵探 | 私家侦探 | 14 |
| sīkǎo | 思考 | 思考 | 7 |
| sīxiǎng | 思想 | 思想 | 8 |
| sìhū | 似乎 | 似乎 | 10 |
| sìmiào | 寺廟 | 寺庙 | 8 |
| sùdù | 速度 | 速度 | 9 |
| sùróng kāfēi | 速溶咖啡 | 速溶咖啡 | 3 |
| sùshí | 速食 | 快餐 | 3 |
| suànmìng | 算命 | 算命 | 8 |
| suànmìng xiānshēng | 算命先生 | 算命先生 | 8 |
| suíshǒu | 隨手 | 随手 | 11 |
| suízhe | 隨著 | 随着 | 3 |

**T**

| | | | |
|---|---|---|---|
| táitóu | 抬頭 | 抬头 | 13 |
| tàijíquán | 太極拳 | 太极拳 | 1 |
| Tàiyǎ | 泰雅 | 泰雅 | 13 |
| tānzi | 攤子 | 摊子 | 2 |
| tán liàn'ài | 談戀愛 | 谈恋爱 | 5 |
| tǎnkè | 坦克 | 坦克 | 9 |
| tànqīn | 探親 | 探亲 | 12 |
| tàng | 趟 | 趟 | 1 |
| tèsè | 特色 | 特色 | 2 |
| tèshū cáinéng | 特殊才能 | 特殊才能 | 7 |
| tí | 提 | 提 | 1 |
| tígāo | 提高 | 提高 | 10 |

| | | | |
|---|---|---|---|
| tíxǐng | 提醒 | 提醒 | 13 |
| tǐxì | 體系 | 体系 | 12 |
| tiānrán zīyuán | 天然資源 | 天然资源 | 14 |
| tiānxià | 天下 | 天下 | 10 |
| tiānzhǔ | 天主 | 天主 | 8 |
| tiānzhǔjiào | 天主教 | 天主教 | 8 |
| tiányāshì | 填鴨式 | 填鸭式 | 7 |
| tiāo | 挑 | 挑 | 2 |
| tiáolì | 條例 | 条例 | 12 |
| tiǎozhàn | 挑戰 | 挑战 | 10 |
| tiàowǔ | 跳舞 | 跳舞 | 1 |
| tíng | 停 | 停 | 6 |
| tíngchēchǎng | 停車場 | 停车场 | 6 |
| tōng háng | 通航 | 通航 | 12 |
| tōnghūn | 通婚 | 通婚 | 13 |
| tōng shāng | 通商 | 通商 | 12 |
| tōng yóu | 通郵 | 通邮 | 12 |
| tǒngzhì | 統治 | 统治 | 14 |
| tóutòng | 頭痛 | 头痛 | 6 |
| tóuzī | 投資 | 投资 | 12 |
| tuántǐ | 團體 | 团体 | 5 |
| tuīdòng | 推動 | 推动 | 14 |
| tuījiàn | 推薦 | 推荐 | 7 |
| tuīxíng | 推行 | 推行 | 13 |
| tuìhuàn | 退換 | 退换 | 2 |
| tuōlí | 脫離 | 脱离 | 14 |
| tùzi | 兔子 | 兔子 | 2 |

## W

| | | | |
|---|---|---|---|
| wàiyù | 外遇 | 外遇 | 10 |
| wánjù | 玩具 | 玩具 | 3 |
| wǎnglái | 往來 | 往来 | 12 |
| wǎngqiú | 網球 | 网球 | 1 |
| wǎngwǎng | 往往 | 往往 | 2 |
| wēixié | 威脅 | 威胁 | 11 |
| wéixiǎn | 危險 | 危险 | 6 |
| wèidào | 味道 | 味道 | 3 |
| wèilái | 未來 | 未来 | 14 |
| wèile | 為了 | 为了 | 7 |
| wēnyì | 瘟疫 | 瘟疫 | 9 |
| wénhuà | 文化 | 文化 | 4 |
| wénjù | 文具 | 文具 | 3 |
| wěn | 穩 | 稳 | 14 |
| wūlóngchá | 烏龍茶 | 乌龙茶 | 4 |
| wūrǎn | 污染 | 污染 | 11 |
| wūshuǐ | 污水 | 污水 | 11 |
| wúfǎ | 無法 | 无法 | 14 |
| wúshù | 無數 | 无数 | 9 |
| wǔhuā bāmén | 五花八門 | 五花八门 | 4 |
| wǔjiàn | 舞劍 | 舞剑 | 1 |

## X

| | | | |
|---|---|---|---|
| xǐjiǔ | 喜酒 | 喜酒 | 5 |
| xìsuǒ | 系所 | 系所 | 7 |
| xīyǐn | 吸引 | 吸引 | 2 |
| xiàle yítiào | 嚇了一跳 | 吓了一跳 | 8 |
| xiàqí | 下棋 | 下棋 | 1 |
| xiǎnrán | 顯然 | 显然 | 10 |
| xiàndài | 現代 | 现代 | 4 |
| xiàndàihuà | 現代化 | 现代化 | 4 |
| xiànrù | 陷入 | 陷入 | 12 |
| xiànxiàng | 現象 | 现象 | 13 |
| xiànzhì | 限制 | 限制 | 10 |
| xiāngdāng | 相當 | 相当 | 8 |
| xiāng | 香 | 香 | 8 |
| xiāngpiàn | 香片 | 香片 | 4 |
| xiāngyīn | 鄉音 | 乡音 | 13 |

| | | | |
|---|---|---|---|
| xiàng | 像 | 像 | 3 |
| xiǎnglè | 享樂 | 享乐 | 14 |
| xiǎngshòu | 享受 | 享受 | 4 |
| xiǎngxiàng | 想像 | 想象 | 14 |
| xiǎngxiànglì | 想像力 | 想像力 | 14 |
| xiǎngxiàng zhōng | 想像中 | 想像中 | 14 |
| xiǎng | 響 | 响 | 9 |
| xiànglái | 向來 | 向来 | 10 |
| xiàngqīn | 相親 | 相亲 | 5 |
| xiàngzi | 巷子 | 巷子 | 3 |
| xiāoshī | 消失 | 消失 | 9 |
| xiāoyè | 消夜/宵 | 消夜/宵 | 3 |
| xiǎo dòngwù | 小動物 | 小动物 | 2 |
| xiǎofàn | 小販 | 小贩 | 2 |
| xiǎojiǎo | 小腳 | 小脚 | 10 |
| xiàoguǒ | 效果 | 效果 | 9 |
| xīnmù | 心目 | 心目 | 4 |
| xīntài | 心態 | 心态 | 14 |
| xīnxiān | 新鮮 | 新鲜 | 1 |
| xìntú | 信徒 | 信徒 | 8 |
| xìnyǎng | 信仰 | 信仰 | 8 |
| xíngrén | 行人 | 行人 | 2 |
| xíngróng | 形容 | 形容 | 6 |
| xíngzhuàng | 形狀 | 形状 | 9 |
| ...xìng | xx性 | xx性 | 8 |
| xìngbié | 性別 | 性别 | 10 |
| xìngbié qíshì | 性別歧視 | 性别歧视 | 10 |
| xìngqù | 興趣 | 兴趣 | 1 |
| xuǎn | 選 | 选 | 2 |
| xuǎnzé | 選擇 | 选择 | 4 |
| xuéshù | 學術 | 学术 | 12 |
| xuéwèn | 學問 | 学问 | 4 |
| xuézhě | 學者 | 学者 | 10 |
| **Y** | | | |
| yālì | 壓力 | 压力 | 7 |
| Yǎměi | 雅美 | 雅美 | 13 |
| yān | 煙 | 烟 | 11 |
| yānhuǒ | 煙火 | 烟火 | 9 |
| yán | 嚴 | 严 | 10 |
| yánjiùsuǒ | 研究所 | 研究所 | 7 |
| Yánshuǐ | 鹽水 | 盐水 | 9 |
| yánzhòng | 嚴重 | 严重 | 11 |
| yāoqiú | 要求 | 要求 | 7 |
| yàojǐn | 要緊 | 要紧 | 5 |
| yèshì | 夜市 | 夜市 | 2 |
| yījù | 依據 | 依据 | 7 |
| yīrán | 依然 | 依然 | 10 |
| yīshēng | 醫生 | 医生 | 10 |
| yíjū | 移居 | 移居 | 13 |
| yíkè | 一刻 | 一刻 | 11 |
| yímín | 移民 | 移民 | 13 |
| yímínrècháo | 移民熱潮 | 移民热潮 | 13 |
| yǐjí | 以及 | 以及 | 6 |
| yǐmiǎn | 以免 | 以免 | 11 |
| yǐshàng | 以上 | 以上 | 1 |
| yǐ...wéiróng | 以…為榮 | 以…为荣 | 13 |
| yìbān | 一般 | 一般 | 2 |
| yìfēn qián yìfēn huò | 一分錢 一分貨 | 一分钱 一分货 | 2 |
| yìjiàn | 意見 | 意见 | 5 |
| yìlì | 毅力 | 毅力 | 14 |
| yìpáng | 一旁 | 一旁 | 1 |
| yìshì | 意識 | 意识 | 11 |
| yìshù | 藝術 | 艺术 | 4 |
| yīncǐ | 因此 | 因此 | 7 |

| | | | |
|---|---|---|---|
| yīnrén éryì | 因人而異 | 因人而异 | 5 |
| yìzhēng chángduǎn | 一爭長短 | 一争长短 | 10 |
| yīnyuè | 音樂 | 音乐 | 1 |
| yǐnliào | 飲料 | 饮料 | 3 |
| yǐnqíng | 引擎 | 引擎 | 11 |
| yǐnshí | 飲食 | 饮食 | 3 |
| yīngyǒu jìnyǒu | 應有盡有 | 应有尽有 | 2 |
| yíng | 贏 | 赢 | 12 |
| yíngyè | 營業 | 营业 | 3 |
| yíngyè shíjiān | 營業時間 | 营业时间 | 3 |
| yǐngxiǎng | 影響 | 影响 | 7 |
| yōngjǐ | 擁擠 | 拥挤 | 11 |
| yǒngyǒu | 擁有 | 拥有 | 14 |
| yòngjù | 用具 | 用具 | 3 |
| yōudiǎn | 優點 | 优点 | 7 |
| yóudiàn | 郵電 | 邮电 | 12 |
| yóuqí | 尤其 | 尤其 | 5 |
| yóuxì | 遊戲 | 游戏 | 2 |
| yóuxíng | 遊行 | 游行 | 9 |
| yóuyǒngchí | 游泳池 | 游泳池 | 1 |
| yóuyú | 由於 | 由于 | 7 |
| yǒulàiyú | 有賴於 | 有赖于 | 14 |
| yǒuxiàn | 有限 | 有限 | 14 |
| yǒuxiàn gōngsī | 有限公司 | 有限公司 | 14 |
| yú | 於 | 于 | 12 |
| yúshì | 於是 | 于是 | 6 |
| yǔ | 與 | 与 | 4 |
| yǔmáoqiú | 羽毛球 | 羽毛球 | 1 |
| yuánlái | 原來 | 原来 | 1 |
| yuánxiāo | 元宵 | 元宵 | 9 |

| | | | |
|---|---|---|---|
| yuánzhùmín | 原住民 | 原住民 | 13 |
| yuǎnjìn chímíng | 遠近馳名 | 远近驰名 | 3 |
| yùndòng | 運動 | 运动 | 1 |
| yùnyòng | 運用 | 运用 | 14 |
| **Z** | | | |
| zài jiāshàng | 再加上 | 再加上 | 6 |
| zǎochū wǎnguī | 早出晚歸 | 早出晚归 | 10 |
| zàochéng | 造成 | 造成 | 5 |
| zàoyīn | 噪音 | 噪音 | 11 |
| zé | 則 | 则 | 8 |
| zérèn | 責任 | 责任 | 10 |
| zēngjiā | 增加 | 增加 | 6 |
| zhá | 炸 | 炸 | 3 |
| zhǎnkāi | 展開 | 展开 | 12 |
| zhàogù | 照顧 | 照顾 | 10 |
| zhèn | 陣 | 阵 | 1 |
| zhēnghūn | 徵婚 | 征婚 | 5 |
| zhěngjié | 整潔 | 整洁 | 11 |
| zhèngcè | 政策 | 政策 | 12 |
| zhèngfǔ | 政府 | 政府 | 14 |
| zhèngmiàn yìyì | 正面意義 | 正面意义 | 7 |
| zhèngquè | 正確 | 正确 | 7 |
| zhèngzhì | 政治 | 政治 | 12 |
| zhímín | 殖民 | 殖民 | 14 |
| zhímíndì | 殖民地 | 殖民地 | 14 |
| zhímín zhèngcè | 殖民政策 | 殖民政策 | 14 |
| zhíwèi | 職位 | 职位 | 10 |
| zhíyè | 職業 | 职业 | 10 |
| zhíyè fùnǚ | 職業婦女 | 职业妇女 | 10 |
| zhǐ | 指 | 指 | 10 |

# Grammar Index

| | | |
|---|---|---|
| yíge yígede | 一個一個的 | 2 |
| yíqiè | 一切 | 14 |
| yízhèn | 一陣 | 1 |
| yǐ...wéi... | 以...為... | 11 |
| yǐ A wéi B | 以A為B | 13 |
| yìbān | 一般 | 2 |
| yīncǐ | 因此 | 12 |
| yóu | 由 | 10 |
| yóuyú | 由於 | 7 |
| yú | 於 | 12 |
| yù A yù B | 愈A愈B | 13 |
| yuánlái | 原來 | 1 |
| zài...xià | 在...下 | 7 |
| zài...xīnmù zhōng | 在...心目中 | 4 |
| zé | 則 | 8 |
| zàochéng | 造成 | 5 |
| zhī + (Noun) | 之 + (Noun) | 12 |
| zhídào...cái | 直到...才 | 3 |
| zhǐyǒu...cái | 只有...才 | 2 |
| zhìyú | 至於 | 5 |
| zhìyú / duìyú / guānyú | 至於、對於、關於 | 13 |
| zhōngyú | 終於 | 7<br>14 |
| zuìhǎo | 最好 | 1 |

# Abbreviations

| | | |
|---|---|---|
| Adv. | Adverb | 副詞（都，大概） |
| B. | Bound Morpheme | 限制詞素（國，著） |
| Coll. | Colloquial | |
| Conj. | Conjunction | 連詞（跟，可是） |
| Det. | Determiner | 限定詞（這，某） |
| Id. | Idiom | 熟語，成語，慣用語（吹牛，一乾二淨） |
| Lit. | Literally | |
| Loc. | Localizer | 方位詞（上，下） |
| M. | Measure | 量詞（個，條；下，次） |
| N. | Noun | 名詞（我，勇氣） |
| Part. | Particle | 助詞（嗎，了） |
| Prep. | Preposition | 介詞（從，對於） |
| Pron. | Pronoun | |
| Usu. | Usually | |
| V. | Action Verb, transitive | 及物動作動詞（買，吃） |
| Vi. | Action Verb, intransitive | 不及物動作動詞（哭，坐） |
| Vaux. | Auxiliary Verb | 助動詞（能，想） |
| V-sep. | Separable Verb | 離合不及物動詞（結婚，生氣） |
| Vs. | State Verb, intransitive | 不及物狀態動詞（好，貴） |
| Vst. | State Verb, transitive | 及物狀態動詞（喜歡，知道） |
| Vs-attr. | State Verb, attributive | 非謂狀態動詞（主要，袖珍） |
| Vs-pred. | State Verb, predicative | 非定狀態動詞（夠，多） |
| Vp. | Process Verb, intransitive | 不及物變化動詞（死，完） |
| Vpt. | Process Verb, transitive | 及物變化動詞（破/洞，裂/縫） |

# Bopomofo–Pinyin Conversion Chart

## 注音：拼音 對照表

**Bpmf–Pinyin Conversion Chart**

| | | | | | | | | | |
|---|---|---|---|---|---|---|---|---|---|
| ㄅb | ㄉd | ㄍg | ㄐj | ㄓzh | ㄗz | ㄚa | ㄞai | ㄢan | ㄦr |
| ㄆp | ㄊt | ㄎk | ㄑq | ㄔch | ㄘc | ㄛo | ㄟei | ㄣen | ㄧi |
| ㄇm | ㄋn | ㄏh | ㄒx | ㄕsh | ㄙs | ㄜe | ㄠao | ㄤang | ㄨu |
| ㄈf | ㄌl | | ㄖr | | | ㄝe | ㄡou | ㄥeng | ㄩü |

**Steps to follow:**

1. Convert Bpmf to Pinyin as shown in the chart above, e.g. ㄊㄞ ㄨㄢ = tai uan, ㄕ ㄈㄢ = sh fan, ㄓㄨㄥ ㄒㄧㄣ = zhung xin.
2. If ㄣ and ㄥ follow another vowel, drop /e/, e.g. ㄧㄣ = ien = in, ㄩㄥ =ueng= ung.
3. If ㄧ, ㄨ, ㄩ occur in the syllable-initial position but before anothervowel, change them (i.e. i, u, ü) into y, w , yu, e.g. ㄧㄚ = ya, ㄨㄛ = wo, ㄩㄣ = yun. If they are alone, add y, w, y, e.g. ㄧ = yi, ㄨ = wu, ㄩ = yu.
4. If ㄧ, ㄨ, ㄩ are the only vowels in a syllable, add y, w, y, e.g. ㄧ = yi, ㄨ = wu, ㄩ = yu.
5. If ㄓ, ㄔ, ㄕ, ㄖ, ㄗ, ㄘ, ㄙ stand alone, add i , e.g. ㄔ = chi, ㄘ = ci, ㄖ = ri.
6. Change the following sequences in all cases: ung = ong, uei = ui, iou = iu.
7. Change ü to u after ㄐ, ㄑ, ㄒ, e.g. ㄒㄩ = xu, ㄑㄩ = qu, ㄐㄩ = ju; but ㄌㄩ = lü, ㄋㄩ = nü.

# Suggested Video Materials

Below is a list of TV documentaries produced by the former Public Television of Taiwan that may be suitable for classroom viewing and discussion. A catalogue was last available from the Broadcasting Development Fund （廣播電視事業發展基金）.

Additional programs about a variety of Chinese/Taiwanese topics are available from Taiwan Public Television Service （公共電視文化事業基金會）. DVDs can be purchased online at http://shopping.pts.org.tw.

Taiwan Public Television Service
No. 50, Lane 75, Kang-Ning Rd., Sec. 3
Taipei 114, Taiwan, R.O.C.
Tel: (886-2) 2633-8037
Fax: (886-2) 2630-1895
http://www.pts.org.tw

Lesson 1. 去公園學功夫

中國武術：太極拳
國術天地：國術運動會
　　　　　洋人愛國術
認識國劇：國劇的武功
新體育－圍棋：泛談圍棋
新聞眼：運動、公園連連看
小戲迷：中國功夫

Lesson 2. 逛夜市

愛的進行式(戲劇)：討價還價擺地攤
大家談：掃除仿冒
百工圖：舊貨商

Lesson 3. 還是小吃好
特別節目：中國美食－英文版(50m)
吃在中國：鍋杓響動滋味來－炒
長短寬窄各有味－麵
吃出鄉情：鹿港情深
從今天到明天：民以食為天吃出品味來速食文化的衝擊
天之美祿：中式速食

Lesson 4. 茶與中國人
款款茶情：臺灣的特色茶臺灣茶館文化臺灣茶藝欣賞與觀摩
文化長廊：茶具
城鄉小調：凍頂茶的故鄉
珍藏天地：茶壺的珍藏

Lesson 5. 我愛紅娘
現代婦女劇場：相親
男女之間（戲劇）：訂婚
生涯路：快樂的單身女郎

Lesson 6. 台北怎麼那麼擠
大家談：停車問題如何解決
新聞眼：現代化都市－交通篇
從今天到明天：城市交通的新寵(捷運) 找回交通的愛

Lesson 7. 熱鍋上的烤生
愛的進行式（戲劇）：補習何時了
空中張老師：聯考之後
百工圖 ：保證升學的人－補習班的老師
校園顯影：「第一名」的陰影
新聞眼：談書包文憑主義、考試、升學與就業

Lesson 8. 大拜拜
認識臺灣－寺廟篇：台北龍山寺
廟會：北港迎媽祖雞籠中元祭土地公祭
愛的進行式（劇場）：算命
大迴響：頭上三尺的神明
快樂童年：神明的家薪火香傳話家祠

Lesson 9. 鹽水的蜂炮
畫我家鄉：鹽水
海濤聲：鹽水的蜂炮
廟會：鹽水武廟慶元宵
中國民俗節令：冬至清明節端午節中秋節
快樂童年：剪紙捏麵人毽子扯鈴陀螺巧手蘭新中國結
靈巧的手：畫糖的水剪紙的手
舞龍的手
大迴響：桃符更新迎新年
歲時人間：中秋之祭古都迎春清明掃墓悠悠江水賽龍舟
民俗藝陣：醒獅（一）

醒獅（二）
高蹺
跳鼓
藝閣

Lesson 10. 女強人
男女之間（戲劇）：請別叫我女強人
愛的進行式（戲劇）：上班媽媽
媽媽的天空：媽媽上班時
現代婦女劇場：家事誰來做
大家談：職業婦女，分身有術
新聞眼：時代女性的新形象

Lesson 11. 帶口罩的騎士
從今天到明天：沒有垃圾戰爭的明天無煙無塵的鄰居
摩登家庭（動畫）：垃圾是寶
路隊長（戲劇）：環保風波
愛的進行式（戲劇）：垃圾之旅
百工圖：環保人員（河殤篇）
大家談：惱人的垃圾看不見的殺手 - 空氣污染
新聞眼：寶特瓶回收傷腦筋

Lesson 12. 海峽兩岸
大家談：開放後的臺灣前途
解嚴後的政治沈思
新聞眼：大陸政策「一國兩制」不可行兩岸關係大陸政策新契機解嚴過後兩岸新情勢(兩岸面對面,華視93-7-19)

Lesson 13. 台灣族群與語言
語文類－壺蓋先講台語山地快樂兒童
藝術與人文類－小鄉土大世界：天生的藝術家—魯凱族客家之音—茶、山歌、三腳採茶平埔夜祭
蘭嶼雅美族—飛魚大餐－山上的孩子

Lesson 14. 台灣的經濟
（無相關影片資訊）

# 練習答案 Key to Exercises

（書面答案僅供參考，答案可異。）
Suggested answers are provided since answers may vary.

## 第一課

（文法）

1.c 今天晚上早一點去休息。
1.d 能去一趟中國。

2.d 週末誰能借我一輛車嗎？
2.e 我能幫你些什麼嗎？

3.c 下了一陣雨以後，空氣真新鮮，
3.d 一陣音樂。

4.c 順著中山路一直走，羽球館就在路左邊。
4.d 我總是順著他們的意見。

5(A)-c 一群小朋友在打籃球。
5(A)-d 就在旁邊，只有十分鐘的路程。

5(B)-c（老）李同學原來對中國沒有什麼認識，去了一趟北京以後，
5(B)-d 小王原來常常生病，

6.c 多半是年紀在六十歲以上的老人。
6.d 其中籃球和羽毛球最受人歡迎。

7.c 如果你喜歡中國音樂，今天晚上你應該去聽那一場音樂會。
7.d 如果已經有太多的人打網球，那麼我就去游泳。

（練習）

1-1（C明白）1-2（F次）1-3（B老是）1-4（E可能）1-5（A清早）
1-6（D如果）1-7（ J 吵鬧）1-8（G討厭）1-9（H黃昏）1-10（ I 老）

2–a 安靜 2–b 男女老少 2–c 抱著 2–d 功夫 2–e 新鮮
2–f 了解 2–g 趟 2–h 球場 2–i 興趣 2–j 群
2–k 原來 2–l 專心

（接字遊戲）

3–a 公園→園林→林場→操場→體操→體育→教育→養育→營養→營火→火災→災難
3–b 打球→球員→員工→工人→人權→權威→威脅→脅迫→緊迫→緊張→張開→開心（以上僅屬舉例，同學可自行創作）

## 第二課

（文法）

1.e 都可以在大學商店裡買到。
1.f 很敏感。
1.g 大部份的水果在台灣都買得到。
1.h 一般說來，百貨公司只有在大城市才找得到。

2.c 警察把所有的車子一輛接著一輛的拖走了。
2.d 他把金魚一隻一隻的放進水族箱裡了。

3.e 都不在乎，就掏出錢想買下它了。
3.f 都掉了，這次他可要挨罵了。
3.g 別擔心，連專家都分不出這是一個仿冒品。
3.h 他已經在香港住了十年了，但是他連用廣東話數數都不會。

4.c 有些寵物，像北京狗，在美國非常昂貴。
4.d 日本商社喜歡在像舊金山、紐約這樣的大城市買房地產。

5.c 噪音也比較多。
5.d 中國菜和法國菜的烹調方法。
5.e 請比較夜市和普通商店的特質。
5.f 白衣服比較適合你。

6.c 容易受騙上當而得不償失。
6.d 比別人早一步得到最新消息。
6.e 人往往看不到自己的弱點。
6.f 較便宜的東西往往品質也比較差。

7.e 我才能買到價廉物美的東西。
7.f 圖書館，才找得到座位。
7.g 只有本地人才能在夜市里擺出攤子。
7.h 只有每天練習中國字，才能記得它們。

（練習）

1-1（c晚上）1-2（f還價）1-3（e假貨）1-4（b選）1-5（d往往）
1-6（a各種）1-7（c整齊）1-8（d冷清）1-9（b小吃）1-10（a不二價）
1-11（e顧客）

2-1 課本，雜誌 2-2 牙刷，毛巾，衛生紙 2-3 迷你褲，牛仔褲
2-4 玫瑰 2-5 白兔，貓，獅子狗 2-6 餃子 2-7 京劇
2-8 蘋果，西瓜 2-9 西洋棋 2-10 乒乓，健美操，棒球

3-a 逛，逛 3-b 擺 3-c 應有盡有 3-d 吸引 3-e 合適 3-f 換
3-g 挑 3-h 特色 3-i 在乎 3-j 耐心 3-k 樂趣 3-l 遊戲
3-m 講價 3-n 滿載而歸

## 第三課

（文法）

1.c 生意每況愈下，
1.d 旅遊資訊發達，
1.e 隨著大陸翡翠逐漸受人喜愛，越來越多的人到博物館去參觀。
1.f 隨著最近經濟的成功，人們享受到更多的政治自由。

2.c 丁小姐常被誤認做是林小姐。

3.e 他另外的一個姊姊還是一個大學學生。
3.f 這家書店的老闆在另外的一所大學裡有一家書店。

4.c 他說的都是真的。
4.d 我親眼看見的。
4.e 他寫一篇報告，關於去年他在中國的所見所聞。
4.f 你所聽到的，只（不過）是真相的一半（而已）。

5.c 我才知道讀書對我很重要。
5.d 我才認識東方的生活哲學。

5.e 直到他上了大學，他才離開家。
5.f 在大城市一些商店直到晚上十一點才關門。

6.c 往往最受人歡迎。
6.d 失去父母照顧

7.c 既不雅觀又不衛生。
7.d 既浪費又傷身體。

（練習）

1–a 主角 zhǔjiǎo, 助教 zhùjiào 1–b 睡覺 shuìjiào, 水餃 shuǐjiǎo
1–c 經濟 jīngjì, 競技 jìngjì 1–d 簡單 jiǎndān, 煎蛋 jiāndàn
1–e 傳統 chuántǒng, 串通 chuàntōng

2–a 速食店，麥當勞 2–b 小吃店 2–c 游泳池 2–d夜市 2–e 夜市，家裡
2–f 床上，沙發上，樹下 2–g 海邊，公園 2–h 銀行，黑市
2–i 路邊，夜市

3–a）3 3–b）2 3–c）2/4 3–d）3 3–e）1 3–f）2 3–g）3 3–h）1
3–i）4 3–j）2

5 g/d/b/a/f/c/e

## 第四課

（文法）

1.c 幾乎都知道水質的重要。
1.d 幾乎趕不上搭早班校車。
1.e 以前在我們班上的每一個人幾乎都曾喝過茉莉花茶。
1.f 瑪麗如此的難過，以致幾乎整晚睡不著。

2.i 我們的每個老師各有各的教學方法。
2.j 為了節省時間，我們就各開各的車吧。

3.d（大陸經濟改革）吸引不少外人設廠投資。
3.e 自從他到中國讀書以來，
3.f（自）過去九個月來，我的老師的英文已經改善很多。
3.g 過去這兩個月來，我一直忙著寫報告。

4.c 成績仍然不見好轉。
4.d 現在很多人已經不喝茶了。
4.e 在北部已經天天在下雨了，然而南部水荒還是很嚴重。
4.f 在城市裡有好幾家百貨公司，然而大部份的人仍然在夜市買東西。

5.c 但對講究喝茶的人來說，那並不是正確的喝茶方式。
5.d 對市井小民來說，的確如此。
5.e 對凡事講求快速的人來說，泡茶、品茶…手續多，
5.f 對愛打麻將的人來說，通宵熬夜打牌，
5.g 對中國人來說，茶是最受歡迎的飲料。
5.h 對學生來說，游泳池比語言實驗室重要。

6.c 非得買一把傘不可。
6.d 非得到當地住一陣子不可。
6.e 既然你主修地理，就非得到中國大陸旅行一趟不可。
6.f 下個月初之前，我們非得收到你的付款不可。

7.e 總統馬英九先生，
7.f 既省油又耐用。

（練習）

1-1）c 1-2）d 1-3）a 1-4）e 1-5）b 1-6）d 1-7）e 1-8）b
1-9）f 1-10）c 1-11）a

2-1）d, n 2-2）a, i 2-3）h, p 2-4）c, j, l, o 2-5）e, g 2-6）b, f, k, m

3-a 泡 3-b 解 3-c 講究 3-d 入 3-e 文化 3-f 流行 3-g 非
3-h 心目 3-i 享受 3-j 藝術

## 第五課

（文法）

1.e 結婚不結婚，
1.f 放在心上。
1.g 無論（他們）是大學生或是高中生，他們都會發現這本漢英字典非常有用。
1.h 無論他畫什麼，他的畫總是供不應求。

3.d 他們相處不甚融洽，但是他們並沒有真正離婚。
3.e 他在德國長大，但是那並不是他每年到那度假的原因。

4.e 在學生活動中心的新自助餐店很受學生的歡迎。
4.f 來自中國的小提琴家逐漸受到西方世界的重視。

5.d 能不能請你把生日蛋糕切成八塊？
5.e 電影院前大排長龍，所以電影我們並沒有看成。

6.c 因為他們父親工作的關係，他們又搬家了。
6.d 許多人在八月結婚，因為那是個吉利的月份。

7.d 我已經把我的信寄到報社去了，至於他們會不會出版它，那得看他們的決定了。
7.e 這個中國家族已經在美國五十年了，至於他們真正來自何處，沒有人有清楚的概念。

（練習）

（2–a）3（2–b）1（2–c）3 or 4（2–d）2（2–e）3（2–f）1（2–g）4（2–h）2（2–i）2（2–j）4

3–a 不久就要舉行婚禮了。
3–b 她的父母都很著急。
3–c 結婚生子仍是人生必經的大事。
3–d 對未來充滿希望。
3–e 依父母之命和張太太結為連理。
3–f 現代人終身不嫁（娶）的想法。
3–g 可遇而不可求的事。
3–h 到法院去公證結婚。
3–i 因為他認為那很難為情。
3–k 錢，他們不能買大的房子。
（以上僅屬舉例，同學可自行創作）

4–a 中國人的家庭觀念重。
4–b 自由戀愛比相親有趣。
4–c 祝那對新人早生貴子。
4–d 許多單身女性都不急著結婚。
4–e 他們不打算在教堂舉行婚禮。

## 第六課

（文法）

1.e 為了閃避車輛而撞上電線杆呢？
1.f 開了一張超速罰單。
1.g 他已經等了兩個鐘頭，但是公車并沒有來，讓他非常生氣。

2.e 連計程車都不見蹤影。
2.f 騎樓下都停滿了（車子）。
2.g 車子停在馬路兩旁，甚至停在人行道上。
2.h 我的機車，甚至我的自行車，昨晚都被偷走了

3.d 於是一些跨國企業紛紛到亞洲設廠。
3.e 於是他搬到學校宿舍去住了。
3.f 報上說，油炸食物有礙健康，於是他再也不吃臭豆腐了。
3.g 所有的班機都被預定一空，於是他取消了他的旅行計畫。
3.h 最近市長辦公室調升交通罰款，於是市區的交通狀況已經改善許多。

4.f 改善校區環境衛生，
4.g 去學游泳，
4.h 將來你希望我如何和你聯絡？
4.i 我們將如何改善我們累贅的交通規則？

5.e 空氣污染問題，全民的共識。
5.f 解決都市交通擁擠的問題。
5.g 有時在台北的行人根本不能順利穿越馬路，到馬路的另一邊去。
5.h 我不知道這件意外是如何發生的，我根本沒有看到其他的來車。

（練習）

2-a 駕，坐／搭 2-b 堵／塞 2-c 騎／開 2-d 觀光 2-e 解決 2-f 發生 2-g 減少 2-h 改善 2-i 做，增加

3（看學生自己如何回答，沒有一定的答案。）

（6-A）2（6-B）3（6-C）3（6-D）1

## 第七課

（文法）

1.e 身體健康狀況很差，
1.f 他一直忘不了他的前任女友。
1.g 由於他的家人，Mike Mei 必須改變他的旅行計畫。
1.h 由於她已經找到一份待遇不錯的工作，Lucy Li 將不去讀研究所。

2.d 王教授是對華語教學很有經驗的老師。
2.e 德國對現代的日本有極大的影響。

3.c 我們在郊區買了房子。
3.d 他們都特別用功。
3.e 為了較好了解中國文化，White先生花了好幾年的時間留在中國偏遠的鄉村。
3.f 爲了能讓他的學生進入一所好大學，老張非常樂意為他的學生做任何事情。

4-d.4 他為了在畢業後容易找到工作而選擇主修工科。
4-d.5 我們今天的旅行，因為天氣不理想而延到下星期。
4-d.6 他們的婚事由於父母不同意而沒有下文。

5.e 在名師的指導下，她已經進步很多。

6.e 被修改了
6.f 專制的作風
6.g 兩年前他們終於提起去他們家鄉的那次不愉快旅行。
6.h 經過她一再的懇求，她父母終于同意了她離婚的要求。

（練習）

1-a 深淺 1-b 高低 1-c 輕重 1-d 長短 1-e 大小 1-f 好壞 1-g 快慢
1-h 濃淡 1-i 難易 1-j 好壞 1-k 成敗 1-l 高矮

2-a早生貴子 2-b上下班 2-c成績 2-d長龍 2-e重考
2-1早班車 2-2考生 2-3望子成龍 2-4放暑假 2-5重視 2-6聯考

## 第八課

（文法）

1.d 嚇了一大跳。
1.e 咬了一口。

2.c 學生，喜愛。
2.d 缺乏愛心
2.e 在許多鄉村，為愛結婚仍不被大部份的人所接受。
2.f 許多宗教活動常為學者批評。

3.e 表示不吉利。
3.f 是一種人倫的主張。
3.g 在英國大部份的人是基督徒，而在另一方面，在愛爾蘭大部份的人是天主教徒。
3.h 佛教徒不崇拜上帝，但大部份的道教廟宇卻擠滿了神明。

4.e 我聽說他現在在南方某一基督教堂工作。

5.f 做了很多重大的改革。
5.g 仍享有很高的聲望。
5.h 我非常不好意思去談論我在經濟上的困難。
5.i 你過去這幾天在工作上還算快樂嗎？

（練習）

1-a上／燒 1-b 解決 1-c 信 1-d 算 1-e 祭拜 1-f 看 1-g 上，做

（3-A） 1 （3-B） 1 （3-C） 2

## 第九課

（文法）

1.g 東京、夏威夷;觀光客。
1.h 牛頓、愛因斯坦;著名

2.d 花錢;受罪
2.e 既可賺錢又可完成學業。

3.c 是用咖啡豆。
3.d 雙方父母介紹認識的。
3.e 大學校長並不是只代表教授們，而是應該代表整個校園。
3.f White先生並不是因為樂趣而到中國旅行，而是為了尋找四十年前的朋友。

4.e 一尊彌勒佛像。
4.f 吃了一塊巧克力蛋糕。
4.g John喜歡打扮得像天主教神父一樣。
4.h Steve唱民謠那麼嚴肅，就好像他在唱國歌一樣。

5.d 他會取消我們的機位。
5.e 下回他們都不來了。
5.f 也許他感覺不舒服，否則他鐵定已經接受邀請了。
5.g 除非明天颱風到來，否則一定是陽光普照的好天氣。

6.d 請假不來上班。
6.e 發生爭吵。
6.f 你才剛從中國旅遊回來，現在你又在計畫到日本旅行？
6.g 你才剛上書法課兩個禮拜，就已經想退掉它？

（練習）

1–a 放 1–b 否則 1–c 中秋節，元宵節 1–d 慶祝，舉行 1–e 消失
1–f 感冒／…，清代 1–g 速度 1–h 形狀

2–a 中國，節慶是春節。
2–b 月餅，中秋節
2–c 在眾人面前捧花向女朋友求婚，
2–d 考試結束了，到郊外
2–e 被熱水燙到了，不要隨便抹上藥膏了事。
2–f 他終於回到了故鄉。
2–g 爸爸生氣的樣子，閃電雷聲
（以上答案僅屬舉例，同學可自行創作）

3–a 行人 3–b 清朝（代） 3–c 海風 3–d 結婚 3–e 效果
3–1 清明節 3–2 結果 3–3 遊行 3–4 人山人海 3–5 風俗習慣

## 第十課

（文法）

1-A.e 政府官員的責任向來就比那些普通百姓來得大。
1-A.f 他向來就不接受別人的禮物，這次是什麼使他改變心意？
1-B.d 蔣太太的工作表現一向第一流的。
1-B.e 顏先生今天一直都沒有抽煙。

2.f 說明事情原委
2.g 公司倒閉
2.h 記者向官員詢問一些非常重要的問題。
2.i 這家雜誌社的發行人向他們展示說明她的公司的組織。

3-B.d 環保的觀念還需要加強。
3-B.e 她仍充滿自信。
3-B.f 下班後如果你還有任何問題，請儘管給我家里打電話。
3-B.g 盡管他獲悉一個更合意的職位，他並不認為他應該去爭取。

4-B.d 父母雙方共同負責。
4-B.e 爺爺奶奶照顧。
4-B.f 現在由王博士報告我們遇到的問題。

（練習）

2.a 教育程度；很多婦女都開始工作了。
2.b 女主外男主內
2.c 裹小腳；中國傳統婦女。
2.d 現代女性；她們更離不開丈夫。
2.e 根本不關心人民；卻說自己是台灣之子。
2.f 照顧父母的責任；長子來承擔。
2.g 社會越來越開放；她們的經濟實力也越來越強。

(3-A)2 (3-B)3 (3-C)2 (3-D)3 (3-E)1

## 第十一課

（文法）

1.d 汽機車廢氣
1.e 機器人將可取代人工，做粗重的工作。
1.f 對大部份的大學生而言，校園宿舍不是理想的居住地方。
1.g 對大部份鄉村農夫而言，參觀大城市的費用太高了。

2.d 關閉游泳池;省水手段。
2.e 家
2.f 鋼琴，大眾所熟知。
2.g 我們店裡主要以翡翠古董為交易。
2.h 在台灣所有的銀行都以日元為標準。

3.d 攜帶的重要證件。
3.e 破壞環境衛生。
3.f 打電話給我。

4.d 小孩子都患感冒了。
4.e 這件工程就此拖延下來了。
4.f 從工廠排放的廢水已經使得黃河受到嚴重污染。
4.g 新的公園和樹木，已經使得我們的城市變成一個更舒適的居住地區。

5.d 很好的機會;知道把握。
5.e 他們仍念念不忘過去經濟艱難的日子。
5.f 即使明天下雨了，那對南部的旱災也沒幫助。
5.g 即使我必須花一個月的時間看完紅樓夢，我一點也不後悔。

6.d 仍繼續製造污染。
6.e 拿不出解決的辦法。
6.f 學校知道水龍頭的髒水，他們卻不願意供應過濾過的水。
6.g 假期中，垃圾在馬路上堆積如山，卻沒有任何行動去改善它。

7.c 環保人士，鼓舞
7.d 市民，惡臭和疾病
7.e 發現石油給這個小國家帶來財富。
7.f 在這地區經濟上的成功，給這個國家的每個人帶來信心。

8.e 經濟的支援，需要人格上的尊重
8.f 危害人類健康，破壞大自然。

8.g 他不只精通歐洲語言，更會說三種非洲方言。
8.h 旅遊業不只能帶來財富，而且能提升國際間的了解。

（練習）

(1–a)1,2,3,4 (1–b) 5 (1–c) 7 (1–d) 9 (1–e) 6 (1–f) 7

2 強調，忽略，結果，整潔，抗議，公德心，郊區，威脅，環境。

## 第十二課

（文法）

1.g 從英國獨立。
1.h 忙碌的教書工作中。
1.i 中國人民共和國於一九四九年建國。
1.j 美國橫貫大陸的鐵路於一八八九年完成。

2.e 靠後天自己的努力。
2.f 還有一位天神的監督。
2.g 在中國三分之二的人說北平話為他們的地方方言。
2.h 在中國總統之下，還有五院院長管理政府裡不同領域的事務。

3.d 國際社會刮目相看。
3.f 讚嘆佩服。
3.g 他的工作表現令那些訓練他的人失望。
3.h 來自台灣的觀光客在大陸上的所作所為，觸犯了當地的政府。

4.d 實際情況
4.e 便攜性上
4.f 好的角度來看。

5.d 因此他更自暴自棄了。
5.e 因此王家取消了這次出國旅行的計畫。
5.f 她現在正在國外旅行，因此她不能參加她室友的婚禮。
5.g John Jiang 在考試當天感到不舒服，因此表現很差。

（練習）

2 c記者，e海峽兩岸，d解除，f終於，a接觸，g態度，i積極，h任何，b赴。

## 第十三課

（文法）

1.d 西北季風。
1.e 他的成功與他的家庭背景無關。
1.f 這件犯罪可能和政治有關。

2.d 我大致上同意你的觀點。
2.e 所有羅馬拼音的系統大致上相同。
2.f 申請手續都完了。

3.e 上海是個高度現代化的都市。
3.f 近代西化運動正在失利中。

4.d 大家都感到相當難過。
4.e 要不要公開道歉。
4.f 台灣原住民文化習俗的書。
4.g 對於這件政治醜聞，我並沒有興趣評論。
4.h 我先研究閩南話，至於客家話我也必須考慮。
4.i 陛下，關於您的私人財產，您希望我們怎麼處理？

5.e 我真的不明白為什麼他把我當作對手。
5.f 由於現在進口啤酒非常便宜，因此他將酒當作水一樣喝。

6.e 現代年輕人的價值觀已經不同以往了。
6.f 鄉土語言這個問題。

（練習）

1 a屬於 b移民 c推行 d重視 e強調 f鄉音 g播放 h消失 i提醒 j包括

2（一）1.× 2.〇 3.× 4.〇 5.〇

## 第十四課

（文法）

1.e domestic market of 3 million PC's annually; 1 million.
1.f only 3 of them have an annual production of 100,000 cars.

2.e finally picked up by the end of the year.
2.f bounced back upward during the first quarter of 2002.

3.e the foundation of all (economic) reforms.
3.f Economy is the life-line of Taiwan; economic development.

4.e businesses; moved their investments abroad.
4.f Affected by a weak demand in consumer goods.

5.e favor implementing changes of policy as quickly as possible favor a more gradual approach
5.f improve our investment climate, so as to increase our international competitiveness in the international business world.

(練習)

1. 經濟奇蹟，環保問題，環境污染，代價，美麗之島，指標意義，象徵。